Policy in Evolution

The U.S. Role in China's Reunification

Policy in Evolution

The U.S. Role in China's Reunification

Martin L. Lasater

Westview Press
BOULDER & LONDON

Westview Special Studies on China and East Asia

Copyright © 1989 by Westview Press, Inc.

Published in 1989 in the United States of America by Westview Press, Inc., 5500 Central Avenue, Boulder, Colorado 80301, and in the United Kingdom by Westview Press, Inc., 13 Brunswick Centre, London WC1N 1AF, England

Library of Congress Cataloging-in-Publication Data
Lasater, Martin L.
  Policy in evolution : the U.S. role in China's reunification / by
    Martin L. Lasater.
    p. cm.—(Westview special studies on China and East Asia)
  Bibliography: p.
  Includes index.
  ISBN 0-8133-7595-9
  1. United States—Foreign relations—China. 2. China—Foreign
relations—United States. 3. United States—Foreign relations—
Taiwan. 4. Taiwan—Foreign relations—United States. 5. Chinese
reunification question, 1949-   . 6. United States—Foreign
relations—1981-   . I. Title. II. Series.
E183.8.C6L37 1989
327.73051—dc19   88-10155
                                                                      CIP

Printed and bound in the United States of America

 The paper used in this publication meets the requirements of the American National
Standard for Permanence of Paper for Printed Library Materials Z39.48-1984.

10   9   8   7   6   5   4   3   2

ST

Contents

Next Step in U.S. Policy, 190
Need for Caution, 191
Notes, 193

Acknowledgments

I am grateful to my parents for making it all possible; to my wife and children for their unfailing support; to Dr. Harold C. Hinton for his academic guidance; and to my many Chinese friends for their patience and understanding. Appreciation is also extended to the Pacific Cultural Foundation of Taipei for a publication grant.

Martin L. Lasater

1

Introduction

The reunification of Taiwan with China is one of the most important policy issues of our time. The issue has broad strategic, political, economic, and moral ramifications for the U.S., as well as for Chinese on both sides of the Taiwan Strait. The People's Republic of China (PRC) has assigned top political priority to reunification and has made the issue a central element of Sino-American relations. Beijing's irritation at continued U.S. support of Taiwan stems from PRC perceptions that Washington stands in the way of an early resolution of differences between the two Chinese sides.

The Republic of China (ROC) on Taiwan also supports reunification, but under democratic rather than communist rule. Taipei relies upon U.S. arms sales, political support, and trade to deter PRC aggression, maintain an international presence, and sustain Taiwan's phenomenal economic growth. Also, U.S. support indirectly strengthens Taiwan's bargaining position with the PRC over the terms and conditions of reunification.

For its part, the U.S. has attempted to downplay the Taiwan issue in Sino-American relations by evolving a finely tuned policy since the early 1970s. A fundamental tenet of that policy is not to become involved in China's reunification, other than to insist that the resolution of mainland-Taiwan differences be made in a peaceful manner. Washington does not state a preference for an outcome of the reunification issue, although various domestic audiences in the U.S. strongly support specific outcomes. Since 1986 the U.S. has supported efforts by both Chinese sides to increase unofficial contact across the Taiwan Strait.

This book examines the origin and development of U.S. reunification policy, focusing on the 1981-1987 period of the Reagan administration. Since U.S. reunification policy is intricately tied to the Taiwan issue, this aspect of Sino-American relations is treated in detail. The direction of future U.S. reunification policy is also examined in view of emerging trends on China and Taiwan.

1

Organization

Chapter 1 contains an executive summary of the book. Chapter 2 discusses the origins of the Taiwan issue in Sino-American relations and traces the evolution of U.S. reunification policy through the normalization of U.S.-PRC relations in 1979 and the enactment of the Taiwan Relations Act. This chapter points to the complex interaction of the many factors which influence U.S. reunification policy, including relations between the Kuomintang (KMT) and Communist Party of China (CPC), the status of U.S.-PRC relations, the Soviet threat, the U.S. commitment to anti-communism, and the domestic debate over China policy which has been a feature of American politics since World War II.

Part 1 (Chapters 3-5) discusses the Reagan administration's initial handling of the Taiwan issue from 1981-1983. Chapter 3 describes how Reagan's presidential campaign statements in support of "official" relations with Taiwan soured Sino-American relations for much of his first term in office. During this period, the issue of U.S. arms sales to Taiwan became the focal point of contention between Washington and Beijing. The origins of this issue are discussed, as well as crucial changes in the PRC's strategic perceptions.

Chapter 4 considers the important issue of China's military threat to Taiwan. Such an assessment is necessary because the Taiwan Relations Act (TRA) requires the U.S. to sell arms to Taiwan to help deter a PRC use of force to achieve reunification. Beijing considers U.S. arms sales "interference in China's internal affairs," while the U.S. regards such sales as a way of maintaining peace and stability in the Taiwan Strait. The military threat to Taiwan is examined both from the military capabilities and political intentions points of view.

Chapter 5 analyzes two critical decisions over arms sales by the Reagan administration in 1982: the January decision not to sell Taiwan an advanced fighter, and the August agreement to a joint communiqué with the PRC in which the U.S. promised to limit future arms sales to Taiwan in exchange for Beijing's pursuit of a peaceful resolution of the reunification issue. These decisions represented major concessions on the part of the Reagan administration to preserve friendly Sino-American relations and to enhance U.S.-PRC strategic cooperation against the Soviet Union.

Part 2 (Chapters 6-8) discusses the reunification policies of Beijing and Taipei. These Chinese policies are important to U.S. reunification policy, because the goal of U.S. policy is a peaceful resolution of differences between China and Taiwan.

Chapter 6 reviews Beijing's proposals for peaceful reunification since 1979, as well as its periodic threats to resolve the issue by force if Taipei does not respond favorably. Chapter 7 examines the ROC's own proposals for reunification. It explains the rationale behind Taiwan's official policy of no contact, no compromise, and no negotiations with the communist regime on the mainland. The growing influence of Taiwanese in ROC politics is assessed for its impact on the reunification issue. Chapter 8 reviews the increased contacts in recent years between the two Chinese sides, a development which influences U.S. policy options.

Part 3 (Chapters 9-11) examines the evolution of U.S. reunification policy from 1984 to 1987. Chapter 9 discusses the impact of the 1984 Sino-British agreement over the future of Hong Kong. This agreement set forth in specific terms Deng Xiaoping's proposal for "one country, two systems" as a solution for China's reunification. Following the signing of the Hong Kong agreement, Deng requested the U.S. to "do something" to help China's reunification. A summary of the resulting review of U.S. policy is included.

Chapter 10 introduces the Soviet factor in U.S. reunification policy. U.S. security concerns over the Soviet penetration of the Asia/Pacific region are noted, as well as the impact of Mikhail Gorbachev's July 1986 speech in Vladivostok. His speech resulted in a further reexamination of U.S. policy toward China and Taiwan. Chapter 11 examines the gradual adjustment of U.S. reunification policy toward more active support for increased contacts between the two Chinese sides.

Part 4 contains concluding Chapters 12 and 13. Chapter 12 considers alternative futures for Taiwan and various U.S. policy options in response to these scenarios. Chapter 13 draws several conclusions which might be useful to U.S. policymakers as they attempt to manage the reunification issue.

Executive Summary

A concise statement of the Reagan administration's policy toward the reunification of China was made by Gaston J. Sigur, Assistant Secretary of State for East Asian and Pacific Affairs, before the World Affairs Council of San Francisco on December 11, 1986. Dr. Sigur said:

> Some have urged the U.S. Government to become involved in efforts to promote peaceful resolution of the differences between Beijing and Taipei. However, there is a real danger that American involvement would be counterproductive. For at least two decades, we have viewed this issue as an internal matter for the PRC and Taiwan to resolve themselves.

We will not serve as an intermediary or pressure Taiwan on the matter.
We leave it up to both sides to settle their differences; our predominant
interest is that the settlement be a peaceful one.[1]

The policy described by Sigur is one of the most delicately balanced
American foreign policy positions to be found on any issue. Since the
early 1970s the U.S. has disclaimed a role in China's reunification and
left the matter for the Chinese to decide. Toward this end Washington
has pursued simultaneously friendly relations with the PRC on the
mainland and with the ROC on Taiwan. After 1979 those relations were
formalized diplomatically with the PRC, and legalized domestically
with the people of Taiwan through the Taiwan Relations Act (TRA).
When President Ronald Reagan assumed office in January 1981, he
maintained existing U.S. China policy, including its policy toward the
reunification of Taiwan and the mainland.

There are many indications which point to the success of U.S.
reunification policy since 1981. American businessmen actively trade
with and invest in both the mainland and Taiwan. Chinese students
and scholars from both sides of the Taiwan Strait routinely meet on
U.S. campuses and in research institutions. The PRC no longer is
considered an enemy of the U.S., and elements of the U.S. Seventh
Fleet have even called at a mainland Chinese port. By insisting that
U.S. interests are tied to a peaceful resolution of the issue, the U.S.
helps to deter a possible PRC use of force against Taiwan and thus
reduces regional tensions. As American friends of the ROC have become
convinced that Taiwan would receive adequate U.S. weapons to defend
itself, China policy has faded as an issue in American domestic politics.
In Asia and throughout most of the world, governments friendly to the
U.S. have adopted models similar to the TRA to serve their political
and commercial interests by maintaining ties with both Chinese governments.

Yet, as Dr. Sigur hinted in his remarks, there are some who advocate
a change in U.S. reunification policy. Arguments for change suggest
that Sino-American relations would improve significantly if Washington
played a more active role in helping to resolve the reunification issue.
Usually this role is described as convincing Taipei to be more receptive
to PRC proposals for peaceful reunification. Ways to do this range from
using friendly persuasion to applying pressure by withholding arms
sales.

Advocacy of a change in U.S. reunification policy has mounted since
1982 when relations between the PRC and the Soviet Union began to
improve. Since 1969 one of the most important U.S. motivations for
normalizing relations with Beijing has been the expectation that a

friendly China would play a larger role in deterring Soviet expansion in Asia. U.S. leaders have hoped to complicate Soviet strategy by confronting Moscow with the possibility of having to fight simultaneously the U.S., China, Japan, and Western Europe. The key steps taken to advance U.S.-PRC relations have been in pursuit of these strategic objectives, including President Richard Nixon's opening to China in 1969-1972; President Jimmy Carter's normalization of diplomatic relations with Beijing in 1978-1979; and President Ronald Reagan's approval of the August 17, 1982, U.S.-PRC Joint Communiqué limiting future U.S. arms sales to Taiwan.

Since about September 1982, the PRC has pursued an "independent" foreign policy calling for the partial cooling of relations with the U.S. and a willingness to improve relations with the Soviet Union. Although Beijing continued to "lean" in the direction of the U.S. because of the more immediate Soviet threat around China's borders, the PRC's adoption of its independent foreign policy resulted in a fairly wide consensus within the U.S. that further concessions over Taiwan should not be made.

But since the December 1984 signing of the Sino-British accord returning Hong Kong to Chinese sovereignty in 1997, the PRC has mounted a sustained effort to convince the Reagan administration to "do something" to help resolve the reunification issue. In early 1985 the Reagan administration seriously considered a message from Chinese leader Deng Xiaoping to this effect. However, little positive response was forthcoming from Washington at that time.

Soviet General Secretary Mikhail Gorbachev's speech in Vladivostok in July 1986 caused another examination of U.S. reunification policy. The Soviet Union launched a series of diplomatic moves designed to match Moscow's military presence in Asia with political and economic influence. A key component of Gorbachev's *glasnost* in Asia was major improvement in Sino-Soviet relations. Several initiatives were made in that direction, particularly on symbolic issues such as border talks, acceptance of the other's system as being truly "socialist," and discussion of the "three obstacles" in Sino-Soviet relations (the Soviet occupation of Afghanistan, Soviet forces along the Sino-Soviet and Sino-Mongolian borders, and Soviet backing of the Vietnamese occupation of Cambodia).

The Soviet peace offensive in Asia raised arguments that Washington should attempt to improve Sino-American relations by removing the Taiwan obstacle. Although most U.S. policymakers rejected the argument, many Chinese analysts on Taiwan and the mainland believed this consideration may have led Secretary of State George Shultz to say in Shanghai on March 5, 1987: "We support a continuing evolutionary process toward a peaceful resolution of the Taiwan issue. . . . We have welcomed developments, including indirect trade and increasing human interchange, which have contributed to a relaxation of tensions in the Taiwan Strait."[2]

The State Department quickly denied that Shultz's remarks implied a change in U.S. reunification policy. Nonetheless, his statement did indicate U.S. approval of increased contact between the two sides. Beijing saw this as a nod in the direction of its proposals for peaceful reunification, while observers in Taipei perceived a subtle hint that the U.S. wanted steps taken to resolve the outstanding differences between the two Chinese sides.

Whether the Secretary's remarks heralded an eventual shift in U.S. reunification policy is difficult to say. Interviews with key government officials closely involved with U.S. China policy suggest that President Reagan will not play a role in China's reunification.[3] But, as the Secretary noted in Shanghai, the situation between the two sides of the Taiwan Strait "has not and cannot remain static." Although Shultz said that "our policy has been constant" and that the pace of the reunification issue "will be determined by the Chinese on either side of the Taiwan Strait, free of outside pressure," the fact remains that U.S. interests require a continuous weighing of the costs and benefits of maintaining current policy.

The analysis presented in the following chapters suggests that U.S. reunification policy will not be changed except under certain circumstances. Principally, these would include a major change in the reunification policy of either Beijing or Taipei. The PRC, for example, might elect to use force to compel Taiwan to negotiate. Under these circumstances, the U.S. might find it appropriate to support a move toward Taiwan's independence. On the other hand, Taipei might request U.S. assistance in arranging a negotiated settlement between the two Chinese sides. In this instance, the U.S. might be willing either to act as a mediator or to guarantee the final reunification settlement. But current trends in the PRC, ROC, and the U.S. suggest that, for the foreseeable future at least, U.S. interests are best served by maintaining its current reunification policy and by sustaining the status quo in the Taiwan Strait.

Notes

1. Gaston J. Sigur, Jr., "China Policy Today: Consensus, Consistence, Stability," U.S. Department of State, *Current Policy,* No. 901 (December 1986), p. 4.

2. "Remarks by the Honorable George P. Shultz, Secretary of State, Shanghai Banquet, Shanghai, China, March 5, 1987," Department of State, *Press Release,* No. 59 (March 10, 1987), p. 3.

3. Interviews by author in Washington, D.C., March 1987.

2

Origins of
U.S. Reunification Policy

This chapter presents a brief historical overview of U.S. relations with China through 1979. It introduces many of the factors which relate to U.S. reunification policy, including the long struggle for control of China between the Nationalist Kuomintang (KMT) and the Communist Party of China (CPC), the history of friendly ties between the U.S. and the Republic of China (ROC), China policy as an issue in U.S. domestic politics, the close relationship between China's domestic and foreign policies, Sino-Soviet relations, and the slow evolution of American perceptions of the People's Republic of China (PRC) from an enemy of the U.S. to a strategic partner to contain Soviet expansion.

The historical record shows a series of twists and turns in U.S. policy toward China and its reunification with Taiwan. This reflects not so much inconsistency on the part of the U.S. as strong disagreement over the proper U.S. relationship with Beijing and Taipei. The origins of this disagreement stem from early U.S. relations with China.

Historical Background

Early U.S.-China Relations

U.S. contact with China dates back to 1784, when the American ship "Empress of China" arrived to trade in the middle of the Qing dynasty (1644-1911).[1] Because the U.S. was a latecomer to the China trade, American interests were in securing equal access to Chinese markets. Decades of effort finally bore fruit during the late nineteenth century, when Secretary of State John Hay played a leading role in the "Open Door Policy" in China. Under the "Open Door," foreign nations received equal opportunity for trade with China and promised to respect China's territorial and administrative integrity.

ι large extent, it was the "Open Door Policy" which prevented
.... from being carved up into several colonies controlled by Europe,
Russia, and Japan. The greatest resistance to the "Open Door" was
Japan. In 1908 and 1909 the U.S. attempted unsuccessfully to convince
Japan to accept the "Open Door" principle in Manchuria. Japan earlier
had seized Korea and Taiwan from China as a result of its victories
in the 1894-1895 Sino-Japanese War.

The desire for trading profits dominated U.S. interests in early relations
with China. But there was a strong moral element to U.S. involvement
with China as well. The first American missionaries arrived in 1811.
Although relatively few in number, they became enormously influential
in Chinese intellectual circles and in forming American perceptions
of China. Virtually every denomination had its China mission society,
and U.S. congregations received periodic missionary reports praising
the good qualities of the Chinese people and pointing to their desperate
need for food, medicine, and modern education. Of particular importance were the many mission-run schools and universities established
throughout China. These schools became the primary means whereby
Chinese intellectuals learned about western thought.

The U.S. military also had a role in early Sino-American relations.
U.S. forces regularly protected American traders and missionaries, and
a sizeable contingent of Marines was deployed to assist in the suppression
of the Boxer Rebellion in 1900. Most of the money received by the
U.S. as indemnity for the Boxer Rebellion was used to educate Chinese
students in the U.S.

The most emotional issue in early Sino-American relations was
Chinese immigration into the U.S. Thousands of Chinese were recruited
to help build the first transcontinental railways across the U.S. during
the 1850s and 1860s. Violent agitation against the Chinese led Congress
in the 1880s to pass a series of laws restricting further immigration
and requiring resident Chinese to register and carry identification.
Angered by this discrimination, Chinese students led boycotts against
American goods in China during the early part of this century.

Founding of the Republic of China

One Chinese student educated in Hawaii was Dr. Sun Yat-sen. After
ten futile attempts, he and other revolutionaries, including a young
military cadet trained in Japan named Chiang Kai-shek, overthrew the
Qing dynasty in October 1911. Dr. Sun was elected provisional president
of the Republic of China in January 1912. He organized the Kuomintang
(KMT) in August to consolidate the various Chinese revolutionary
parties then in existence.

The KMT's ideology was Dr. Sun's *San Min Chu-i,* or Three Principles of the People (nationalism, democracy, and social welfare). The structure of the government was a mixture of western institutions (executive, legislative, and judicial branches) and traditional Chinese institutions (examination branch to select the civil service and control branch to enforce standards of behavior among officials). Dr. Sun theorized that the ROC would go through three stages of development: military dictatorship, political tutelage under the KMT, and constitutional democracy.

A few months after being named provisional president, Dr. Sun resigned to allow a central government to be formed in Beijing under warlord Yuan Shih-kai. Yuan became a dictator and attempted to reestablish the monarchy with himself as emperor. He dissolved the KMT and sent its members into exile. Yuan died in 1916, but most western governments, including the U.S., recognized the Beijing regime as the legitimate government of China.

During World War I, the U.S. tried to help Beijing reject the Twenty-One Demands of Japan, which would have made China a Japanese protectorate. The Chinese government secretly accepted Japan's claim to Shandong province, however. When this became public at the close of the war, massive student protests against the Beijing government and the Japanese occurred on May 4, 1919. The May Fourth Movement rekindled enthusiasm for Dr. Sun's republican revolution, but led other Chinese to explore communism as a solution to China's problems.

Not finding support for his cause among the western democracies, Dr. Sun turned to the newly established Soviet Union. In 1923 Michael Borodin and other Soviet Comintern agents arrived to assist both the KMT and the recently founded Communist Party of China (CPC). At Soviet urging, the KMT and CPC entered into their first period of cooperation from 1923-1927 to defeat the warlords and unite China. The Soviet advisers sent Chiang Kai-shek to Moscow for military training. Chiang returned to China late in 1923 and established the Whampoa Military Academy in Guangzhou, the seat of the KMT-CPC alliance. Chiang became head of the KMT following Dr. Sun's death in 1925 and relocated the ROC capital to Nanjing.

Chiang moved against the northern warlords in 1926, gradually expanding ROC control over most of the country. In June 1928 Beijing was captured by the Nationalists. On June 25, 1928, the U.S. became the first country to recognize Chiang's Nanjing government as the national government of the Republic of China. Unification of the country under the ROC was completed by the end of the year.

In 1927 Chiang decided to rid the KMT of the communists. He launched a series of campaigns which nearly destroyed the CPC. Chiang's relentless attacks forced the communists to undertake the arduous Long March of 1934-1935, in which a small remnant under Mao Zedong finally escaped to Yan'an (Yenan) in southern Shaanxi province. While Mao worked out his ideology and gradually expanded his base of support, Chiang turned to the new threat from Japan.

Japanese Invasion of China

In 1931 Japan initiated its seizure of Manchuria. The following year Manchukuo was declared an independent state under Japan's protection. The U.S. refused to recognize the territorial change. Undeterred by American protests, the Japanese moved to establish a demilitarized area in China stretching from the Great Wall to the outskirts of Beijing and from the coast 250 miles inland. Full-scale war between China and Japan broke out in July 1937, following a clash of troops at the Marco Polo Bridge outside of Beijing.

In December 1936 Chiang Kai-shek was kidnapped by one of his generals and held captive in Xian to force him to work with the communists to fight the Japanese. Chiang finally agreed, and from 1937-1945 the KMT and CPC had a second period of cooperation. Throughout the war with Japan, however, the KMT and CPC attacked each other as well as the Japanese.

The internecine struggle between the Chinese was a source of great frustration to the U.S., which entered the war against Japan in December 1941. Throughout the war, one of the aims of the U.S. was to bring about a cessation of hostilities between the Nationalists and the communists.

Despite disagreement with Chiang over how to deal with the communists, the U.S. and the ROC became firm allies during World War II. U.S. military aid began in February 1942. In January 1943 the U.S. relinquished extraterritorial and related rights in China, and in December President Franklin D. Roosevelt repealed discriminatory legislation aimed at Chinese immigration. At U.S. insistence, China was accepted as a "great power" in Allied strategy. In the Cairo Declaration of December 1943, the ROC was promised that Manchuria, Formosa (Taiwan), and the Pescadores would be returned to China at the conclusion of the war. The Republic of China became one of five permanent members of the Security Council of the United Nations, formed in June 1945.

But American decisions in Asia were not always beneficial to the ROC. In the February 1945 Yalta agreement the U.S. ceded Outer Mongolia to the Soviet Union, along with strategic ports and railroads in Manchuria, in exchange for Moscow's entering the war against Japan.

The ROC was not party to the Yalta agreement, but accepted it following the Japanese surrender on August 14. Port Arthur became a Soviet naval base. The decision to allow Moscow to manage Manchurian railways proved costly to the war-torn Nationalist government. The Soviets stripped Manchuria of its industrial equipment and allowed the Chinese communists to arm themselves with the military equipment surrendered by the Japanese.

Resumption of the Chinese Civil War

Despite a brief truce arranged by the U.S. in October 1945, fighting resumed between the Nationalists and the communists at the close of World War II. In November U.S. Ambassador Patrick J. Hurley resigned to protest a U.S. decision to stop military aid to Chiang in an attempt to end the civil war. Hurley later testified to Congress that several members of the State Department supported the communists in China and worked to undermine U.S. China policy. Also in November, President Harry S Truman appointed General George C. Marshall as his special representative to China.

Marshall negotiated another truce between the two sides in early 1946. However, fighting broke out in Manchuria as Soviet troops withdrew. Throughout the year, U.S. mediated truces were broken repeatedly. When Chiang convened a National Assembly in Nanjing in November 1946 to adopt a ROC constitution, the communists boycotted the meeting. Their chief negotiator, Zhou Enlai, told Marshall that the CPC would not negotiate with Chiang until the Assembly was dissolved and Nationalist troops withdrawn to earlier positions. Marshall tried unsuccessfully to convince Chiang that a military victory was impossible and that the only way to bring peace to China was through a negotiated settlement.

In January 1947 Truman recalled Marshall and named him Secretary of State. Marshall reported that the breakdown in KMT-CPC negotiations had been caused by mutual suspicion and radicals on both sides. The U.S. announced that its efforts to mediate a settlement would cease and that all remaining U.S. military personnel would be withdrawn from China. During the remainder of the year, the U.S. cut and then resumed military aid to the Nationalists several times.

The situation in China became increasingly desperate. Hyperinflation completely undermined the ROC economy. In December 1946 it took more than 1 million Chinese yuan to buy what had cost 1 yuan in 1937. By December 1947 the cost was nearly 17 million yuan. The following December the cost was 21.5 billion yuan. In March 1949 it took 2.4 *trillion* yuan to purchase the equivalent of 1 yuan in 1937.[2] In the face of this economic disaster, U.S. aid was insignificant.

The Nationalists suffered repeated military defeats in 1948 as the communists seized the offensive and annihilated ROC divisions in Manchuria and other parts of Northern China. Chiang asked for much greater U.S. military and economic assistance. After review, the U.S. concluded that the cost to rescue the Nationalists would be too great, even if the estimated $5 billion were properly utilized. The ROC had received more than $2.5 billion in U.S. aid since World War II, but had not listened to Marshall and other American advisers. Moreover, the Nationalist armies seemed to be demoralized. Only direct U.S. military intervention would save the ROC and this the U.S. was unwilling to do.

In January 1949 the Nationalists appealed to the U.S. and other western governments to mediate peace with the communists. The U.S. refused to become involved, and the communists announced in any case that they intended to finish the fight rather than negotiate. Beijing fell the same month. The Yangtze River was crossed in April; Nanjing, Wuhan, and Shanghai fell in April and May. On October 1, 1949, Mao announced the establishment of the People's Republic of China (PRC) with Beijing as its capital. Later that month Canton fell, and Chongqing fell in November. In late December Chiang Kai-shek arrived in Taiwan to join the remnants of his military and civilian government. It appeared certain that the communists would soon attack Taiwan and destroy the Nationalists altogether.

Controversy over U.S. China Policy, 1949-1950

In the face of this disaster, an acrimonious debate broke out between the Truman administration and Congress over who was at fault for the "loss" of China. In August 1949 the State Department issued a White Paper on China policy in which it blamed the collapse of the Nationalist regime to inefficiency on the part of the Chiang government. The State Department said no amount of U.S. aid could have deterred a communist victory. The State Department released a further memorandum in December which stated that Taiwan was of no military significance to the U.S.

In January 1950 Truman announced that no additional U.S. aid would be sent to the Nationalists on Taiwan. Also in January Secretary of State Dean Acheson defended his China policy and declared that the U.S. was willing to defend a line which ran from the Aleutian Islands to Japan, the Ryukyu Islands, and the Philippines. Excluded were both Taiwan and Korea. Meanwhile, the administration sent several signals to the PRC that it would consider establishing diplomatic relations.

The State Department's China policy came under heavy attack in the Congress, which appropriated emergency funds for the Nationalists. Individual congressmen pleaded that American troops be sent into China to stop the communists. Many congressmen urged the President not to recognize the new Beijing government because of a series of incidents involving American diplomatic personnel. In April 1949 communist troops pulled U.S. Ambassador John Leighton Stuart out of his bed at the Embassy for questioning. They also held American Consulate General Angus Ward in Mukden under house arrest for nearly a year. In January 1950 the communists seized the American consulate in Beijing.

Congress stepped up its criticism of U.S. China policy after a 30-year Sino-Soviet Treaty of Friendship, Alliance, and Mutual Assistance was signed in February 1950. The following month, Senator Joseph R. McCarthy began to attack by name alleged communists in the State Department and in the American academic community he felt were responsible for the loss of China to the communists.

These recriminations were overshadowed dramatically on June 25, 1950, when North Korea launched a surprise invasion of South Korea. Later that afternoon, while the Soviet Union boycotted Security Council meetings in an attempt to have the PRC seated in place of the ROC, the U.N. Security Council adopted a resolution calling for a cease fire and withdrawal of North Korean troops. The resolution also called on member nations to assist the U.N. in the implementation of the resolution.

Two days later, prompted by concerns that the Korean War might expand and that Beijing might use Taiwan to threaten the U.S. position in Japan, Truman sent the Seventh Fleet into the Taiwan Strait to prevent either Chinese side from attacking the other. In his statement of June 27, 1950, Truman said:

The attack upon Korea makes it plain beyond all doubt that communism has passed beyond the use of subversion to conquer independent nations and will use armed invasion and war. It has defied the orders of the Security Council of the United Nations issued to preserve international peace and security. In these circumstances, the occupation of Formosa by communist forces would be a direct threat to the security of the Pacific area and to the United States forces performing their lawful and necessary functions in that area.

Accordingly, I have ordered the Seventh Fleet to prevent any attack on Formosa. As a corollary of this action, I am calling upon the Chinese Government on Formosa to cease all air and sea operations against the mainland. The Seventh Fleet will see that this is done. The determination of the future status of Formosa must await the restoration of security in the Pacific, a peace settlement with Japan, or consideration by the United Nations.[3]

Truman's decision to interpose the Seventh Fleet between Taiwan and China was a crucial turning point in U.S. policy toward China. Immediately following Chiang's retreat to Taiwan, the U.S. determined that an invasion of Taiwan by the communists was imminent and that American forces would not intervene in that outcome. With the outbreak of the Korean War, however, Taiwan instantly became important to protect the southern flank of U.S. war efforts in Northeast Asia. For the next several decades, the prevention of Beijing's takeover of Taiwan became an important element of U.S. global strategy to contain communism.

Taiwan and the U.S. Strategy of Containment

With the entry of the PRC into the Korean conflict in October 1950, U.S. hostility toward Beijing became firm policy.[4] In December 1950 Truman froze PRC assets in the U.S. and imposed an embargo on U.S. trade with China. The embargo remained in effect until 1971 when it was lifted by President Nixon.

As part of its strategy to contain the PRC, Washington increased political, economic, and military ties to Taiwan. Total U.S. aid from 1949 exceeded $5.9 billion, including $1.7 billion in economic assistance and $4.2 billion in military assistance.[5] The United States ended economic assistance to the ROC in 1965 and phased out all military aid in the mid-1970s.

In April 1951 the U.S. appointed a Military Assistance Advisory Group for Taiwan and resumed direct military aid to the Nationalists. In May Assistant Secretary of State for Far Eastern Affairs Dean Rusk told Congress that the U.S. recognized the ROC as the legitimate government of China, not the Beijing regime. But Truman was careful not to widen the war in Asia. He turned down Chiang's offer to send Nationalist troops to help fight in Korea and rejected General Douglas MacArthur's suggestion that Chiang be allowed to attack Chinese positions on the mainland. MacArthur was a strong advocate of the strategic importance of Taiwan to the U.S. He urged that Taiwan be turned into a U.S. defense stronghold and called Taiwan an "unsinkable aircraft" carrier.

China policy was a heated issue in the 1952 presidential campaign, as it was during the campaigns of 1956, 1960, 1964, 1968, and 1980. (The issue was muted in the presidential elections of 1972, 1976, 1984, and 1988.) Truman's policy toward China in the late 1940s, his pursuit of limited objectives in the Korean War, and his unpopular dismissal of General MacArthur in April 1951 led to intense criticism of his foreign policy. Congress held several hearings on U.S. Asian policy denouncing the administration's record. China's image in the U.S. was further blackened by the 1950-1951 invasion of Tibet and Beijing's statements at the U.N. to the effect that it intended to "liberate" Taiwan and to aid the communists in Indochina, the Philippines, and Japan.

The Republicans under Dwight D. Eisenhower campaigned on a tough anti-communist theme, winning the presidency and both Houses of Congress. President Eisenhower announced in his first State of the Union Message that the Seventh Fleet no longer would prevent the Nationalists from attacking the mainland. This announcement, coupled with his July 1953 threat to use nuclear weapons against China, were thought to pressure Beijing into signing a July 27 armistice ending the Korean War.

As the Korean War ended, however, a new crisis arose in French Indochina. The communist Viet Minh launched their attack against French forces at Dienbienphu in March 1954 and overran the garrison in May. Although the U.S. funded much of the French effort in Indochina, the Eisenhower administration turned down French requests to intervene militarily. Nonetheless, the Viet Minh victory in Indochina was viewed as a threat to U.S. security interests in Southeast Asia. In September 1954 Secretary of State John Foster Dulles, after participating in the Geneva Conference ending the French Indochina War, helped to create the Southeast Asian Treaty Organization (SEATO, or the Manila Treaty). The alliance, designed to shore up the defenses of Southeast Asia against communist expansion, was part of U.S. efforts to isolate and contain China.

Taiwan was brought formally into the U.S. collective defense system and made part of U.S. containment strategy in December 1954, when the two countries signed the U.S.-ROC Mutual Defense Treaty. The treaty followed similar agreements with the Philippines, South Korea, and Japan. The U.S.-ROC treaty was signed in response to a September 1954 PRC attack against Quemoy and other offshore islands. The treaty gave the U.S. "the right to dispose such land, air and sea forces in and about Taiwan and the Pescadores as may be required for their defense." In an exchange of notes in January 1955, the ROC assured the U.S. that it would not attack the mainland without prior consultation with Washington.

The ROC territory defined under the Mutual Defense Treaty included the islands of Taiwan and the Pescadores (Penghu), but did not include the offshore islands of Quemoy (Kinmen) and Matsu (Mazu). The exclusion of these small islands, located a few miles off the coast of

China, reflected U.S. reluctance to go to war with the PRC over Quemoy. In fact, the U.S. attempted unsuccessfully to convince Chiang Kai-shek to abandon the islands.

On January 29, 1955, Congress passed the Formosa Resolution. Until its repeal in 1974, this resolution gave the President the authority to defend Quemoy and Matsu if he felt it necessary for the security of Taiwan and the Pescadores. In practice, the U.S. has viewed any attack against Quemoy and Matsu as a threat to Taiwan. American support was given to the ROC during the Quemoy crises of 1954, 1958, and 1962.

The U.S. response to the 1958 Chinese attack was decisive. Six aircraft carriers were deployed to the region and nuclear capable howitzers were sent to the Quemoy garrisons. Soon thereafter, the PRC commenced shelling of Quemoy on alternate days. Unlike the first Quemoy crisis, the U.S. did not pressure the ROC to abandon the offshore islands. It did, however, secure from Chiang a pledge to use political rather than military means to recover the mainland.

During the 1962 Quemoy crisis, President John F. Kennedy reaffirmed U.S. policy to "defend Quemoy and Matsu if there were an attack which was part of an attack on Formosa and the Pescadores."[6]

Taiwan and the Vietnam War

Like many other aspects of U.S. foreign policy, the Vietnam War proved to be a turning point in U.S. policy toward China and Taiwan. Prior to the war, the U.S. considered its relations with Taiwan to be essential to American objectives to contain China. By the war's conclusion, the U.S. had come to view friendly relations with the PRC as a strategic asset in U.S.-Soviet competition. This was an era in which the U.S. attempted to pursue a "two Chinas" policy recognizing both Beijing and Taipei as legitimate governments of two separate nations.

In 1961 the U.S. had 685 military advisers in South Vietnam, but assessments of Saigon's ability to handle the growing communist threat were pessimistic. As the U.S. military buildup continued in 1962, the Chinese began to warn that the American military presence in South Vietnam was a threat to Hanoi and seriously affected China's security. The Kennedy administration replied that it was drawing the line in South Vietnam against communist expansion in Asia and that the war was one the U.S. could not afford to lose. Following Kennedy's assassination in 1963, President Lyndon B. Johnson increased the U.S. military commitment to Saigon. By 1964 more than 21,000 U.S. troops were in the country. China again warned that any attack against North Vietnam would threaten Chinese security and that China would defend North Vietnam.

In the wake of the August 1964 Tonkin Gulf incident, the U.S. began a massive buildup in Indochina and commenced periodic bombing against North Vietnam. Taiwan at this time became an important logistics and recreation and rehabilitation center for U.S. war efforts, as well as a key listening post for gathering intelligence on the PRC. The U.S. called the Vietnam conflict the key to stopping communist expansion in Asia. Richard Nixon said the war was between the U.S. and China. Johnson described the war as part of China's larger purposes to spread violence on every continent. For its part, Beijing pictured the U.S. war effort as being directed primarily against China and argued that Vietnam was a testing ground for people's war. Although neither the U.S. nor China wanted to fight each other, each saw the Vietnam conflict as a test of its will. By the end of 1965 the U.S. troop commitment was over 70,000.

The rapid military buildup in Indochina and the bombing of North Vietnam sparked domestic criticism of U.S. policy in Asia. Since one of the main objectives of the U.S. war effort was to contain China, considerable attention focused on American policy toward China.

In March 1966 the Senate Foreign Relations Committee held hearings on U.S. China policy. The conclusion of most witnesses was that the U.S. policy of containing China in the hope of bringing about a collapse of the communist regime had failed. Strong recommendations were made that the U.S. should begin to look for ways to increase non-diplomatic contact with the PRC as a way of bringing China out of isolation into the international community. Some scholars felt that China should be seated in the U.N. and that official U.S. relations with the PRC should be established. Few argued, however, that U.S. ties to Taiwan should be severed.

During these hearings, Secretary of State Dean Rusk listed key elements of U.S. China policy. These included: firmness in assisting allied nations against Chinese aggression; honoring commitments to defend the ROC; prevention of the expulsion of the ROC from the U.N. and opposition to the PRC's membership; assurance to Beijing that the U.S. did not intend to attack the mainland; enlargement of possibilities for unofficial contact between the U.S. and China; and continued diplomatic contact with the PRC in ambassadorial talks in Warsaw.

In response to increased pressure for a change in policy toward the PRC, the administration sought alternative suggestions. One of the most popular ideas was that the U.S. should follow a "two Chinas" policy of dual diplomatic recognition and dual representation in the

U.N. The objective was to bring China out of isolation yet maintain U.S. commitments to Taiwan. When the suggestion of "two Chinas" was raised to the Chiang government, however, the ROC rejected the idea.

In 1967 the Warsaw meetings increased in frequency, as both the U.S. and China clarified their objectives in Vietnam so as to avoid an unintentional Sino-American war. But all U.S. efforts to increase academic and other exchanges with China were rejected by Beijing, which was in the throes of the Cultural Revolution.

The year 1968 was critical to the evolution of U.S. China policy. In January the Tet Offensive was mounted, causing President Johnson to announce that he would not run for reelection. The offensive gave the North Vietnamese a major psychological victory by disproving administration claims that the war was winding down. Domestic opposition to the war swelled on campuses around the nation. Presidential candidates from both parties urged China to change its isolationist policy and said that they were eager to have more contact with China. This in fact is what President Richard Nixon did after assuming office in January 1969.

Before examining Nixon's historic overtures to China in 1969-1972, however, it is important to note two factors which had enormous impact on U.S. China policy: the close relationship between China's domestic and foreign policies, and the Sino-Soviet split. Certain conditions had to exist in both of these areas before Sino-American rapprochement was possible.

PRC Domestic and Foreign Policies

There generally is a close correlation between Chinese internal politics and its external policies, particularly in regards to Sino-American relations and the Taiwan issue. This certainly was the case between 1949 and 1968.

From the founding of the PRC in 1949 through the Korean War and the 1954 Quemoy crisis, China viewed the U.S. as its principal enemy and pursued a policy of military liberation of Taiwan. This was a period of intense persecution of the bourgeoisie on the mainland and successive campaigns to eliminate all opposition to communist rule.

From 1955 to the second Quemoy crisis in 1958, the PRC entertained relatively moderate policies both internally and externally. This was particularly true in 1956 when Beijing introduced the "Hundred Flowers" policy in which criticism of the CPC and alternative policy suggestions were encouraged. Major efforts by Secretary-General Deng Xiaoping were made to bring intellectuals into the government and party. Chinese leaders were shocked by the extent of the criticisms, however, and by 1957 renewed the anti-rightist campaigns.

During the "Hundred Flowers," China's moderate domestic policies were reflected in a more moderate foreign policy. In April 1955 China participated in the Bandung Conference in Indonesia. Zhou Enlai enunciated the "Five Principles of Peaceful Coexistence," earlier agreed to by India and China in 1954. The "Five Principles," which later were incorporated in U.S. communiqués with China, included mutual respect for each other's territorial integrity and sovereignty; non-aggression; non-interference in each other's internal affairs; equality and mutual benefit; and peaceful coexistence.

From 1955 until 1958, China expressed a desire to negotiate with the U.S. to reduce tensions in Asia. The U.S. response was favorable, but only if the talks included the ROC as an equal participant. Beijing rejected this condition as one leading to "two Chinas." However, the U.S. and China agreed to meet privately at the ambassadorial level in Geneva and later in Warsaw. In the discussions both sides expressed a desire to renounce the use of force in the region. The U.S. intended that to include Taiwan, but the PRC specifically excluded Taiwan because it was an "internal affair." Given this fundamental disagreement, little progress was made in the ambassadorial talks, although the PRC referred to the "peaceful liberation" of Taiwan rather than its "military liberation."

One effect of the more moderate PRC foreign policy was U.S. domestic pressure on Dulles to allow American reporters to visit China. A few calls for admission of China into the U.N. were heard as well, along with proposals to lift the U.S. trade embargo and to establish diplomatic relations with Beijing.

China's renewed anti-rightist campaigns in 1957 and the introduction of the disastrous "Great Leap Forward" economic policy in 1958-1960 made the U.S. cautious about moving too quickly toward improved relations with Beijing. The Chinese attack against Quemoy in August 1958 reinforced this caution. During the "Great Leap Forward," in which the PRC tried to communize China overnight, Beijing's policies were intensely anti-American. Chinese relations with the Soviet Union began to deteriorate as well.

Between 1961 and 1965 China attempted to recover from the ill-effects of the "Great Leap Forward." Deng in particular played an important role in improving the quality of party leadership. Relations with the U.S. were strained over the growing American presence in Indochina and by the third Quemoy crisis in 1962. Nonetheless, the U.S. and China maintained a dialogue in Warsaw which increased mutual understanding and helped clarify each other's intentions in

Indochina. China was active in international affairs during this period. Although little movement occurred in Sino-American relations, the U.S. opened the door to the possibility of improved relations if China would change its policies. By late 1963 the U.S. concluded that its policy of isolating China had not worked and that the communist regime would not collapse. During this period the idea of "two Chinas" gained strong support in the U.S.

Hope for improved Sino-American relations were dashed during the "Great Proletarian Cultural Revolution," which began in 1966. China isolated itself during the initial stages of this upheaval, withdrawing all but one of its ambassadors from abroad. During the domestic crisis, the PRC's political and economic systems were nearly destroyed, as well as the communist party itself. Although the U.S. by this time was willing to help China end its isolation, chaos on the mainland prevented meaningful dialogue. The U.S. became more firmly in favor of a "two Chinas" policy. For its part, China became very bellicose against the U.S. and Taiwan, as well as toward the Soviet Union.

In 1968 the Chinese Army began to take over the administrative functions of running China. They put down the radical Red Guards and gradually restored order. The army was under the direction of Defense Minister Lin Biao, who supported wars of national liberation in the Third World to defeat the U.S. Lin was opposed by the more moderate Premier Zhou Enlai. One of the key issues between Lin and Zhou was how to handle the superpowers. Lin wanted to confront militarily both the U.S. and the USSR. Zhou felt that the more dangerous Soviet threat could be blunted through improved relations with the U.S. Mao seemed to vacillate between his two principal advisers, but leaned increasingly in the direction of Zhou.

Chinese foreign policy gradually became more moderate after 1968. By 1971 the PRC press was justifying improving relations with the U.S. on the grounds that the U.S. was now the secondary enemy of China, while the Soviet Union was the primary enemy. As part of its united front strategy, China was ready to ally with all countries opposed to the Soviet Union, including the U.S. Shortly before the trip of President Nixon to China in February 1972, Lin Biao reportedly was killed in an airplane crash attempting to escape from a failed coup attempt against Mao.

Improved Sino-American relations were impossible as long as China pursued radical anti-American policies. The moderation of those policies was made imperative by the growing hostility between China and the Soviet Union.

The Sino-Soviet Split

The breakup of the Sino-Soviet alliance of the early 1950s and the antagonism that developed between the two socialist countries during the 1960s and 1970s were two of the most important geopolitical developments in the post World War II period. They eventually led to the normalization of Sino-American relations in 1979 and the severing of U.S. diplomatic ties to the ROC. In the process, U.S. policy toward China's reunification changed considerably, from recognition of the ROC as the legitimate government of China, to a "two Chinas" policy, to the recognition of the PRC as the sole legal government of China, of which Taiwan was acknowledged to be a part. In the latter policy, the U.S. insisted only that the resolution of the future of Taiwan be achieved peacefully by the Chinese themselves.

The Sino-Soviet split frequently is traced to February 1956, when Soviet First Secretary Nikita S. Khrushchev delivered two important speeches to the 20th Soviet Party Congress. The speeches created a major ideological dispute between Moscow and Beijing. In his February 14 speech Khrushchev said war with the imperialists was no longer inevitable. Instead, the Soviet leader argued that Moscow would use "peaceful coexistence" as the road to power. This contradicted Mao's doctrine of the inevitability of armed struggle between the forces of socialism and imperialism. In his February 24 speech Khrushchev delivered a detailed denunciation of the late Joseph Stalin and his policies. Mao interpreted this as indirect criticism of his own leadership. From 1956 until the early 1980s, the two communist parties bitterly debated which side was the true heir of Marx and Lenin and which was undermining the socialist movement.

In 1958 Moscow became worried that Chinese policies toward the Taiwan issue might draw the Soviet Union into a war with the U.S. Khrushchev refused to support China during its large-scale attack against Quemoy in August 1958. The following year, the Soviets withdrew their 1957 offer to help the PRC develop nuclear weapons. In mid-1960 the Soviet Union began to pull out its advisers from China and terminate joint projects. Moscow refused to help China in its 1962-1963 war with India.

In 1966 Moscow demanded that Beijing allow Soviet arms shipments to pass through Chinese territory on the way to North Vietnam. At first China refused, but the PRC finally agreed when the USSR began to build up its troops along the 7,000 mile Sino-Soviet border. Periodic border skirmishes occurred during the Cultural Revolution. A major military confrontation seemed imminent in 1969. Some 400 border clashes occurred, including serious incidents in March on Zhenbao (Damansky) island in the Ussuri River in which the two sides exchanged ambushes with heavy casualties. To defuse tensions somewhat, China agreed to border talks in October 1969.

In June 1969 the Soviets called for the formation of an Asian collective security system aimed at limiting Chinese influence in Southeast and South Asia. Between 1971-1972 the Soviet Union increased the number of its divisions stationed along the Sino-Soviet border from 30 to 49, nearly one-third of the Soviet army.

China took Soviet efforts to contain the PRC seriously. In 1968 the Soviet Union had invaded Czechoslovakia to bring that country back into the Soviet camp. Soviet leader Leonid Brezhnev spoke of the doctrine of "limited sovereignty," which justified Soviet intervention in fraternal socialist countries when socialism itself came under attack. The Chinese were concerned that the chaos resulting from the Cultural Revolution might led to a Soviet invasion of their own country.

At the same time that Sino-Soviet relations were reaching a point of dangerous confrontation, President Nixon announced that the U.S. was making a fundamental shift in its foreign policy away from confrontation in Asia. In June 1969 Nixon started withdrawing troops from Vietnam. He announced in Guam in July that the U.S. no longer would play the role of global policeman, that the U.S. would reduce its military presence on the Asian mainland, and that it would provide Asian nations with the means to defend themselves. One of the major signals of the end of American animosity toward Beijing was the U.S. refusal to join the Soviets in a preemptive strike against China's nuclear facilities in 1969. Instead, the U.S. warned the Soviets against such a move.

It was the immediacy of the Soviet threat that led Chinese leaders, especially Zhou Enlai, to conclude that China should take advantage of the U.S. willingness to improve relations with the PRC. The strategic aspects of Sino-American relations became paramount in the 1968-1979 period of gradual normalization, although diplomatic relations could not be exchanged for nearly a decade due to domestic political considerations.

Nixon's Overtures to Beijing

One of Nixon's first acts as President was to direct National Security Adviser Henry Kissinger to review U.S. China policy with a view to possible rapprochement. In April 1969 Secretary of State William Rogers announced that the U.S. had come to accept the existence of a communist regime on the mainland and a Nationalist regime on Taiwan as facts of life which the U.S. would not attempt to change. Rogers said that the Nationalists did not represent all of China. He said that the U.S. would take initiatives to begin to improve relations with the mainland.

Despite disagreements over Taiwan, both the U.S. and the PRC decided to make Taiwan a secondary issue and to concentrate instead on the strategic interests of the two countries. The U.S. took several initiatives in 1969 and 1970 to signal its desire to improve relations with China. In July 1969 travel and trade restrictions were eased. A total trade embargo had been in effect since 1950. In November the regular Seventh Fleet patrol of the Taiwan Strait, maintained since June 1950, was ended. In 1970 the Warsaw talks were resumed and trade and travel restrictions eased further. And in a speech in early 1971, Nixon referred to Communist China for the first time by its official name, the People's Republic of China, saying that the U.S. would welcome a constructive role played by the PRC in the international community.

The Chinese demonstrated a willingness to improve relations with the U.S. by a surprise invitation in April 1971 to an American table tennis team to visit China. Most significant was Henry Kissinger's secret trip to China in July 1971, after which Nixon announced that he would visit Beijing at the invitation of the Chinese government in early 1972. Kissinger returned to Beijing in October 1971, at the same time that the U.N. General Assembly voted to expel the ROC and seat instead the PRC.

Not surprisingly, Taipei was very nervous about the turn of events in the Nixon administration. The U.S. kept the ROC in the dark about its specific intentions, but did seek President Chiang Kai-shek's agreement to seat both Chinas in the U.N. According to one ROC diplomat, Chiang was willing to do this,[7] although publicly both Beijing and Taipei harshly criticized the U.S. "two Chinas" policy. In any event, "two Chinas" was short-lived as a policy option after the ROC was expelled from the U.N.

As a result of the U.N. vote and trends toward improved U.S.-PRC relations, most nations switched recognition from Taipei to Beijing. Many countries followed the British model of "acknowledging" rather than "recognizing" the PRC position that Taiwan is part of China. Another innovation was the Japanese model of creating private offices staffed by regular diplomats on temporary leaves of absence to handle unofficial Japan-Taiwan relations after Tokyo severed diplomatic ties with Taipei in 1972.

President Nixon had many incentives to improve Sino-American relations. He believed that an isolated China would be more dangerous to world peace than if it were involved in international affairs. Since

China had joined the nuclear weapons club in 1964, it was felt that Beijing had to be drawn into international disarmament talks. It also appeared as if improved relations with the PRC would permit the U.S. to withdraw more easily from Vietnam. Nixon's Guam Doctrine, which postulated a reduced U.S. military role in the Far East, required that China play a more constructive role in the region. And Nixon believed that China in the future could be an important trading partner of the U.S. in the Asia-Pacific region.

However, as noted by both Nixon and Kissinger, the driving force behind Washington and Beijing's determination to improve bilateral relations in the early 1970s was a common perception of a growing Soviet threat. In reflecting upon this period ten years later, Nixon wrote:

> The key factor that brought us together ten years ago was our common concern with the Soviet threat, and our recognition that we had a better chance of containing that threat if we replaced hostility with cooperation between Beijing and Washington. This overriding *strategic* concern dominated our dialogue, and our relationship, during the first decade.[8]

Henry Kissinger, also reflecting a decade later, described the strategic perspective of the Nixon administration in this way:

> What brought the two nations together was not sentiment but awareness of a common threat. . . . There were powerful incentives for a rapprochement with China: to balance the Soviet Union, either to restrain it or to induce it to negotiate seriously; to isolate Hanoi to give it an incentive to end the Vietnam War; to maintain American self-assurance amid our messy withdrawal from Indochina by demonstrating our continuing capacity for major positive initiatives.[9]

From the outset of Sino-American discussions aimed at normalization of relations, it was clear that Taiwan would be an issue over which little agreement could be found. The reunification issue was central. At the time, the U.S. openly favored a "two Chinas" solution and supported Taiwan's right to claim independence as a separate nation. Richard Nixon in his memoirs noted that as late as August 1971 "we had . . . indicated our support of the concept of the 'two Chinas,' Chiang Kai-shek's Republic of China on Taiwan and the communist People's Republic of China, each to have membership" in the United Nations.[10]

Despite fundamental disagreement over the future of Taiwan, the Chinese were careful not to allow the Taiwan issue to spoil the delicate opportunity to improve Sino-American relations after twenty years of mutual hostility. During Nixon's February 1972 trip to China, Mao Zedong and other Chinese leaders conveyed the impression that the Taiwan issue, while important to China, could wait a considerable length of time before resolution. Kissinger wrote in his memoirs:

> [Mao] delicately placed the issue of Taiwan on a subsidiary level, choosing to treat it as a relatively minor internal Chinese dispute; he did not even mention our military presence there. . . . Neither then, nor in any subsequent meeting, did Mao indicate any impatience over Taiwan, set any time limits, make any threats, or treat it as the touchstone of our relationship. 'We can do without them for the time being, and let it come after 100 years.' 'Why such great haste?' 'This issue is not an important one. The issue of the international situation is an important one.' 'The small issue is Taiwan, the big issue is the world.' These were Mao's thoughts on Taiwan as expressed to us on many visits. (These were also the view of Zhou Enlai and Deng Xiaoping.) But Mao, like Zhou and Deng, spent very little time in our talks on this issue.[11]

Kissinger also reported that Zhou Enlai told Nixon just prior to his departure from China on February 28, 1972: "We, being so big, have already let the Taiwan issue remain for twenty-two years, and can afford to let it wait there for a time."[12]

Although the Taiwan issue was handled carefully by both sides in discussions, the issue proved to be very difficult when it came to agreeing to language in a joint communiqué issued at the conclusion of the Nixon trip. Normally, communiqués contain language on which both sides agree. Over the Taiwan issue, there remained major unresolved differences. As Nixon said: "Taiwan was the touchstone for both sides. We felt that we should not and could not abandon the Taiwanese; we were committed to Taiwan's right to exist as an independent nation. The Chinese were equally determined to use the communiqué to assert their unequivocal claim to the island."[13]

After several evenings of intense negotiations, a formula was worked out whereby the two sides finally agreed to disagree by setting forth their respective positions without any attempt at compromise. In important statements of policy which remain at the bedrock of Sino-American understanding on the Taiwan issue today, the February 28, 1972, Shanghai Communiqué read:

> The Chinese side reaffirmed its position: The Taiwan question is the crucial question obstructing the normalization of relations between China and the United States; the Government of the People's Republic of China is the sole legal government of China; Taiwan is a province of China which has long been returned to the motherland; the liberation of Taiwan

is China's internal affair in which no other country has the right to interfere; and all U.S. forces and military installations must be withdrawn from Taiwan. The Chinese Government firmly opposes any activities which aim at the creation of "one China, one Taiwan," "one China, two governments" or advocate that "the status of Taiwan remains to be determined."

The U.S. side declared: The United States acknowledges that all Chinese on either side of the Taiwan Strait maintain there is but one China and that Taiwan is a part of China. The United States Government does not challenge that position. It reaffirms its interests in a peaceful settlement of the Taiwan question by the Chinese themselves. With this prospect in mind, it affirms the ultimate objective of the withdrawal of all U.S. forces and military installations from Taiwan. In the meantime, it will progressively reduce its forces and military installations on Taiwan as the tension in the area diminishes.

Other sections of the Shanghai Communiqué set forth the major principles governing relations between the U.S. and the PRC. The communiqué acknowledged:

There are essential differences between China and the United States in their social systems and foreign policies. However, the two sides agreed that countries, regardless of their social systems, should conduct their relations on the principles of respect for the sovereignty and territorial integrity of all states, non-aggression in the internal affairs of other states, equality and mutual benefit, and peaceful coexistence. International disputes should be settled on this basis, without resorting to the use or threat of force. The United States and the People's Republic of China are prepared to apply these principles to their mutual relations.

With these principles in mind, the two sides stated that progress toward the normalization of U.S.-PRC relations were in the interests of all countries; that both wished to reduce the danger of international military conflict; and that neither sought hegemony in the Asia-Pacific region nor supported efforts by other countries to establish such hegemony.

Interim Years, 1973-1979

It was expected that Nixon would normalize U.S.-PRC relations during his second term in office. But domestic political problems in both the U.S. and China, as well as the difficulty in finding an acceptable solution to the Taiwan issue, delayed the establishment of diplomatic relations until the end of the decade.

In February 1973 the two governments established liaison offices in each other's capitals and gave officials diplomatic immunities and privileges. Shortly thereafter, Beijing invited Taipei to begin discussions aimed at reunification. This type of appeal for a negotiated settlement had not been heard since the 1950s. Indicating internal disagreement over the Taiwan issue, a tougher stance was assumed by the PRC in 1974, but then the softer line reappeared in 1975.

Taipei, however, firmly rejected all PRC appeals to come to the negotiating table. Taiwan repeatedly protested improving relations between the U.S. and China, but Taipei's political position both in the U.S. and in the international community rapidly eroded following Nixon's visit to the PRC.

Surprising to many Americans at the time but in a negotiating style that has since been noted by analysts,[14] the PRC used the Shanghai Communiqué as a platform from which to demand further concessions from the U.S. over the Taiwan issue. In the spring of 1973 the PRC set three conditions for the normalization of relations with the United States: (1) termination of official U.S. relations with the Republic of China; (2) termination of the 1954 U.S.-ROC Mutual Defense Treaty; and (3) withdrawal of American troops and military installations from Taiwan.

The demands were unacceptable to Nixon and had the effect of dampening efforts toward normalization, already slowed as the result of the President's difficulties with the Watergate scandal. By April 1973, four of Nixon's chief advisers had resigned because of their implications in a cover-up of the June 1972 Watergate break-in. Nixon himself resigned in August 1974.

President Gerald Ford sent Secretary of State Kissinger to Beijing in November 1974 and October 1975 to explore normalization. Kissinger found Vice Premier Deng Xiaoping and other Chinese leaders to be inflexible on the Taiwan issue and stern on China's three conditions for normalization. Ford's own trip to China in December 1975 was uneventful. This effectively closed the door for normalization of Sino-American relations under a Republican administration, already stung by the fall of Cambodia to the Khmer Rouge on April 18, 1975, the surrender of Saigon to the Viet Cong on April 30, and the takeover of Laos by the Pathet Lao on August 23. In September 1975 it was announced that SEATO would be dissolved, marking the end of the U.S. collective defense security system in Asia.

China had political difficulties of its own. Mao remained number one in the Chinese hierarchy, with Zhou number two; but Wang Hongwen became number three. Wang, along with Zhang Chunqiao, Jiang Qing, and Yao Wenyuan, comprised the radical "Gang of Four."

They criticized Zhou for improving relations with the U.S. and argued that China must prepare for an attack from both superpowers. As Mao became increasingly unable to direct affairs of state because of illness, the radicals launched serious attacks against Zhou and Deng.

But there were signs of moderation in Chinese policies as well. In January 1975 Zhou called for the modernization of agriculture, industry, national defense, science and technology. Deng Xiaoping said he recognized the importance of the U.S remaining in Asia as a counterweight to the Soviet Union, and expressed his willingness to accept the "Japanese model" for unofficial relations between Washington and Taipei. Deng criticized the U.S. for being naive in pursuing detente with the Soviet Union.

The internal struggle between the moderates and radicals went on until the death of Zhou in January 1976, at which time the "Gang of Four" gained the ascendancy. Deng was purged in April. The power of the radicals was made stronger following the death of Mao in September. But in October Premier Hua Guofeng arrested the "Gang of Four" and rehabilitated Deng in July 1977.

From 1973 until 1977 China was unable to take major steps to improve relations with the U.S., although trends toward moderation in both domestic and foreign policies could be seen. Beginning in 1977, the PRC began to liberalize its economic and social systems. Also starting in 1977, PRC leaders began to press for normalization of Sino-American relations.While refusing to rule out the use of force to resolve the Taiwan issue, Beijing became less threatening toward Taiwan. At the same time, more public attention was placed on the need to counter the Soviet Union.

Normalization of Sino-American Relations

As political and economic pragmatism resurfaced in China, an opportunity was presented to the United States, now under the administration of President Jimmy Carter, to pursue normalization. Carter entered the presidency determined to establish diplomatic relations with China, and he brought into his administration individuals sharing this commitment.[15] Carter sent Secretary of State Cyrus Vance to Beijing in September 1977 to propose that an American embassy be established in Beijing and that a liaison office, similar to that existing in Beijing since 1973, be established in Taipei. The Chinese, considering this to be a step backward in Sino-American relations, rebuffed Vance. Henceforth, the pivotal contact with the Chinese during the Carter administration became National Security Adviser Zbigniew Brzezinski.

Brzezinski visited China in May 1978 to lay the groundwork for diplomatic recognition. (His visit coincided with Chiang Ching-kuo's inauguration as ROC President and was taken as an insult by Taipei.) In views similar to those of Nixon and Kissinger, Brzezinski believed that strategic cooperation with the PRC to counter the Soviet Union served critical U.S. security interests. The Chinese were arguing strongly along the same lines at the time. The geopolitical pressures to normalize Sino-American relations increased in January 1978 when Vietnam invaded eastern Cambodia, China's ally, in response to a previous Khmer Rouge attack against Vietnam's Tay Ninh Province. In April Vietnam and China were clashing along their common border. The Soviet Union also began to deploy modern weapons along the Sino-Soviet border, including SS-20 mobile intermediate range ballistic missiles.

According to President Carter's memoirs, during the Huang Hua-Leonard Woodcock talks held later that year in Beijing to work out the details of normalization, the United States did not press the Chinese for a pledge of nonuse of force against Taiwan. The U.S. did, however, state its intention to continue supplying defensive arms to Taipei. Carter also informed the Chinese that the United States would maintain the Mutual Defense Treaty with Taiwan until it was terminated according to its provisions. He further insisted that Beijing not contradict U.S. statements that the Taiwan issue should be settled peacefully and with patience. According to Carter, in late November 1978 the Communist Party Central Committee met to consider his proposal for normalization, along with two other key issues: the final consolidation of Deng Xiaoping's control and possible military action against Vietnam.[16]

The Chinese at least partially agreed to Carter's conditions, because in December the PRC softened its rhetoric directed toward Taipei and started to call for peaceful "reunification" instead of "liberation." Carter noted that during Deng Xiaoping's visit to the United States in January 1979, the Chinese leader said that "the only two circumstances under which they would not resolve the issue peacefully and be patient were if there was an extended period of no negotiation or if the Soviet Union entered Taiwan."[17]

On December 15, 1978, the United States and the People's Republic of China announced they would exchange diplomatic recognition on January 1, 1979. It was clear that in the normalization process the U.S. had abandoned the "two Chinas" policy believed possible at the time of the 1972 Shanghai Communiqué.

In his televised explanation to the American people, President Carter reaffirmed the principles in the Shanghai Communiqué and emphasized that "the Government of the United States of America acknowledges the Chinese position that there is but one China and Taiwan is part of China." He went on to say:

> As the United States asserted in the Shanghai Communiqué of 1972 . . . we will continue to have an interest in the peaceful resolution of the Taiwan issue. I have paid special attention to ensuring that normalization of relations between our country and the People's Republic of China will not jeopardize the well-being of the people of Taiwan. The people of our country will maintain our current commercial, cultural, trade, and other relations with Taiwan through nongovernmental means.[18]

The Taiwan question was also addressed in the official U.S. statement accompanying the joint communiqué released December 15. The statement said that "as of January 1, 1979, the United States of America recognizes the People's Republic of China as the sole legal government of China." On the same date, the document continued, the U.S. would terminate diplomatic relations with the ROC, give the required one year's notice of termination of the Mutual Defense Treaty, and withdraw remaining American personnel from the island. Regarding U.S. relations with Taiwan, the statement explained: "In the future, the American people and the people of Taiwan will maintain commercial, cultural, and other relations without official government representation and without diplomatic relations." To accomplish this, the administration would seek necessary changes in existing law. Regarding the future of Taiwan, the statement concluded: "The United States is confident that the people of Taiwan face a peaceful and prosperous future. The United States continues to have an interest in the peaceful resolution of the Taiwan issue and expects that the Taiwan issue will be settled peacefully by the Chinese themselves."

For its part, the PRC expressed confidence that the Taiwan issue had been resolved in principle, but refused to rule out the use of force as a means of bringing Taiwan back to the control of the mainland. In its official statement on the establishment of diplomatic relations, the PRC said:

> As is known to all, the Government of the People's Republic of China is the sole legal government of China and Taiwan is a part of China. The question of Taiwan was the crucial issue obstructing the normalization of relations between China and the United States. It has now been resolved between the two countries in the spirit of the Shanghai Communique and through their joint efforts, thus enabling the normalization of relations so ardently desired by the people of the two countries. As for the way of bringing Taiwan to the embrace of the motherland and reunifying the country, it is entirely China's internal affair.[19]

Also at the time of normalization, the PRC set the next marker for negotiations with the U.S. over Taiwan: the issue of arms sales to Taiwan. On December 16, 1978, Hua Guofeng said:

In the course of negotiations, the U.S. side mentioned that it would continue to sell arms to Taiwan for defense purposes after normalization. We can absolutely not agree to this. During the discussion, we made our position clear on many occasions. On this question, continued sale of arms to Taiwan after normalization does not conform to the principles of normalization, is detrimental to a peaceful settlement of the Taiwan question and will exercise unfavorable influence on peace and stability in the Asia-Pacific region and the rest of the world.[20]

The Taiwan Relations Act

As promised in his announcement of the establishment of Sino-American diplomatic relations on December 15, 1978, President Carter submitted to the Congress draft legislation designed to handle future relations with Taiwan.[21] After considerable revision by the Congress, this legislation became the Taiwan Relations Act (TRA). While generally in favor of normalized relations with Beijing, Congress was displeased by the administration's decision to abrogate the U.S.-ROC Mutual Defense Treaty without prior consultation. In July 1978 the Senate had requested by unanimous vote consultation before any action was taken by the administration on the treaty. That request was written into an amendment to the 1979 security aid authorization bill signed by Carter in September 1978.

In its hearings on Carter's draft legislation, Congress voiced major concerns over the administration's lack of attention to the PRC threat to Taiwan.[22] However, the administration insisted that Taiwan's security was not at risk. Indeed, the U.S. had proceeded with normalization because China was willing to resolve the reunification issue by peaceful means. Deputy Secretary of State Warren Christopher told the Senate Foreign Relations Committee on February 5, 1979: "A peaceful resolution of the Taiwan issue is a fundamental part of the structure of normalization." He explained:

. . . any effort by the People's Republic of China to resolve the Taiwan issue by other than peaceful means would be inconsistent with its evident desire to have better relations with the United States and our allies and friends. . . . A decision by China to use force against Taiwan would, in effect, be a decision to renounce good relations with these nations and hence to abandon the program of modernization and growth.[23]

Christopher also addressed the question of U.S. policy regarding China's reunification: "It is our position that if there is to be a reunification, it is of great importance that it be peaceful and not be destabilizing in the area. But we do not have a position of encouraging the people on Taiwan to do something against their will."[24]

After extensive hearings, Congress rewrote major portions of the President's draft legislation in ways favorable to Taiwan and passed S. 245/H.R. 2479 by more than two-thirds of both Houses in late March 1979.[25] President Carter signed the revised TRA bill on April 10, 1979.

In the absence of diplomatic relations and the Mutual Defense Treaty, the TRA has become the principal legal framework for U.S.-Taiwan relations. The TRA specifically links the future of Taiwan with U.S. security interests in the Far East. Section 2 of the Act states: "The Congress finds that the enactment of this Act is necessary . . . to help maintain peace, security, and stability in the Western Pacific." Section 2 further states that U.S. policy in the Western Pacific is designed:

(1) to preserve and promote extensive, close, and friendly commercial, cultural, and other relations between the people of the United States and the people on Taiwan, as well as the people on the China mainland and all other peoples of the Western Pacific area;

(2) to declare that peace and stability in the area are in the political, security, and economic interests of the United States, and are matters of international concern;

(3) to make clear that the United States decision to establish diplomatic relations with the People's Republic of China rests upon the expectation that the future of Taiwan will be determined by peaceful means;

(4) to consider any effort to determine the future of Taiwan by other than peaceful means, including by boycotts or embargoes, a threat to the peace and security of the Western Pacific area and of grave concern to the United States;

(5) to provide Taiwan with arms of a defensive character; and

(6) to maintain the capacity of the United States to resist any resort to force or other forms of coercion that would jeopardize the security, or the social or economic system, of the people on Taiwan.

Section 3 of the Taiwan Relations Act gives specific instructions on the implementation of the above policy. Especially important are the provisions for arms sales to Taiwan.

(1) In furtherance of the policy set forth in section 2 of this Act, the United States will make available to Taiwan such defense articles

and defense services in such quantity as may be necessary to enable Taiwan to maintain a sufficient self-defense capability.

(2) The President and the Congress shall determine the nature and quantity of such defense articles and services based solely upon their judgment of the needs of Taiwan, in accordance with procedures established by law. Such determination of Taiwan's defense needs shall include review by United States military authorities in connection with recommendations to the President and the Congress.

(3) The President is directed to inform the Congress promptly of any threat to the security or the social or economic system of the people on Taiwan and any danger to the interests of the United States arising therefrom. The President and the Congress shall determine, in accordance with constitutional processes, appropriate action by the United States in response to any such danger.

The TRA was in some respects more specific than the 1954 Mutual Defense Treaty in stating how threats to Taiwan would be against U.S. interests. Nonetheless, the Chinese reaction to the TRA was moderate at the time. This was primarily due to President Carter's promise to implement the TRA in a way consistent with the normalization communiqué. He stated when signing the TRA bill into law on April 10:

The act is consistent with the understandings we reached in normalizing relations with the Government of the People's Republic of China. It reflects our recognition of that Government as the sole legal government of China. . . . In a number of sections of this legislation the Congress has wisely granted discretion to the President. In all instances, I will exercise that discretion in a manner consistent with our interest in the well-being of the people of Taiwan and with the understandings we reached on the normalization of relations with the People's Republic of China as expressed in our joint communiqué of January 1, 1979.[26]

The President also unilaterally imposed a one-year moratorium on arms sales to Taiwan. This action, plus his promise to implement the TRA in a way consistent with previous communiqués, mollified the Chinese. Moreover, the strategic environment at the time—the Vietnamese occupation of Cambodia in December 1978; the retaliatory Chinese incursion into northern Vietnam in February 1979; increased Soviet access to Cam Ranh Bay shortly thereafter; and the Soviet invasion of Afghanistan in December 1979—was so threatening to Chinese security interests that Beijing had to focus on solidifying its relationship with Washington. During 1979 Deng Xiaoping was openly calling for a "united front" between China, Japan, Europe, and the United States to counter Soviet hegemony. The Chinese leader told *Time* magazine in February 1979:

> After setting up this relationship between China, Japan and the U.S., we must further develop the relationship in a deepening way. If we really want to be able to place curbs on the polar bear [Soviet Union], the only realistic thing for us is to unite. If we only depend on the strength of the U.S., it is not enough. If we only depend on the strength of Europe, it is not enough. We are an insignificant, poor country, but if we unite, well, it will then carry weight.[27]

Deng's efforts in 1979 to form a strategic alliance with the U.S. to contain Soviet expansion in Asia strongly influenced U.S. perceptions of Sino-American relations for the next decade. Since the Soviet Union was the principal enemy of the U.S. and the sole country able to threaten U.S. national survival, strategic planners in Washington diligently pursued Deng's tantalizing offer. In this larger geopolitical calculation, Taiwan seemed to lose importance to U.S. interests. Although American commitments to Taiwan were thought sustainable, there was considerable willingness on the part of the Carter and Reagan administrations to narrow those commitments in order to secure China's strategic cooperation.

The following section (Chapters 3-5) examines the close relationship between U.S. strategic perceptions and American concessions to the PRC over arms sales to Taiwan. The arms sales issue is central to U.S. reunification policy, because Taiwan's ability to field a deterrent has a direct relationship to the peaceful or forceful resolution of China's reunification.

Notes

1. Numerous books have discussed U.S. relations with China during the Qing dynasty and the era of the Republic of China on the mainland. Particularly useful in this chapter's summarization have been Frederick H. Chaffee and others, *Area Handbook for the Republic of China* (Washington, D.C.: Government Printing Office [GPO], 1969); *China: U.S. Policy Since 1945* (Washington, D.C.: Congressional Quarterly, Inc., 1980); and Frederica M. Bunge and Rinn-Sup Shinn, *China: A Country Study* (Washington, D.C.: GPO, 1981).

2. *China: U.S. Policy Since 1945* (Washington, D.C.: Congressional Quarterly, Inc., 1980), pp. 81, 83, 85-86.

3. *American Foreign Policy, 1950-1955: Basic Documents, II* (Washington, D.C.: GPO, 1957), p. 2467.

4. For a detailed chronology of U.S. policy from 1949-1980, see *China: U.S. Policy Since 1945,* pp. 75-264. An excellent overview of U.S. involvement with

Taiwan from 1950 until the late 1970s can be found in Ralph N. Clough, *Island China* (Cambridge, MA: Harvard University Press, 1978).

5. *U.S. Overseas Loans and Grants and Assistance from International Organizations* (Washington, D.C.: Agency for International Development, 1984), p. 83.

6. "President Kennedy's Statement on the Taiwan Strait, June 27, 1962," *Current History,* 43 (September 1962), p. 178.

7. For a discussion of the ROC's view of Sino-American normalization, see James C.H. Shen, *The U.S. & Free China: How the U.S. Sold Out Its Ally* (Washington, D.C.: Acropolis Books, 1983).

8. Richard M. Nixon, "America and China: The Next Ten Years," *New York Times,* October 11, 1982, p. A19.

9. Henry A. Kissinger, "Mr. Shultz Goes to China," *Washington Post,* January 30, 1983, p. C8.

10. Richard M. Nixon, *RN: The Memoirs of Richard Nixon* (New York, NY: Grosset and Dunlap, 1978), p. 556.

11. Henry A. Kissinger, *White House Years* (Boston, MA: Little, Brown and Co., 1979), p. 1062.

12. Ibid., p. 1087.

13. Nixon, *RN,* p. 70.

14. See, for example, Richard H. Solomon, *Chinese Political Negotiating Behavior: A Briefing Analysis* (Santa Monica, CA: Rand Corporation, December 1985) and Lucian W. Pye, *Chinese Commercial Negotiating Style* (Cambridge, MA: Oeleschlager, Gunn and Hain Publishers, 1982).

15. For Carter's views on relations with China, see Jimmy Carter, *Keeping Faith: Memoirs of a President* (New York, NY: Bantam Books, 1982), pp. 186-211.

16. Ibid., p. 197.

17. Ibid., pp. 209-210.

18. The text of President's Carter's speech may be found in *Public Papers of the Presidents of the United States: Jimmy Carter, 1978, Book II* (Washington, D.C.: GPO, 1979), pp. 2264-2266.

19. New China News Agency (NCNA), December 16, 1978, in Foreign Broadcast Information Service, *Daily Report: China,* December 18, 1978, p. A2. Hereafter cited as *FBIS-China.*

20. Ibid., p. A5.

21. The President's draft legislation, along with documentation on the reaction of Members of Congress, can be found in Robert L. Downen, *The Taiwan Pawn in the China Game: Congress to the Rescue* (Washington, D.C.: Georgetown University, 1979).

22. One of the most useful collections of information about Taiwan and related U.S. interests can be found in the Senate hearings on the Taiwan Relations Act. See U.S. Congress, Senate, Committee on Foreign Relations, *Taiwan* (Washington, D.C.: GPO, 1979).

23. Ibid., pp. 16-17.

24. Ibid., p. 64.

25. An excellent account of the congressional handling of the TRA can be found in Lester L. Wolff and David L. Simon, *Legislative History of the Taiwan Relations Act* (New York, NY: American Association for Chinese Studies, 1982).

26. Office of the White House Press Secretary, "Statement by the President on Public Law 96-8 (H.R. 2479)," April 10, 1979.

27. *Time,* February 5, 1979, p. 34.

PART ONE

Reagan and the
Taiwan Issue, 1980-1983

3

Early Confrontation
with China over Taiwan

Because of the threatening international environment, both Washington and Beijing tacitly agreed in 1979 to set aside the Taiwan issue in the interest of strategic cooperation against the Soviet Union. The PRC did not feel it necessary at the time to challenge U.S. policy toward Taiwan, because the momentum for Taiwan's eventual reunification with the mainland appeared unstoppable: Taipei was increasingly isolated in the international community; its people and government were demoralized in the wake of the sudden U.S. derecognition; and Beijing had seized the initiative with proposals for peaceful reunification which had won worldwide recognition.

Nonetheless, Sino-American relations soon chilled rapidly over the Taiwan issue from mid-1980 to late 1982. Although U.S. reunification policy was not the direct cause, certain related aspects of U.S. policy toward Taiwan were more directly involved. Chief among these were Ronald Reagan's strong public support of Taiwan during the 1980 presidential campaign and the question of U.S. arms sales to Taiwan. Another development, only indirectly related to the Taiwan issue, was Beijing's determination that a strategic relationship with the U.S. was no longer necessary or in its interest. This reassessment of PRC foreign policy enabled Chinese leaders to assume a harder line on Taiwan than might otherwise have been possible.

Reagan's 1980 Campaign Speeches

The most frequently cited cause for the worsening of Sino-American relations from 1980 to 1982 was Ronald Reagan's 1980 campaign speeches calling for "official" U.S. relations with Taiwan. It was an article of faith among Reagan's conservative supporters that Taiwan had been treated unfairly by President Jimmy Carter. Throughout the campaign,

Reagan promised to correct the injustice and to recognize as "official" the U.S. relationship with Taiwan. Many American friends of Taiwan assumed this meant the reestablishment of diplomatic ties with the ROC.

Recognizing that Reagan was far more supportive of Taiwan than Carter, Beijing feared that a Reagan presidency would reverse the trend toward improved Sino-American relations and would sell Taiwan advanced weapons for its defense. As a result of this increased support, Beijing reasoned, Taipei would see no reason to respond favorably to China's appeals for a negotiated settlement of the reunification issue. The PRC decided that its best strategy under these circumstances was to directly challenge Reagan during the presidential campaign over the issue of "official" relations with Taiwan.

China's official news agency *Xinhua* responded to a June 13 Detroit speech by Reagan: "Reagan's position runs diametrically opposite to the principles governing the establishment of diplomatic relations between China and the United States." The commentary warned, "Reagan's declaration for the reestablishment of 'official relations' with Taiwan is obviously a great retrogression. It reflects an attempt among certain short-sighted people in the United States to revive their own dream of 'two Chinas.' Whatever the supporting arguments, his position, if carried into practice, would wreck the very foundation of Sino-U.S. relations."[1]

An even more strongly worded commentary appeared the next day in China's official newspaper *Renmin Ribao:*

> If the United States reestablished "official relations" with Taiwan according to the policy announced by Reagan, it would imply that the very principle which constitutes the foundation of Sino-U.S. relations is thoroughly destroyed and that Sino-U.S. relations will retrogress against the will of the two peoples. As for the absurd calls for a return of the U.S. military presence on Taiwan and a revival of the U.S.-Taiwan "Mutual Defense Treaty," they constitute brazen interference in China's internal affairs.[2]

Reagan's foreign policy advisers were caught somewhat in a dilemma. On the one hand, conservative supporters of Reagan demanded that he rectify what they considered to be President Carter's betrayal of the Republic of China. On the other hand, there were influential Republicans (Nixon, Kissinger and Alexander Haig, for example) who stressed that U.S. interests were served by friendly Sino-American relations because of the growing Soviet threat in Asia. To reconcile these views, Reagan sent advisers George Bush and Richard Allen to the PRC and Japan in August 1980 for extensive consultations. Upon their return, Reagan gave an important speech in Los Angeles on August 25 in which he set forth five principles of his China policy:

> First, U.S.-Chinese relations are important to American as well as Chinese interests. Our partnership should be global and strategic. In seeking improved relations with the People's Republic of China, I would extend the hand of friendship to all Chinese. . . . I would continue the process of expanding trade, scientific and cultural ties.
>
> Second, I pledge to work for peace, stability and the economic growth of the Western Pacific area in cooperation with Japan, the People's Republic of China, the Republic of Korea, and Taiwan.
>
> Third, I will cooperate and consult with all countries of the area in a mutual effort to stand firm against aggression or a search for hegemony which threatens the peace and stability of the area.
>
> Fourth, I intend that United States relations with Taiwan will develop in accordance with the law of our land, the Taiwan Relations Act. This legislation is the product of our democratic process, and is designed to remedy the defects of the totally inadequate legislation proposed by Jimmy Carter. . . . Fifth, as President I will not accept the interference of any foreign power in the process of protecting American interests and carrying out the laws of our land. . . .
>
> It is my conclusion that the strict observance of these five principles will be in the best interests of the United States, the People's Republic of China and the people of Taiwan.[3]

Reflecting the opinion of many conservatives, Reagan harshly criticized the manner in which Carter had broken diplomatic relations with Taipei. In his Los Angeles speech, Reagan argued "that a condition of normalization—by itself a sound policy choice—should have been the retention of a liaison office on Taiwan of equivalent status to the one which we had earlier established in Beijing." Reagan went on to say that the Congress, in correcting "the inadequate bill which Mr. Carter proposed," provided in the TRA "adequate safeguards for Taiwan's security and well-being" and provided "the official basis for our relations with our long-time friend and ally. . . . And, most important, it spells out our policy of providing defensive weapons to Taiwan." Reagan then asked rhetorically: "You might ask what I would do differently. I would not pretend, as Carter does, that the relationship we now have with Taiwan, enacted by our Congress, is not official."

Reagan's position disappointed many conservatives, who had hoped the presidential candidate would reestablish diplomatic relations with Taipei if elected. Nonetheless, Beijing reacted strongly to Reagan's August 25 policy guidelines. A commentary in *Renmin Ribao* set the tone for much of the first two years of the Reagan presidency. The article criticized Reagan for "his erroneous stance on the Taiwan question" and his advocacy of the "establishment of 'official relations' with Taiwan."[4] The commentary said of Reagan's interpretation of the TRA:

> It is known to all that the "Taiwan Relations Act" is nothing but a domestic act of the United States. It can in no way serve as a legal basis for handling U.S.-Chinese relations. It should be pointed out that many parts of the Act, including its claim to reserving the United States' right to continue interfering in the Taiwan problem, run counter to the fundamental principles of the communiqué on the establishment of diplomatic relations between China and the United States. Therefore, the Chinese Government has more than once made clear its solemn stance against the Act and demanded that the U.S. have the overall interests of Sino-U.S. relations in mind and strictly abide by the principles of the Sino-U.S. agreement and truly respect China's sovereignty and territorial integrity.

The commentary pointed out that the correct approach to the TRA was the one adopted by President Carter whereby the Act would be implemented in accordance with the normalization agreement. The commentary said: "It must be pointed out what is really intolerable is the attempt to make Sino-U.S. relations retrogress by imposing on China a U.S. domestic act which is harmful to the political foundations on which China and the United States established diplomatic relations." The commentary noted that Reagan had gone even further than the Taiwan Relations Act by insisting on the restoration of "official relations" between the United State and Taiwan. "This is not a matter of 'semantics' but an overt call for 'two Chinas'," the article said. "Should Reagan's erroneous proposition be put into practice, it would inevitably lead to grave retrogression in Sino-U.S. relations."

Renmin Ribao then warned that U.S. strategic interests would be damaged if the U.S. followed Reagan's position on Taiwan:

> China takes Sino-U.S. friendly relations seriously and does not wish to see the relations impaired. This is actuated not only by her own interests, but more importantly by the overall interests of safeguarding world peace and opposing hegemonism. It has been proved that the normalization of Sino-U.S. relations is not only in the interests of the Chinese and American peoples but is also conducive to stabilizing the world situation. Thus, when China evaluates the U.S. Government's strategic decisions and foreign policy, she regards its China policy as one of the most important criteria; for what is involved is global strategy, not a problem of a local nature.

Any action detrimental to Sino-U.S. relations will have serious adverse effect on the struggle against hegemonism and for safeguarding world peace. . . . It would be impossible for any American statesman to possess a correct strategic viewpoint and pursue a wise foreign policy if he fails to handle Sino-U.S. relations from the viewpoint of overall interests, or worse, if he causes harm to Sino-U.S. relations. . . . Reagan's erroneous stand on the Taiwan question has a vital bearing on the strategic situation in the world. . . . Whither goes Reagan, we shall wait and see.

Following the protests over Reagan's campaign statements, the PRC hardened its position on the Taiwan issue with the U.S. In October 1980 the American Institute in Taiwan (AIT) and the Coordination Council for North American Affairs (CCNAA)—the two private corporations established by the U.S. and Taiwan respectively to handle relations between the two countries in the wake of derecognition—signed an agreement giving each other's representatives diplomatic privileges and immunities. When this occurred, the PRC complained that Washington was extending "official status to the two organizations." *Renmin Ribao* warned: "Clearly a question of major importance for the leaders of the United States is whether to pursue [U.S.-PRC] relations further or to reverse them."[5]

Thus, when Ronald Reagan assumed office in January 1981, the PRC already was angry at what it perceived to be retrogression in Sino-American relations. Beijing's strong reaction to Reagan's calls for "official" relations with Taipei convinced many analysts that it was the inept handling of the Taiwan issue by Reagan's campaign staff that caused the souring of Sino-American relations during the 1980-1982 period. In reality, however, two other factors contributed to this development: U.S. arms sales to Taiwan and Beijing's reevaluation of the regional correlation of forces in the wake of the U.S. response to the Soviet invasion of Afghanistan.

U.S. Arms Sales to Taiwan

Despite Carter's insistence that the U.S. would continue selling defensive arms to Taiwan, the Chinese were not seriously offended, since the President unilaterally imposed a one-year moratorium on arms sales to Taiwan immediately after recognizing the PRC as the sole legal government of China. However, in June 1980 the State Department decided to permit Northrop and General Dynamics to go to Taiwan to discuss the sale of their versions of a new fighter, the so-called "FX."[6]

The FX was designed by both companies with Taiwan specifically in mind. Taipei wanted to modernize its air force with purchases from the U.S., but nothing in the U.S. inventory was thought to be suitable because of its offensive capability. The U.S. did not want to sell Taiwan weapons posing a threat to the PRC for fear of jeopardizing Sino-American relations. The Department of Defense and State Department approached Northrop and asked that company to design a new fighter with limited range and ground attack capability for export to Taiwan and similar countries.

Northrop designed the F-5G (or F-20, as it later became known) as a follow-on model to the F-5E/F fighters it coproduced on Taiwan. The F-5G sale was approved in principle by both the Department of Defense and State Department, but the sale was delayed because Congress wanted to give General Dynamics an opportunity to compete for the potentially lucrative contract. General Dynamics' version of the FX, the F-16-J79, was a lower performance version of the U.S. Air Force's front line fighter, the F-16A.

The PRC interpreted U.S. efforts to sell an advanced fighter to Taiwan as a serious threat to Beijing's efforts to achieve reunification. Taipei had rejected the PRC's calls for negotiations leading to peaceful reunification (see Chapters 6 and 7). Beijing feared that if Taiwan acquired the advanced interceptor, it would be able to delay reunification indefinitely by means of the island's enhanced deterrent capabilities. In July 1980 Premier Zhao Ziyang told a visiting congressional delegation: "The Chinese people feel strongly against the U.S. Government's handling of its relations with Taiwan and particularly its continued sales of weapons to Taiwan." These actions, Zhao said, "are incompatible with the principles as outlined in the communiqué on the establishment of diplomatic relations between China and the United States. They are likely to produce an unfavorable impact on the stability of the Asia-Pacific region."[7]

In a move generally described as "killing the chicken to scare the monkey," the PRC used the occasion of the Netherlands' decision to sell Taiwan two Zwaardvis submarines in November 1980 as an opportunity to frighten the U.S. out of selling the FX to Taiwan. Beijing strongly protested the submarine sale, calling it "detrimental to the peaceful unification of Taiwan and the mainland and only [serving] to increase tension in the Taiwan Strait area." It added, "No country friendly to China should make such a decision which is absolutely unacceptable to the Chinese people."[8]

Throughout December 1980 and January 1981 the PRC warned that if the submarine sale were allowed to go forward, relations between Beijing and The Hague would suffer seriously. When the Netherlands decided to proceed with the sale in mid-January, the Chinese Foreign Ministry notified the Dutch government that their relations would be downgraded to the level of charge d'affaires.

PRC statements at the time indicated that Beijing's actions were directed as much toward Washington as toward The Hague. After pointing to the numerous Chinese warnings about selling arms to Taiwan, *Xinhua* asked: "Why, then, is the Netherlands' Government insisting on doing this stupid thing despite the opposition by both the Chinese and Netherlands people?" The commentary went on:

> The answer has to be found in U.S. backstage support. . . . The United States . . . told the Netherlands that the U.S. Government itself was also planning to sell weapons to Taiwan. . . . Some advisers of U.S. President-elect Reagan . . . said that the attitude of the new U.S. President toward Taiwan would be even more active than the present President, Carter. Obviously, the adverse current now emerging in a number of countries to create "two Chinas" and interfere in China's internal affairs originates from the pro-Taiwan forces in the United States. We sternly warn those attempting to create the adverse current of "two Chinas" in the international community that the Chinese people will not tolerate them, be they small countries, big powers or superpowers, or whether they choose to use "two Chinas" or "one China, one Taiwan" or other forms of "two Chinas."[9]

The PRC reacted strongly to the submarine sale because of great concern in Beijing that, once in office, the Reagan administration would approve the FX sale to Taiwan. Air superiority had long been identified as the key to Taiwan's security, and the sale of the FX would give Taipei that superiority for the foreseeable future. Recognizing this fact, conservative backers of Reagan had pointed to the sale of the FX as the single most important step the President-elect could take to protect his friends on Taiwan. Many in the Congress believed that Carter had deliberately withheld the sale of advanced weapons to Taiwan to smooth Sino-American relations. One Senate Foreign Relations Committee report concluded, for example, that "the failure to approve or even address Taiwan's top priorities—an advanced fighter (the FX), the Harpoon (naval) missile and the Standard (air defense) missile—raised questions about the willingness of the United States to improve and modernize Taiwan's defensive military capabilities."[10]

Beijing's anger over U.S. handling of the Taiwan issue arose because of Reagan's references to reestablishing "official" relations with Taipei and the high probability that the incoming Reagan administration would proceed with the FX sale. Having isolated Taiwan from the U.S. through Sino-American normalization, the PRC now saw these gains being lost because of the strong support for Taipei evinced by the incoming Republican administration. However, Beijing's anger could not have been translated into threats to downgrade U.S.-PRC relations unless it felt confident that the threat posed to its security by the Soviet Union was manageable.

China's Independent Foreign Policy

To counterbalance the Soviet threat, PRC leaders had been willing to overlook objectionable U.S. policies toward Taiwan on several occasions in order to move Sino-American relations forward. Indeed, as noted by Nixon and others, U.S.-PRC relations until the early 1980s were dominated by anti-Soviet strategic concerns. In fact, as late as Deng Xiaoping's visit to the U.S. in January-February 1979, the Chinese were calling for strategic cooperation with the U.S. against the Soviet Union.

However, the strong U.S. response to the Soviet invasion of Afghanistan in December 1979 convinced the Chinese that Washington would no longer tolerate Soviet encroachments in Asia. Increased hostility between the superpowers meant that Soviet attention would focus more on the U.S. and Southwest Asia than on China. This tended to diminish somewhat the immediate Soviet threat to the PRC, giving Beijing increased political flexibility on issues such as Taiwan.

There were several indications of this shift in China's assessment of the regional balance of power. In October 1980 Deng Xiaoping noted for the first time the possibility of improved Sino-Soviet relations if Moscow took steps to reduce its threat to China. In an interview with the *Christian Science Monitor* Deng said:

> If the Soviet Union changes its global strategy and social-imperialist policy, Sino-Soviet relations can be changed right away, and there is no reason for us to wait for a few years. The Soviet Union must prove with concrete action that it has changed its global strategy and abandoned its hegemonism by reducing its one million troops [along the Sino-Soviet border] to at least the same number as that under Khrushchev [ten divisions].[11]

But the best evidence of a PRC reassessment of the strategic balance of power and the increased flexibility this gave to Chinese foreign policy was a December 1983 statement by Huan Xiang, director of China's Institute for International Affairs. In response to questions from *Der Spiegel* as to why China was pursuing an "independent" foreign policy when in 1979 Deng had been calling for "coordinated measures" with the U.S. against Moscow, Huan explained:

> What has changed is the international situation. In the early seventies the Soviet Union had very strongly expanded toward the outside militarily and had become a threat to everybody. For this reason China offered cooperation to each state that felt threatened by the Soviet Union.
>
> Near the end of the Carter administration's term and at the beginning of the term of the Reagan administration, the Americans determinedly and energetically put up a front against the Soviet Union politically and militarily in the struggle for superiority in nuclear armament, in the matter of the European intermediate range weapons, in the Caribbean region, in the Middle East and, finally, also in Asia.
>
> This stopped the Soviet Union, and the rivalry of the two superpowers considerably intensified throughout the world. It seems that the Russians still do not feel strong enough to react to the U.S. offensive. In our view, a certain balance between the two has emerged, especially in the military field.[12]

Valuable insight into the reasoning behind Beijing's decision to move away from a policy of strategic alignment with the U.S. to improved relations with the USSR was also found in a top secret Chinese Communist Party document obtained by Japan's Foreign Ministry. As summarized by *Yomiuri Shimbun,* this document concluded:

1. The two superpowers—the United States and the Soviet Union—are contending with each other in pursuit of hegemony. Militarily, the Soviet Union stands in an offensive position and the United States is relatively inferior. The potential strength of the United States, however, should not be underestimated.
2. The United States normalized its diplomatic relations with China. But it did so for the purpose of compensating for its military inferiority to the Soviet Union and because it thought that normalization would be of benefit to itself. In deciding on normalization, the United States recognized "one China" but it still continues its commitment to Taiwan. This constitutes an intervention in China's internal affairs and, for the development of U.S.-China relations, it is undesirable for the United States to continue such a policy.
3. The Soviet Union has lately been making overtures to China for a rapprochement. This is also intended for the Soviet Union's own benefit. Although militarily it is relatively superior to the United States, the Soviet Union is isolated internationally and faces economic difficulties domestically and, therefore, it thinks that easing tension with China will be of benefit to itself.

4. In the final analysis, both the United States and the Soviet Union are trying to use China as a card in the process of seeking hegemony. The fact that the Soviet Union desires a rapprochement with China does not alter the intrinsic nature of Soviet hegemonism or big-power chauvinism. Nevertheless, the Soviet Union was a friend of China for a long time. An excessive confrontation with the Soviet Union is ill-advised for China as well.[13]

It was this reassessment of the balance of power between the U.S. and the USSR which led to China's determination, announced formally at the 12th Party Congress in September 1982 by General Secretary Hu Yaobang, to pursue improved relations with the USSR as part of China's new "independent" foreign policy. In his address to the Congress, Hu said that it would be possible for Sino-Soviet relations to move forward if Moscow took meaningful steps to remove three threats to China's security. These became known as the "three obstacles" and included: large Soviet military deployments along the Sino-Soviet and Sino-Mongolian borders; Soviet assistance to Vietnam's invasion and occupation of Cambodia; and the Soviet invasion and occupation of Afghanistan. Addressing the issue of Sino-Soviet relations, Hu said:

The relations between China and the Soviet Union were friendly over a fairly long period. They have become what they are today because the Soviet Union has pursued a hegemonist policy. For the past twenty years, the Soviet Union has stationed massive armed forces along the Sino-Soviet and Sino-Mongolian borders. It has supported Vietnam in the latter's invasion and occupation of Kampuchea [Cambodia], acts of expansion in Indochina and Southeast Asia and constant provocations along China's border. Moreover, it has invaded and occupied Afghanistan, a neighbor of China, by force of arms. All these acts constitute grave threats to the peace of Asia and to China's security. We note that Soviet leaders have expressed more than once the desire to improve relations with China. But deeds, rather than words, are important. If the Soviet authorities really have a sincere desire to improve relations with China and take practical steps to lift their threat to the security of our country, it will be possible for Sino-Soviet relations to move toward normalization. The friendship between the Chinese and Soviet peoples is of long standing, and we will strive to safeguard and develop this friendship, no matter what Sino-Soviet state relations are like.[14]

The following month the PRC embassy in Washington issued a statement explaining China's independent foreign policy:

China opposes anyone who seeks hegemony, and at any place. This is the independent stand of China. On the Afghanistan and Kampuchean issues, both China and the United States oppose the armed invasions by the Soviet Union and Soviet-backed Vietnam. However, the United States met with opposition from both China and the Soviet Union in its support for Israeli aggression and for the racist regime in South Africa. As can be seen, this by no means indicates that China "enters into alliance" with the United States in one case and becomes a partner of the Soviet Union in another. But it does prove that first, China is independent of any superpower, and secondly, while the Soviet Union and the United States are contending with one another for world hegemony, China may, toward certain issues, adopt an attitude similar to that of one of the superpowers. But the "rendezvous" are carried out from different points of departure.[15]

There is considerable irony surrounding the evolution of China's independent foreign policy. The Reagan administration, determined to counter the growing Soviet threat, pursued a strategic relationship with the PRC for the first two years of its term even more vigorously than the Carter administration. Secretary of State Alexander Haig was instrumental in this policy, and it resulted in important U.S. concessions over arms sales to Taiwan. Most notable of these were certain provisions within the August 17, 1982, U.S.-PRC Joint Communiqué limiting future weapons transfers to Taipei.

The conservative Reagan administration was willing to make these concessions, painful as they were to individuals generally sympathetic to the Nationalist Chinese on Taiwan, because of the mistaken belief that PRC strategic cooperation could be gained once Chinese confidence in the U.S. had been restored. Due to Chinese anger over Reagan campaign rhetoric about reestablishing "official" relations with Taipei, there existed in the minds of many U.S. China experts a belief that "we owed the Chinese one" over the Taiwan issue.

U.S. Concessions over Taiwan

Thus, at the beginning of the Reagan administration's first term in office, a remarkable coincidence of strategic, political, and psychological factors arose which made concessions over Taiwan appear to be in the U.S. interest. The incoming administration believed the Soviet threat to be rising and America's strength to be inadequate to meet the challenge unilaterally. Friendly relations with the PRC were thought necessary for vital strategic reasons. This perception supported those arguing for limited concessions over Taiwan in order to demonstrate to Beijing that Reagan was sincere in wanting to maintain friendly Sino-American relations.

While the U.S. was seeking to improve relations with the PRC, China was in the process of downgrading its assessment of the immediate Soviet threat. The principle reason for this was U.S. determination to counter continued Soviet hegemonism following the invasion of Afghanistan. China no longer had to be in the forefront of anti-Soviet united front activity; the U.S. assumed this activist role. As the U.S. strengthened its deterrent posture in Asia to counter the Soviets, the PRC found it enjoyed increased diplomatic flexibility. Both superpowers wanted to solidify their relations with China in order to concentrate on Soviet-American rivalries.

Weighing the U.S. and Soviet foreign policies, Beijing concluded that Chinese interests would best be served by a more independent foreign policy that would pursue simultaneously friendly relations with both superpowers. The PRC took advantage of U.S. and Soviet desires to improve relations with Beijing to strengthen its bargaining position over "obstacles" in Sino-Soviet and Sino-American relations. In the case of the Soviet Union, China demanded concessions on the "three obstacles" as the price for normalization of relations. In the case of the U.S., China demanded concessions on U.S. relations with Taiwan, particularly arms sales.

Thus, China's willingness to enter into strategic cooperation with Washington faded at precisely the time the Reagan administration most wanted to pursue that objective. Apparently, the administration did not correctly perceive this fundamental shift in Chinese assessments of PRC interests until at least 1983. Official U.S. statements from 1980-1982 routinely called for a strategic relationship with the PRC. The Fiscal Year 1984 Defense Posture Statement, for example, listed as one of the U.S. security objectives in Asia "to build toward a durable strategic relationship with the People's Republic of China."[16] And in explaining why he had approved the August 17, 1982, U.S.-PRC Joint Communiqué, President Reagan said:

> Building a strong and lasting friendship with China has been an important foreign policy goal of four consecutive American administration. Such a relationship is vital to our long-term national security interests and contributes to stability in East Asia. It is in the national interests of the United States that this important strategic relationship be advanced.

The U.S. pursuit of a strategic relationship with the PRC, at the very time that China had decided that its security interests were best served by reducing tensions with the USSR, gave Beijing tremendous leverage over U.S. Taiwan policy. The PRC, already angry at Reagan for suggesting an "official" relationship with Taiwan, decided to teach the administration a bitter lesson by threatening to downgrade Sino-American relations unless the U.S. made concessions over Taiwan. Although Beijing's hardened position troubled American policymakers at the time, the Chinese seizure of an advantage should not have been surprising. As Henry Kissinger noted, one of China's most pronounced characteristics in dealing with foreigners has been the willingness of its leaders to use foreign perceptions to China's advantage. In his memoirs, Kissinger writes of Mao Zedong and Zhou Enlai:

> For all their charm and ideological fervor, the Chinese leaders were the most unsentimental practitioners of balance-of-power politics I have encountered. From ancient times Chinese rulers have had to contend with powerful non-Chinese neighbors and potential conquerors. They have prevailed, often from weakness, by understanding profoundly—and exploiting for their own ends—the psychology and preconceptions of foreigners.[17]

The PRC was able to achieve two significant gains in reducing American support for Taiwan before Washington assimilated the implications of the shift in Chinese strategic thinking. These were the Reagan administration's determination not to sell Taiwan an advanced replacement fighter and the signing of the August 17 Communiqué. Neither decision changed U.S. reunification policy, which remained constant throughout this period, but the decisions did make it more difficult for Taiwan to defend itself against the PRC and for the U.S. to argue that it was not involved in the reunification issue. The FX decision and August 17 Communiqué will be discussed in Chapter 5.

Before turning to that discussion, however, we need to examine the nature of the PRC military threat to Taiwan. Such an assessment plays an important role in U.S. reunification policy, because the level of U.S. arms sales to Taiwan is determined by U.S. perceptions of Beijing's intention to use force to achieve reunification. As stated in the Shanghai Communiqué and reaffirmed at the time of the normalization of Sino-American relations, a peaceful settlement of the Taiwan issue lies at the heart of U.S. reunification policy.

Notes

1. *Xinhua,* June 13, 1980, in *FBIS-China,* June 16, 1980, p. B3.
2. *Renmin Ribao,* June 14, 1980, in *FBIS-China,* June 16, 1980, p. B4.
3. "Ronald Reagan on U.S. Policy Toward Asia and the Pacific," Reagan for President Press Release, Los Angeles, CA, August 25, 1980.
4. *Renmin Ribao,* August 28, 1980, in *FBIS-China,* August 28, 1980, p. B1.

5. *Renmin Ribao,* October 9, 1980, in *FBIS-China,* October 9, 1980, p. B1.

6. For background on the fighter sale issue, see Robert G. Sutter and William deB. Mills, "Fighter Aircraft Sales to Taiwan: U.S. Policy," Library of Congress, Congressional Research Service, *Issue Brief,* IB81157 (October 28, 1981).

7. *Xinhua,* July 8, 1980, in *FBIS-China,* July 9, 1980, p. B2.

8. *Xinhua,* December 3, 1980, in *FBIS-China,* December 4, 1980, p. G1.

9. *Xinhua,* January 17, 1981, in *FBIS-China,* January 19, 1981, p. G2.

10. U.S. Congress, Senate, Committee on Foreign Relations, *Implementation of the Taiwan Relations Act; the First Year: A Staff Report* (Washington, D.C.: GPO, June 1980), p. 10.

11. *Xinhua,* November 24, 1980, in *FBIS-China,* November 24, 1980, p. L18.

12. *Der Spiegel,* December 26, 1983, in *FBIS-China,* December 29, 1983, pp. A7-A8.

13. *Yomiuri Shimbun,* November 30, 1982, pp. 1-2.

14. Hu Yaobang, "Create a New Situation in All Fields of Socialist Modernization," *The Twelfth National Congress of the CPC* (Beijing: Foreign Languages Press, 1982), pp. 58-59.

15. Embassy of the People's Republic of China, Press Release, No. 82/019, n.d., p. 4.

16. U.S. Department of Defense, *Annual Report to the Congress, Fiscal Year 1984* (Washington, D.C.: GPO, 1983), p. 17.

17. Henry A. Kissinger, *White House Years,* pp. 1087-1088.

4

Assessing China's
Military Threat to Taiwan

U.S. policy toward the reunification of China has stressed three points since the early 1970s: that Chinese on both sides of the Taiwan Strait should resolve the issue themselves; that the U.S. would not become involved; and that the sole U.S. interest is in the peaceful settlement of the issue. The U.S. supports a peaceful resolution of the Taiwan issue because U.S. national security interests are involved. Two interests loom of major importance: the need to maintain U.S. credibility in East Asia and the need to maintain peace and stability in the region.

U.S. Security Interests

U.S. credibility as a dependable ally is a vital factor in the Taiwan issue. The ROC government remained a staunch U.S. ally throughout World War II until the breaking of diplomatic relations in January 1979. Even today, Taipei has let it be known through various channels that its air and port facilities are available for use by American military forces in the event of an international crisis. Asian nations understand the strategic reasons why the U.S. switched official relations from Taipei to Beijing. But they also recognize Taiwan's loyalty to the Free World, a loyalty which deserves consideration in U.S. policy decisions. To a certain extent, how the U.S. treats Taiwan is taken as a sign of the degree of American commitment in terms of U.S. involvement in Asia and the credibility of that commitment. An abandonment of Taiwan would severely undermine the value of the U.S. commitment to other Asian nations. In a period of increased Soviet political and military activity in the region, the U.S. can ill afford a weakening of American credibility in Asia.

U.S. reunification policy also serves national security interests by helping to maintain peace and stability in the Taiwan Strait region.

Taiwan sits astride critically important sea lines of communication essential for the conduct of trade in East Asia as well as the movement of major navies of the world, especially those of the U.S. and the USSR. In the event of an outbreak of violence in the Taiwan Strait, trade would be disrupted and the warships of the superpowers might be affected. Taiwan's close proximity to Japan and the Philippines means that these two U.S. allies would consider instability in the Taiwan Strait of grave concern to their own security interests. Most importantly, tensions in the Taiwan Strait would call into operation the security provisions of the Taiwan Relations Act. Since the Korean War, the U.S. has sought to avoid a military confrontation with China. A war in the Taiwan Strait carries high risk that U.S. and PRC forces would come into direct conflict.

Because of these security concerns, the U.S. would prefer that Taiwan remain under the control of a friendly government and that any resolution of the Taiwan issue be peaceful. During the 1950s and 1960s, when Beijing was hostile to Washington, the U.S. perception was that Taiwan should be separate from the mainland. The U.S. was willing to recognize Taiwan as an independent country, but this option was rejected by the ROC because the Nationalists laid claim to all of China, not just Taiwan. Since the 1970s, the PRC has become increasingly less hostile toward the U.S. Under these conditions, the U.S. no longer seeks to prevent reunification of Taiwan and the mainland, but rather to ensure that the reunification process takes place peacefully over time.

The sale of U.S. arms to Taipei since 1979 has been justified on the ground that the best way to ensure a peaceful settlement of the Taiwan issue is to make sure that Taipei fields an adequate deterrence against any likely PRC use of force. This policy enjoys wide political support in the U.S., particularly from those friends of Taiwan who reject any suggestion that the people of Taiwan should be subjected to Beijing's rule against their wishes. Thus, the sale of defensive arms to Taiwan has become institutionalized as part of U.S. China policy for both security and moral reasons.

There is a fine line for U.S. policy, however, between not becoming involved in the reunification issue and providing arms to Taiwan to defend itself against the PRC. China has been quick to point out this potential contradiction in U.S. reunification policy. Beijing realizes that if Taipei is able to deter a PRC attack, Taiwan is far less likely to agree to change the favorable existing status quo. The PRC feels that if its threat to Taiwan lacks credibility, then Taipei can accept or reject PRC proposals for reunification at will. For nationalistic as well as bargaining reasons, Beijing has consistently viewed U.S. arms sales as interference in the reunification process.

As the importance of Sino-American relations has grown since 1969, the U.S. has had to be careful in managing the arms sales issue. A balance has to be maintained between two sets of American security interests. On the one hand, arms sales to Taiwan should not be allowed to undermine the strategically important Sino-American relationship. On the other hand, adequate arms have to be sold to Taiwan to enable it to field a credible deterrence against the PRC.

The difficulty in maintaining this balance is revealed clearly in the processes behind the FX decision and August 17 Communiqué, discussed in the next chapter. But in these and other arms sales decisions, a careful assessment of the actual PRC threat to Taiwan has to be made. These threat assessments contain two elements: an assessment of the relative capabilities of the two Chinese armed forces and the likely outcome of various scenarios of conflict between the two sides; and an assessment of the intentions of both sides actually to call their respective armed forces to battle. In the case of Taiwan since 1978, the U.S. threat assessment has been weighed heavily on the side of PRC political intentions as opposed to PRC military capabilities.

Low U.S. Assessments of PRC Threat

U.S. assessments of the PRC threat to Taiwan have been consistently low since the normalization of Sino-American relations. In part this reflects the apparent commitment by Beijing since late 1978 to pursue a policy of peaceful reunification instead of military "liberation" with respect to Taiwan. In part it also reflects hesitancy in Washington to focus public attention on the PRC threat to Taiwan. Such attention would cause supporters of Taiwan to challenge the improvement of U.S. relations with China and also generate demands that more advanced weapons be sold to Taipei. The issue could threaten Sino-American relations in general, as indeed it did during the 1980-1982 period.

The low assessment of the PRC threat to Taiwan has enabled the U.S. to develop an effective "dual-track" China policy, wherein friendly official relations are pursued with Beijing and friendly unofficial relations are maintained with Taipei. These low threat assessments were especially important during the sensitive 1978-1979 period of normalization of Sino-American relations, when the Carter administration had to convince Congress that the shifting of diplomatic relations from Taipei to Beijing did not harm Taiwan's security.

Secretary of Defense Harold Brown assured members of the Senate Foreign Relations Committee during the 1979 hearings on the Taiwan Relations Act (TRA) that "for a variety of reasons PRC military action against Taiwan is extremely unlikely for the foreseeable future."[1]

Chairman of the Joint Chiefs of Staff, General David Jones, told the committee: "Our estimates are that Taiwan does have the capability to deter any attack by the People's Republic of China now and for a considerable time into the future."[2]

During subsequent hearings on the implementation of the TRA, spokesmen for the Carter administration continued to reassure Congress that the PRC did not threaten Taiwan. On June 11, 1980, for example, Assistant Secretary of State Richard Holbrooke told the House Subcommittee on Asian and Pacific Affairs: "I can report to you today that a variety of political and military factors continue to render unlikely any PRC action against Taiwan."[3]

Although it was expected that the Reagan administration, because of its friendly ties to Taiwan, would reassess upward the PRC threat to Taipei, assessments made from 1981 to 1987 paralleled those made by the Carter administration. The most significant assessment was made in January 1982, when the Reagan administration announced that it was not selling an advanced fighter to Taiwan because "no military need for such aircraft exists."[4] In March 1982, as Sino-American negotiations were underway on the August 17 Communiqué, Assistant Secretary of State John Holdridge told the Congress: "Tensions in the Taiwan Strait are at a 30-year low. We are quite certain that Taiwan is under no imminent threat of attack, and we believe we would have considerable lead-time—perhaps as much as five years—if there should be a shift in Beijing's intentions."[5]

On August 18, 1982, the day after the communiqué's announcement, Holdridge explained to the House Committee on Foreign Affairs that the U.S. was willing to sign the agreement limiting future arms sales to Taiwan because China had promised to pursue a peaceful resolution of the Taiwan issue. Holdridge said that if Beijing changed its policy, the U.S. reserved the right to increase arms sales to Taiwan. Holdridge explained:

> China has announced a fundamental policy of pursuing peaceful means to resolve the longstanding dispute between Taiwan and the mainland. Having in mind this policy and the consequent reduction in the military threat to Taiwan, we have stated our intention to reduce arms sales to Taiwan gradually. . . . While we have no reason to believe that China's policy will change, an inescapable corollary to these mutually interdependent policies is that should China change its policy, we will reassess our policy.[6]

Low U.S. estimates of the PRC threat have continued throughout the Reagan administration. In April 1986, for example, Deputy Assistant

Secretary of State James Lilley told the Senate that Beijing would not likely use force against Taiwan because such a move would not serve Chinese interests. Lilley said:

> Even though the situation has occasionally been tense in the Taiwan Strait, it has been basically peaceful for nearly thirty years. This can only be explained by a complex set of factors, political, economic, and psychological, as well as military. We believe that this realistic appraisal is shared by the government in Beijing. . . . Although there have been occasional, troubling remarks suggesting possible future military actions and Beijing declines to renounce formally the use of force to resolve what it considers to be an internal matter, we believe that Beijing shares our view that the use or threat of force could complicate this issue rather than facilitate its settlement.[7]

As indicated by Lilley, the PRC is deterred from using force against Taiwan for several pragmatic reasons, including various military factors. The next section of this chapter will consider the military balance between the two Chinese sides as it existed at the end of 1987. The analysis shows that while the probability of Beijing attacking Taiwan is low in the near-term, the probability may increase in the future if China gains a decisive advantage in critical areas such as blockade capabilities or air superiority.

Military Capabilities

In terms of total military capabilities, the PRC clearly enjoys superiority over Taiwan in most crucial categories. Only in destroyers does Taiwan have an advantage over the mainland (26 vs. 15).[8] Fairly close numbers are found between Taipei and Beijing for frigates (9 vs. 31), minesweepers (8 vs. 33), amphibious ships (451 vs. 613), and fighters that can operate in a ground attack mode (377 vs. 500). But in all other areas Taiwan is vastly outnumbered, frequently by a ratio of 10 to 1 (for example, total armed forces, total troops, infantry divisions, total naval personnel, submarines, fast attack craft, air force personnel, total combat aircraft, and fighter/interceptors). In several categories, Beijing enjoys a monopoly on weapons systems (including all strategic nuclear forces, naval bombers and fighters, and air force bombers). It seems clear that in a major military confrontation between the two armed forces, Taiwan would face almost certain defeat barring outside intervention on its behalf or the collapse of political will to pursue the struggle on the part of the PRC.

But since the PRC must be concerned not only with Taiwan but also with threats from the Soviet Union, India, and Vietnam, a more realistic assessment of the threat to Taiwan must focus on forces deployed in the Taiwan Strait region. The first threat to be considered is an amphibious invasion of Taiwan. The PRC naval and air threats also will be discussed.

In terms of army personnel, some 24 regular army divisions (535,000 troops) are deployed in the Nanjing Military Region, facing Taiwan's 22 divisions (340,000 troops). The PRC also has some 90,000 Marines deployed throughout its three fleets. Taiwan's Marines total about 20,000.

Estimates of the number of divisions required to invade Taiwan successfully range upward of 40 or more. In its hearings prior to the enactment of the Taiwan Relations Act, the Senate Foreign Relations Committee found that the U.S. during World War II estimated that it would take 300,000 American troops to defeat 32,000 Japanese ground forces then occupying Taiwan.[9] Given the fact that the PRC and ROC ground forces in the Strait region are in rough parity, and that the People's Liberation Army (PLA) is known to suffer major weaknesses (including lack of mobility and mechanization, poor logistics, limited power projection capability, obsolescent weapons, and weak command and control capabilities), it would seem that currently the PLA army does not have the power to threaten the security of Taiwan. The PLA might be able, however, to seize the islands of Kinmen (Quemoy) and Matsu just off the coast of Fujian province, because of their close proximity to the mainland.

Other than threatening the offshore islands, the PLA would have to engage in a massive mobilization and buildup in the region before attempting an invasion of Taiwan. This could be seen by U.S. and Taiwan intelligence far in advance of any immediate threat, giving both Washington and Taipei adequate time to formulate an appropriate response.

A contributing factor to the low probability of a PRC invasion of Taiwan is the lack of Chinese amphibious capabilities. It was estimated in 1979 that PRC naval vessels, including motorized junks, would be able to transport only 100,000-150,000 troops to Taiwan.[10] Troubling to Taipei, however, is the PRC's new emphasis on marine-type forces and the construction of at least thirty new landing vehicles since 1979. But U.S. analysts believe these to be intended for use in the South China Sea, where Beijing has several territorial disputes in the Paracel and Spratly islands with Vietnam and other countries, rather than against Taiwan.

Although the threat of an amphibious invasion of Taiwan is low, a more complex and less assuring picture emerges when considering

PLA naval and air deployments in the Taiwan region. The PRC East Sea Fleet has some 750 vessels, 350 of which are over 100 tons, including 5 destroyers, 16 frigates, and 40 submarines. At least 90 missile-equipped fast patrol craft are also assigned to the East Sea Fleet.

ROC naval officers are concerned about the PRC surface fleet, particularly the many small missile attack craft that pose a formidable challenge to the larger, slower destroyers carrying Taiwan's flag. Neither side possesses advanced electronic countermeasures. A missile exchange between the Russian-style Styx surface-to-surface missile (SSM) carried by PRC vessels and the Israeli-designed Gabriel-type SSM carried by Taiwan's ships would likely be determined by the number of ships and missiles brought into play. Existing ratios point to a clear PRC advantage, despite construction in recent years of up to 50 missile-equipped fast attack craft by Taipei. Both sides are upgrading their antiship missiles.

PRC submarines pose an even greater threat to Taiwan. Only ten of the fourteen "Gearing"-type destroyers in the ROC navy have been equipped with anti-submarine rockets. The remainder are armed with anti-submarine torpedoes of approximately the same range as the torpedoes carried by PRC submarines. Although Taiwan's anti-submarine warfare (ASW) capabilities are being upgraded with the addition of improved sonar, S-2E anti-submarine aircraft, ASW helicopters, two ASW submarines, and several FFG-7 frigates, the ability of Taiwan's fleet to survive submarine attack is questionable.

The greatest naval threat to Taiwan is a blockade. As noted by Admiral Edwin K. Snyder in his testimony before the Senate Foreign Relations Committee during its 1979 hearings on the TRA:

> The most dangerous action that the PRC could participate in right now is the declaration of an embargo on all commerce into Taiwan. She could state that Taiwan is a province of China, and that henceforth all deliveries to her "province" must clear customs through one of her seaports. She can back this declaration up by stating that a blockade exists, and any ship entering her sovereign waters—including those surrounding Taiwan—are subject to boarding and inspection. . . . I don't foresee any threat of invasion of Taiwan. Invasion is unnecessary if you can destroy your enemy by starving him economically.[11]

Assessments vary as to whether a PRC blockade of Taiwan would be successful in forcing Taipei to the negotiating table.[12] Without question, such a blockade would severely damage Taiwan's economy given its heavy dependence on trade. On the other hand, the island is self-sufficient in food production, and critical resources such as petroleum are held in three or more months' reserves. In all likelihood, a blockade's success or failure would hinge on the political will of Beijing and Taipei respectively.

Although a blockade would be relatively easy for Beijing to declare in effect, and the deployment of submarines to demonstrate a determination to enforce the blockade would unquestionably be within the capabilities of the PRC, a successful sustained blockade might be very difficult to execute without enormous expenditure of resources. For one thing, Taiwan plans to respond to a high intensity blockade—the only type likely to be effective—with an immediate escalation of the conflict. This would include the use of Taiwan's air force against mainland shipping and port targets, as well as the mining of PRC ports such as Shanghai.[13]

Yet another factor escalating the cost of a PRC blockade of Taiwan would be the adverse reaction of the United States, Japan, Western Europe, and perhaps even the Soviet Union if their trade and ships were interfered with in a blockade of the Taiwan Strait and Bashi Channel. These are international waterways of great importance in shipborne traffic between Northeast and Southeast Asia, as well as between the Indian and Pacific Oceans. Moreover, given the close interdependence of world trading partners—which increasingly includes the PRC— a blockade of Taiwan would hurt the interests of far more countries than the ROC. The PRC in effect would also be blockading itself.

Moreover, it would not be easy to stop ships calling on Taiwan. In 1984, for instance, more than 34,000 ships carrying cargoes from more than 100 nations went in and out of Taiwan's ports. The total tonnage of these ships was nearly 350 million tons. The difficulty in strangling Taiwan economically becomes obvious when one considers that in all of World War II, the U.S. sank only 8 million tons of Japanese ships.[14]

In summary, the naval threat to Taiwan from the PRC is much higher than the amphibious threat, although it is still relatively low given the high risks to PRC surface ships and submarines should Beijing attempt to destroy the ROC navy or blockade the island.

In terms of the air threat to Taiwan, it must be recognized that the most important single key to Taiwan's deterrence is the maintenance of qualitative air superiority over the Taiwan Strait. Air superiority would enable Taipei to exact prohibitively high costs on PRC aircraft, ships, and amphibious forces in case of an assault on the island. Under optimum conditions, air superiority might enable Taiwan to defeat attacking mainland forces.

ROC strategists believe that Taiwan's security depends on an ability to thwart a limited PRC air-sea-land attack on the island. This can be achieved through both offensive and defensive tactical air operations, until the loss of essential materiel and bases halt the PRC offensive. This strategy is based on three key assumptions. First, competing pressures on Beijing would prevent the PRC from concentrating all of its offensive power against Taiwan. Second, as the time and costs of the operation escalated, PRC planners would find the military option less and less attractive. Third, the U.S. and other powers would aid Taiwan diplomatically and perhaps militarily in a limited way.

The air balance in the Taiwan Strait is difficult to calculate with exactitude. In general terms, however, Taiwan has approximately 560 combat aircraft, of which 225 are F-5Es. Other combat aircraft include 30 F-5F, 42 F-100A/D, 15 F-104A, and 80 F-104G. All of these aircraft would be involved in the defense of Taiwan. The PRC, on the other hand, has some 6,100 naval and air force combat aircraft, including 170 medium H-6 bombers, 630 light H-5 bombers, 500 ground attack fighters (MiG-15 and Q-5), and 4,600 fighters. Of the latter, the J-6/B/D/E are the most important interceptors, totalling some 3,000 aircraft.

According to ROC sources, within 750 nautical miles of Taiwan the PRC stations 358 bombers, 2,855 fighters, 410 transport planes, 209 helicopters, and 134 other planes. Within 600 nautical miles there are 215 bombers, 100 ground-attack fighters, 1,100 interceptors, and 60 reconnaissance aircraft. At least seven major air bases are within 250 nautical miles of Taiwan, placing aircraft stationed there within five to seven minutes of their targets on the island.[15]

Most analysts assume that the PRC would lose at least 500 aircraft in a battle for air superiority over the Taiwan Strait. Some estimates range much higher. As to the outcome of such an air battle, some sources predict that within two or three weeks the ROC air force "would be neutralized."[16] ROC planners believe that the PRC would have to commit around 4,000 aircraft to overwhelm Taiwan's air defenses, and that each aircraft "would last for only about four missions—a very high rate of attrition."[17]

What quickly becomes apparent in any assessment of the PRC air threat to Taiwan is the importance of technology. In the past the ROC has maintained a high degree of technological advantage over the Chinese air force. However, with the modernization of the PLA, including some Western assistance, and the restrictions on U.S. arms sales to Taiwan by the August 17 Communiqué, Taipei's qualitative advantage is at risk.

This issue was highlighted by the controversy surrounding the 1986 U.S. sale to the PRC of $550 million of advanced avionics for the supersonic J-8-II interceptor. U.S. officials insisted that the sale would not adversely affect the qualitative balance of air power in the Taiwan

Strait, whereas critics of the sale and Taiwan military officials noted that the avionics package would give the PRC all-weather, day-night fighting capabilities not possessed by Taiwan.[18]

Since the mainstay of Taiwan's air deterrent is the 1950s-1960s technology found in the F-5E and F-104, Taipei has placed high priority on the acquisition of a replacement fighter. Until the FX decision and the August 17 Communiqué, Taiwan had assumed that such an aircraft could eventually be purchased from the U.S. But to avoid disrupting U.S.-PRC relations, Washington excluded the possibility of selling Taiwan an advanced fighter. Taipei thus has looked to third countries and domestic production to supply its air defense needs.

For a variety of reasons, Taiwan has been unable to purchase an advanced fighter from third countries. This has forced Taiwan to adopt the costly option of domestically designing and producing an indigenous fighter (IDF), the first prototypes of which may be flying in the early to mid-1990s. Limited assistance for the IDF program has come from U.S. aircraft manufacturers on a commercial sales basis. Whether the IDF will meet Taiwan's air defense needs in the 1990s is unknown at this time.

Weighing these factors, one has to conclude that the air threat to Taiwan is higher than either the land or sea threat. One critical factor as to whether the air threat will increase to dangerous levels is the outcome of the race between the two Chinese governments to modernize their fighters. If Taiwan can maintain its qualitative edge, then the costs involved in attempting to resolve the Taiwan issue by force will likely remain prohibitively high. However, if the PRC is able to neutralize Taiwan by superior fighters, then Taipei's deterrence will be seriously weakened and the military option may become more viable to Beijing's leaders.

Overall, a comparison of the military capabilities of China and Taiwan reveals a clear, but not decisive advantage for the PRC. A conclusion reached by both American and Chinese analysts is that Beijing could defeat Taipei if it is willing to pay a high enough cost. The military balance remains somewhat fluid, however, because the two Chinese sides are rapidly modernizing their respective armed forces. A technological race is underway in the Taiwan Strait, the outcome of which carries major implications for the future of Taiwan and U.S. reunification policy.

Political Intentions

As important as military capabilities are in assessing the PRC threat to Taiwan, of greater importance still is the question of Beijing's intentions to use force against Taipei. PRC leaders have stated repeatedly that they will not rule out the use of force to resolve the Taiwan issue. But more careful analysis reveals both incentives and disincentives for the PRC to choose a military option. Among the major disincentives to the use of force, the following may be considered.

First, the use of force would probably cause the U.S., Japan, Western Europe, ASEAN, and other countries to reassess their policy of friendly, constructive ties with China. Because of the Taiwan Relations Act and the many influential friends of Taiwan in and out of the U.S. government, the possibility exists that Washington would intervene in some meaningful way on Taipei's behalf. Economic and technological assistance to China from the U.S., Japan, and Western Europe would certainly be adversely affected, and ASEAN would likely slow the pace of improved relations with the PRC. China has gained considerable international prestige as a result of its attempt to find a peaceful solution to the difficult Taiwan question; that prestige would be undermined if force was used against Taiwan.

Second, an attack against Taiwan might not be successful. War under any conditions is a risky affair, and the spectacle of massive China floundering in a prolonged, expensive war with Taiwan would undermine the PLA's credibility throughout Asia. Moreover, Taiwan's strategy of expanding the war and prolonging it indefinitely might succeed. As time passes, the cost to the PRC in terms of manpower, equipment, foreign exchange, and international prestige would increase dramatically. A point could be reached where Beijing would have to cut its losses and end the conflict short of its objectives. Also, a prolonged conflict might increase world sympathy for Taiwan and enhance Taipei's prestige in the international community. Certainly, the U.S. is not presently inclined to support Taiwan's independence, but many Americans would view a PRC attack as justification for the people of Taiwan to pursue their own future separate from the mainland.

Third, the political crisis introduced on Taiwan in the wake of an attack or threat of force could work against long-term PRC interests. The lifting of martial law on Taiwan in July 1987 led to the creation of several new political parties, including some which contain substantial numbers of Taiwanese supporting an independent Taiwan. Presumably, an increased threat of force against the island would bring to the surface strong sentiment for Taiwan to become a separate, sovereign nation. These sentiments would make any negotiated settlement with the mainland extremely difficult.

Fourth, given Taipei's strategy of escalation, an attack against Taiwan would result in widespread destruction on the island. Its ports, transportation system, power grids, and other infrastructure would be heavily damaged. Loss of life would be substantial, particularly if the people of Taiwan decided to fight a guerrilla war against occupying mainland forces. This would not serve the PRC's interests because of the negative international image that such destruction would generate, the high cost of reconstruction on the island once resistance had subsided, and the loss of Taiwan's potential contribution to the mainland's development in terms of a trading partner and source of investment capital. No doubt, such a display of destruction would also sour much of the current enthusiasm of the Overseas Chinese to help develop the Chinese motherland.

Fifth, an attack against Taiwan could cause a shift in the regional balance of power along lines detrimental to China's interests. Many ASEAN states, for example, might be willing to accept the presence of the Soviet Union in the region as a deterrence against future Chinese uses of force. The U.S. would be forced to reconsider its strategic and military cooperation with Beijing. Hostile PRC action against Taiwan would greatly upset Japan, which traditionally has viewed a friendly government in Taiwan as essential to the security of Japan's southern flank. A substantial increase in Japanese defense expenditures might result. And even the Soviet Union, although publicly supportive of Beijing's position on Taiwan, would note the PRC's use of force and ensure that its own position was militarily unassailable in the Far East.

The above disincentives to the use of force against Taiwan are so compelling that most American analysts tend to discount the possibility of Beijing reversing its current policy of peaceful reunification. Nonetheless, there are powerful historical, strategic, economic, political, and bureaucratic forces at work within the PRC which might make the military option more viable in the future. These incentives to the use of force against Taiwan may include the following.

Historically, the Chinese have viewed a united nation as proof of the strength and durability of the country's regime. China suffered terribly under foreign occupation during the last two centuries, and Taiwan's separation from the mainland—and the colonial status of Hong Kong and Macao—reflect the remnants of foreign intervention in the affairs of a weakened China. Although the relative priority of reunification has varied at times in Beijing since 1949, the eventual goal of reunification has never been questioned as a policy. The strong sense of nationalism felt by the Chinese, the consistent policy objective of national reunification, and the historic responsibility to unify China felt by all rulers in Beijing point to the necessity of eventually resolving the reunification issue. The stronger the PRC becomes, the more weighty becomes its leaders' responsibility to bring Taiwan back to the "embrace of the motherland." In past periods of China's division, reunification has almost always occurred by force of arms. Given the importance of reunification in the Chinese sense of history, Beijing may feel it has no choice but to employ force against Taiwan in the future if it appears that other approaches to reunification have failed.

Strategically, the island of Taiwan is vital to China's long-term security. Given its strategic location off Fujian province, a military presence on the island by either of the superpowers would give Washington or Moscow tremendous leverage over China in case of war. If Taiwan were controlled by the mainland, Beijing would have a significant advantage in that the island controls access to both the Taiwan Strait and Bashi Channel, key choke points through which Soviet or American fleets must sail to establish their presence in East Asia. Japan is dependent on ships passing through these channels to fuel its economy. If China controlled Taiwan, then Beijing would have a significant lever with which to influence Japanese policies along lines serving China's interests. Moreover, if in the future China wants to play a role in Pacific economic cooperation and to deploy a "blue-water" fleet of its own in the Pacific, then Taiwan is excellently situated to further these goals. Hence, for strategic reasons, China cannot permit Taiwan to become an independent state or enter into alliances with either of the super-powers. To prevent these developments from occurring, Beijing may feel it has to use force to bring about reunification.

Economically, Taiwan has great potential for aiding the modernization of the mainland. Although commercial ties are indirect and limited by Taipei to mostly transshipment through Hong Kong, a natural symbiotic relationship exists. If the PRC continues its present course of socialist modernization, Beijing will have great need for investment capital, skilled managers, technicians, scientists, engineers, and others talented and experienced in the difficult process of modernization. Taiwan possesses these financial and human resources in abundance. It has the significant advantage of being a Chinese society. The mainland offers vast markets for Taiwan's consumer and industrial products, as well as rich natural resources needed by the island's industries. The obvious benefits of this economic relationship might precipitate a decision in Beijing to end the separation quickly by force, if it appeared possible to conduct the operation surgically and with minimal damage to Taiwan's economy.

Politically, Taiwan is a major source of embarrassment to Beijing. The fact that the Taiwan issue remains unresolved after nearly 40 years demonstrates the limits of PRC power. From the perspective of the mainland, the U.S. involvement in Taiwan smacks of humiliating foreign intervention in China's domestic affairs. The economic success and progress toward democracy on Taiwan contrasts starkly with the mixed results of modernization on the mainland. Lifestyles on Taiwan exceed in every imaginable way the style of life experienced on mainland China. The opening of the PRC since 1978 has given its citizens an opportunity to learn about Taiwan and its standard of living. This learning curve has sharpened since 1987, when Taipei began permitting its citizens to visit relatives on the mainland. The inevitable comparisons between the "two Chinas" has engendered problems for Beijing because the unavoidable inference is that, since both are Chinese societies, the difference in lifestyles must be attributed in part to their respective political systems. Of all crimes in a communist society, none is more serious than challenging the right of the communist party to rule. Yet the very existence and success of the KMT on Taiwan provides an alternative to communism that every Chinese—whether on Taiwan, the mainland, or in overseas communities—must consider. Given the long history of China and the successive rise and fall of governments, the Communist Party of China (CPC) cannot be complacent about its hold on the strings of power until the CPC co-opts or eliminates its KMT rival on Taiwan. If a peaceful strategy proves unworkable, then the elimination of the KMT by force may be the only alternative for Beijing.

From a bureaucratic perspective, the problem of how to handle Taiwan is a delicate issue. The timetable for regaining control of the island varies, as do the policies advanced for achieving that goal. Since 1978, Deng Xiaoping has convinced his colleagues that a peaceful approach to national reunification best serves China's interests. But that approach appears to be part of a larger policy package which includes the opening to the West for trade, technology, and investment capital; the introduction of market incentives into the rural and urban economies; the replacing of an aging and ideologically-motivated cadre with younger, more technology-minded leaders; limited political reform, such as a less intrusive role for the CPC in day-to-day affairs of the government, economy, and lives of the people; and less material support for revolutions abroad. The overall policy package has been described as "pragmatic," but it lacks a binding ideological justification. As American scholars Michel Oksenberg and Richard Bush noted: "Until a consensus on ideology exists, it is improbable that China's political system will be fully stable."[19]

Veteran CPC leader Chen Yun's criticism of certain aspects of Deng's economic reforms before the National Congress in September 1985 demonstrated that a consensus did not then exist.[20] Moreover, the forced resignation of Hu Yaobang in January 1987, the campaign against "bourgeois liberalization," and the increased emphasis on ideological purity in education and the media—all in response to student demonstrations in December 1986—strongly suggest that some PRC officials are not satisfied with the political and economic liberalization policies introduced by the reformists. For purposes of maintaining a consensus on other key issues, or if the reformists' policy package runs into trouble, China's leaders may be forced to assume a more militant position on reunification.

The above list of incentives for the PRC to use force against Taiwan is sufficiently compelling to take seriously PRC threats against Taipei. A few examples of these threats, given since the 1978 implementation of Beijing's peaceful reunification policy, are reminders that the PRC's refusal to rule out the use of force may not be merely for bargaining purposes. Under certain circumstances, Beijing probably would use force against Taiwan.

Deng Xiaoping told U.S. Senators Sam Nunn, John Glenn, Gary Hart, and William Cohen in January 1979 that China would use force against Taiwan under three conditions: "Taipei refuses over a long period to negotiate with the mainland, the ROC proclaims Taiwan an independent state separate from mainland China, or the Soviet Union tries to 'interfere' in Taiwan."[21]

A few days later Deng told another visiting congressional delegation that, regarding Taiwan, "the Chinese people are very patient but their patience is not limitless."[22] Also in January, Deng told Hedley Donovan of *Time* magazine that "ten years is too long a time" to wait for reunification.[23] In May 1979 PRC official Liao Chengzhi said:

> We will strive for a settlement of the Taiwan question through peaceful means. But, if some countries arm Taiwan in their own interests, and make the Taiwan authorities become self-conceited and disregard the common wish of the entire Chinese people, then we cannot assure definitely not to use means other than peaceful ones.[24]

In January 1981 *Beijing Review* editorialized: "If we are driven by the Taiwan authorities' adamant refusal to resort to non-peaceful means to solve the issue, that is entirely China's internal affair which the United States has no right to meddle in."[25] And in July, Chinese sources told the *New York Times* that the long-term continued supply of U.S. weapons might provoke PRC military action.[26] In November 1981 the author was told in Taipei that PRC officials had warned privately that the development of a nuclear bomb by Taiwan would also be considered justification for the use of force.

Such warnings have continued to the present, although their frequency trailed off considerably after 1985. During that year various PRC spokesmen warned Taiwan several times that force may be necessary to achieve reunification if peaceful means fail.

In March 1985 Li Shenzhi, Director of the Center for American Studies, Chinese Academy of Social Sciences, distributed a paper prepared for the Atlantic Council in which he said: "The Chinese Government has never committed itself to peaceful solution under *any* circumstance. It has made known its position that reunification is the major premise, and that it reserves the right to resort to non-peaceful means when all roads to peaceful solution are barred and when it is left with no other choice."

Li went on to describe a situation in which the PRC might elect to use force: "A Taiwan out of control because of the lack of a successor [to President Chiang Ching-kuo], with different political forces rivaling for power, thus leading to a chaotic situation and even violence and bloodshed." Li said a declaration of Taiwan independence was "another form of chaos." Under these circumstances, according to Li, Beijing would use force to gain control of Taiwan because "any Chinese in power who show weakness or hesitancy on this point will be rejected by the people." Li acknowledged that such a course might interrupt the Four Modernizations or result in unfavorable reactions from abroad, but noted that these costs would be bearable to China given the alternative of an independent Taiwan.[27]

One of the most explicit threats to use force against Taiwan was General Secretary Hu Yaobang's comments to *Pai Hsing* editor Lu Keng on May 10, 1985. China cannot renounce the use of force, Hu said, "because if we make such a promise KMT authorities will be all the more free from anxiety."[28] The General Secretary admitted that China was too weak presently to use force against Taiwan, but that over a period of four to ten years the PRC economy would develop to the point where the PLA would be strong enough to take action against Taiwan. Hu stated: "If we are economically powerful in seven, eight, or ten years, we shall be in a position to modernize our national defense. If the broad masses of the Taiwan people wish to return and a small number of people do not wish to return, it will be necessary to use some force."

In the interview Lu Keng noted that Deng Xiaoping had mentioned the possibility of imposing a blockade around Taiwan. Hu Yaobang responded: "That depends. If we have the strength to enforce a blockade and if Taiwan vehemently opposes reunification, we shall have to consider enforcing a blockade."

Foreign policy specialist Huan Xiang said in June 1985, "We must turn down the demand of the United States that we openly commit ourselves to giving up the use of armed force in the settlement of the Taiwan issue because it would not be possible to realize the reunification of the mainland and Taiwan if we make such a commitment." Huan went on to say:

> We want to warn the Taiwan authorities that we have an alternative to a peaceful reunification. We will be patient enough to wait for the realization of the peaceful reunification, but if the peaceful reunification cannot be realized in the next 20 or 30 years we will have to consider other ways to reunify the motherland. . . . We should reserve a military option in case peaceful reunification becomes hopeless.
>
> In this sense, [the refusal to rule out the use of force] is not only a warning, but is also a potential possibility. . . . We are telling the world that we have the right to choose different ways to settle the Taiwan issue and that we will not allow any people, including the United States, to impose their opinions on us.

Regarding the circumstances under which China might use force against Taiwan, Huan noted, "It would not be tolerable if Taiwan enters into an alliance with the Soviet Union, nor would it be tolerable if Taiwan tries to become independent."[29]

Unlike previous years, during 1986 and 1987 few public threats toward Taiwan were issued by Beijing. In February 1986, however, *Xinhua* warned the KMT that its time was running out to make a settlement favorable to itself: "The world is changing rapidly, and people should make careful plans. It is better to help yourself than to have others help you. Friend or foe, we both spring from the same roots. Dilatoriness is fraught with dangers, present obstinacy spells future ruin."

The commentary went on: "It is our sincere hope that the Kuomintang authorities understand their position and role in history well and, balancing advantages and disadvantages and considering their own future, do things that suit the development of events and meet popular demand. . . . It is the only way to ensure the well-being of the Kuomintang authorities."[30]

In June 1986 Deng Xiaoping told Philippine Vice President Salvador Laurel that, regarding the Taiwan issue, "problems can be postponed but they cannot be ignored forever. When patience runs out and peaceful compromise is refused, there is no other way but force."[31] In October 1986 Hu Yaobang again reiterated, "We strive to settle the question of Taiwan through peaceful reunification, [but] we do not exclude other ways of settling this question."[32]

Vice Premier Yao Yilin's comments in March were typical of the restrained attitude of the PRC during 1987. He said: "As for whether China's reunification will be completed in the next ten years or so, or how it will be achieved, I cannot predict. What I can say is that we hope Taiwan will be reunited with the mainland as soon as possible. We wish to resolve the Taiwan issue through peaceful means, but non-peaceful means cannot be excluded."[33]

One of the best summaries of the circumstances under which the PRC said it would use force against Taiwan appeared in the summer 1985 issue of *Foreign Affairs.* Chinese scholar Huan Guo-cang listed five conditions under which Deng Xiaoping had said China would attack Taiwan: "If Taibei leaned toward Moscow instead of Washington; if Taibei decided to develop nuclear weapons; if Taiwan claimed to be an independent state; if Taibei lost internal control as a result of the succession process; or if Taibei continued to reject reunification talks for 'a long period of time'."[34]

Taiwan has also documented several instances of threatening statements from PRC leaders. One unpublished Taipei source has recorded the following incidents:

- Teng Hsiao-ping [Deng Xiaoping] in Tokyo following his [1979] trip to the United States said: "Do not rule out the possibility of liberating Taiwan by force."
- In May and July 1980 the Central Military Committee gave these instructions to the Fukien [Fujian] Military District: "Aiming at the defense characteristics, organization and equipment of ROC troops on Taiwan and other islands, you must hasten the joint combat training of various armies and services. . . . The war status on the Fukien front has never been altered; the whole army must be fully prepared to liberate Taiwan."
- In January 1981 the Fukien front command sent an officer to attend a militia conference in Amoy. He delivered this instruction from the Party Central: "Use force to liberate Taiwan if necessary."
- On April 4, 1981, Li Hsien-nien [Li Xiannian] told the president of the European Democratic League that the PRC "will never rule out [the possibility] of unifying Taiwan by force."
- In April 1981 the Central Military Committee sent this order to Fukien forces: "To liberate Taiwan, the air force should be able to fly under any weather conditions and the army should strengthen landing operations training."

It is believed in Taipei that the current low-key posture adopted by Beijing on reunification has specific objectives in mind. According to the unpublished document cited above, these include:

- creating a false image of peaceful intentions to isolate the Republic of China, in particular to persuade the Reagan administration not to sell arms to Taiwan;
- weakening the anti-communist will of the mainland people by creating the impression that KMT-CPC talks are about to get underway;
- softening the anti-communist determination of the ROC by making nice-sounding, but unrealistic offers.

According to the same document, if Taiwan continues to refuse to negotiate, Beijing will carefully time an attack against Taipei on the basis of such considerations as:

- when international developments are favorable to Peking [Beijing];
- when Washington-Peking cooperation does not irritate Moscow, Soviet expansion into Indochina slows down, and Sino-Soviet border tensions are at a low point;
- when Peking-Hanoi ties are temporarily improved;
- when Peking's activities to isolate the ROC internationally have had an effect;
- when the United States adopts a passive attitude on arms sales to the ROC;
- when Chinese communist war preparations are completed;
- when the Chinese communists can hope for support from dissidents in Taiwan.

No doubt, other PRC incentives and disincentives for the use of force against Taiwan to achieve reunification could be listed. But the above are sufficient to suggest that, while the probability of force being used against Taiwan in the immediate future is small, that probability could increase under certain circumstances. These circumstances might include:

- an attempt by Taiwan to declare its independence;
- an attempt by either superpower to establish a military presence on the island;
- a change in PRC reunification policy resulting from impatience over Taiwan's refusal to negotiate or from internal developments on the mainland;
- a collapse of KMT control on Taiwan or the collapse of political will to resist among the people there resulting from political or economic disruption;

- the establishment of clear PRC military superiority in the Taiwan Strait region;
- a determination by Beijing that U.S. or other international intervention on Taiwan's behalf is no longer credible.

An historical analysis of the use of force by Beijing indicates that the military is regarded as a deliberate instrument of politics by leaders in the PRC.[35] Even during the heightened revolutionary fervor of the Cultural Revolution, Beijing made no attempt to use the military to achieve a major foreign policy objective. Tensions along the Sino-Soviet border caused by the 1969 Ussuri River incident were quickly cooled; and the PLA prevented radical Red Guards from moving into Hong Kong. This leads one to the conclusion that Beijing probably will not attempt to use force to achieve reunification with Taiwan unless it is virtually sure of success and sees no other less costly option.

Hu Yaobang's May 1985 interview with Lu Keng supports this thesis. Hu said: "The first of Chairman Mao's 16 military principles is do not fight a battle without preparation, and do not fight one in which the outcome is uncertain. If you fight, you must be sure of victory. Therefore, we have not underestimated Taiwan." Hu specifically cited the following factors as contributing to Taiwan's strength:

- China's military strength was weak because its economy was weak;
- the majority of the people of Taiwan do not as yet want to reunite with the mainland;
- the possibility exists of foreign intervention on Taiwan's behalf;
- Taiwan's armed forces, military installations, economy, and political system remain strong; and
- the United States continues to strongly support Taiwan.

Of these factors, Hu said, U.S. support for Taiwan was "the most important point."[36] It is for this reason that demonstrations of continued U.S. support for Taiwan play a crucial role in whether the resolution of the Taiwan issue will be peaceful or violent. One of the most demonstrable expressions of U.S. support is the sale of modern weapons to Taipei. As long as Beijing sees adequate levels of arms sold to Taiwan to ensure that a minimal ROC deterrence is maintained in the Taiwan Strait, the probability of the use of force by the PRC will remain small—even if China's political intentions change in favor of using force.

Because of the delicate nature of this calculation, the U.S. decisions in 1982 to deny Taiwan a replacement fighter and to sign the August 17 Communiqué limiting future arms sales to Taiwan presented serious problems to Taiwan's security. The complex maneuvering behind these controversial decisions are discussed in the next chapter.

Notes

1. U.S. Congress, Senate, Committee on Foreign Relations, *Taiwan,* p. 36.

2. Ibid., p. 740.

3. U.S. Congress, House of Representatives, Committee on Foreign Affairs, Subcommittee on Asia and Pacific Affairs, *Implementation of the Taiwan Relations Act* (Washington, D.C.: GPO, 1980), p. 28.

4. "No Sale of Advanced Aircraft to Taiwan, Department Statement, January 11, 1982," *Department of State Bulletin,* 82, 2059 (February 1982), p. 39.

5. U.S. Congress, House of Representatives, Committee on Appropriations, Subcommittee on Foreign Operations, *Foreign Assistance and Related Programs, Appropriations for 1983, Part 4* (Washington, D.C.: GPO, 1982), p. 326.

6. U.S. Congress, House of Representatives, Committee on Foreign Affairs, *China-Taiwan: United States Policy* (Washington, D.C.: GPO, 1982), p. 5.

7. "Opening Statement by Deputy Assistant Secretary James R. Lilley, Senate Foreign Relations Committee, April 29, 1986," pp. 6-7, ms.

8. The comparison between PRC and Taiwan military forces is taken from *The Military Balance: 1986-1987* (London: International Institute for Strategic Studies, 1986), pp. 142-145; 169-170.

9. "Legislative History, P.L. 96-8 (Taiwan Relations Act)," *U.S. Code Congressional & Administrative News,* No. 4 (June 1979), 96th Cong., 1st sess., p. 661.

10. Ibid.

11. *Taiwan,* p. 653-654.

12. For an extensive discussion of a potential PRC blockade of Taiwan, see Martin L. Lasater, ed., *Beijing's Blockade Threat to Taiwan* (Washington, D.C.: The Heritage Foundation, 1986).

13. Ibid., pp. 6-15.

14. Ibid., p. 13.

15. For a more comprehensive examination of the air balance in the Taiwan Strait, see Martin L. Lasater, *Taiwan: Facing Mounting Threats* (Washington, D.C.: The Heritage Foundation, 1987), pp. 18-24.

16. Admiral Edwin K. Snyder in *Taiwan,* p. 586.

17. Admiral Ko Tun-hwa in *Beijing's Blockade Threat to Taiwan,* pp. 8-9.

18. See the remarks of Department of Defense official Edward Ross and subsequent discussion in Martin L. Lasater, ed., *The Two Chinas: A Contemporary View* (Washington, D.C.: Heritage Foundation, 1986), pp. 83-95.

19. Michel Oksenberg and Richard Bush, "China's Political Evolution: 1972-82," *Problems of Communism,* September-October 1982, p. 19.

20. For the text of Chen Yun's speech, see *Beijing Review,* September 30, 1985, pp. 18-20.

21. Quoted in William M. Carpenter and others, *Long Term Strategic Forecast for the Republic of China* (Arlington, VA: SRI International, November 1980), p. 31-32.

22. *Yomiuri Shimbun,* January 15, 1979, in *FBIS-China,* January 18, 1979, p. B2.

23. *Washington Star,* January 29, 1979, p. 1.

24. *Xinhua,* May 21, 1979, in *FBIS-China,* May 24, 1979, p. D8.

25. *Beijing Review,* January 12, 1981, p. 9.

26. *New York Times,* July 4, 1981, p. A3.

27. Li Shenzhi and Zi Zhongyun, "Taiwan in the Next Decade," unpublished paper presented to the Atlantic Council, Washington, D.C., March 11, 1985.

28. For the text of the remarkable interview, see *Pai Hsing,* June 1, 1985, in *FBIS-China,* June 3, 1985, pp. W1-W35.

29. *Wen Wei Po,* June 22, 1985, in *FBIS-China,* June 24, 1985, pp. W3-W5.

30. "Both Sides of the Strait Work Together to Invigorate China," Embassy of the People's Republic of China, Press Release, February 8, 1986, pp. 5-6.

31. *South China Morning Post,* June 22, 1986, p. 1.

32. *Liaowang,* October 13, 1986, in *FBIS-China,* October 29, 1986, p. U2.

33. *Beijing Review,* April 6, 1987, p. 17.

34. Guo-cang Huan, "Taiwan: A View from Beijing," *Foreign Affairs,* 63, 5 (Summer 1985), p. 1068.

35. See Allen S. Whiting, *The Chinese Calculus of Deterrence: India and Indochina* (Ann Arbor, MI: University of Michigan Press, 1975). Also, Ellis Joffe, *The Chinese Army After Mao* (Cambridge, MA: Harvard University Press, 1987).

36. The list was summarized from *Pai Hsing,* June 1, 1985, pp. W7-W11.

5

U.S. Concessions
on Arms Sales to Taiwan

As noted in Chapter 3, Sino-American relations during the first two years of the Reagan administration were very rocky because of the Taiwan issue. The PRC was concerned that Reagan's support of Taiwan might undermine Beijing's success in isolating Taiwan under the Carter administration. From China's point of view, the isolation and demoralization of Taipei were essential to compel the Kuomintang (KMT) to negotiate reunification with the Communist Party of China (CPC). For the first time in a decade, a U.S. administration was coming into office calling for improved relations with Taiwan.

Rather than passively watch its position erode, Beijing directly confronted the Reagan administration over its Taiwan policy. After a series of probes to determine where flexibility existed in the U.S. position, the PRC focused its attention on U.S. arms sales to Taiwan.

China strongly opposed arms sales since American weapons formed the backbone of Taiwan's defensive capabilities. Without U.S. arms, Taipei would be in a much weakened position and might not be able to withstand PRC pressure to enter into negotiations. For both Chinese sides, the arms sales question was crucial to their respective positions regarding China's eventual reunification.

There were at least three reasons why the Reagan administration was vulnerable on the arms sales issue. First, the U.S. wanted to maintain friendly relations with China for vital strategic interests. Second, U.S. assessments of China's military threat to Taiwan were low in view of the PRC's policy of "peaceful reunification." Third, the international security environment provided China with a degree of flexibility in its relations with the superpowers.

The latter point is important because it gave Beijing an excellent bargaining position on the arms sales issue. It will be recalled from Chapter 3 that following the strong American response to the Soviet

Union's invasion of Afghanistan, the PRC grew more confident in U.S. opposition to Soviet expansion in Asia. Also beginning about that time, Moscow began to seek improved relations with China.

Since the U.S. considered relations with China vital to American security interests, Washington believed the PRC threat to Taiwan was low, and the Chinese perceived the immediate Soviet threat to China to be diminished somewhat, Beijing was able to threaten to downgrade relations with the U.S. if advanced arms sales to Taiwan were continued. In this way, the PRC forced the Reagan administration to choose between strategic ties to Beijing and advanced weapons sales to Taipei.

From the 1978-1979 normalization of Sino-American relations until the signing of the August 17, 1982, U.S.-PRC Joint Communiqué, the U.S. did not support the reunification of China. Rather, U.S. policy was that if reunification did occur, it should take place peacefully. No pressure was exerted on Taiwan to accept Beijing's offer for peaceful reunification.

The August 17 Communiqué made the U.S. a more active participant in China's reunification. By linking arms sales to the level of the Chinese military threat to Taiwan, the U.S. obligated itself to reduce weapons sales as long as China pursues peaceful reunification.

The effect of this obligation was to limit U.S. and Taiwan flexibility on the reunification issue. The communiqué gave the PRC a role in determining future U.S. arms sales to Taiwan. The communiqué made it more difficult for the U.S. to support a continuation of the status quo in the Taiwan Strait. The communiqué weakened Taiwan's military deterrence, and it may contribute to a decisive tilt in the military balance of power in the Taiwan Strait region. The communiqué weakened Taiwan's bargaining position vis-à-vis the PRC; it limited the possibility of Taiwan eventually declaring independence; and it made Taipei more subject to PRC threats and intimidation.

To its credit, the Reagan administration attempted to redress the worse aspects of the August 17 Communiqué by applying quanitative and qualitative indexes to arms and technology sold to Taiwan. But whether future administrations will continue this practice is unknown.

The FX Fighter Issue

U.S. Dilemma over Arms Sales to Taiwan

Although initially approved by the Carter administration, the FX sale to Taiwan was delayed because of the normalization of U.S.-PRC relations, congressional insistence that General Dynamics' F-16-J79 be given an opportunity to compete with Northrop's F-5G, and Taipei's indecision in choosing one of the two FX versions. When the Reagan administration assumed office in January 1981, it was widely believed that it would proceed expeditiously with the FX sale. Instead, the administration moved very cautiously because of its concern that the sale might undermine the U.S.-PRC quasi-alliance against the Soviet Union in Asia.By the end of its first year in office, the Reagan administration concluded that the advanced fighter should not be sold to Taipei.

The steps leading up to this decision, and the subsequent August 17, 1982, U.S.-PRC Joint Communiqué, are important to review because they illustrate a difficult dilemma faced by the U.S. in its reunification policy: how to help Taiwan field an adequate self-defense capability, yet not allow U.S. arms sales to wreck the strategically important U.S. relationship with Beijing.

Secretary of State Alexander Haig, convinced that Sino-American strategic cooperation was both desirable and possible, played an instrumental role in the FX decision and the August 17 Communiqué. In June 1981 Haig travelled to China in an attempt to soothe Chinese feelings over Reagan's campaign statements calling for "official" relations with Taiwan. Haig assured Beijing that the Reagan administration intended to treat China as an important and valuable friend for global strategic reasons. He said that "a fundamental strategic perspective" governed Reagan's Asian policy and that a key element was the Soviet threat. To demonstrate the new administration's desire to improve relations with the PRC, Haig announced that, for the first time, the U.S. would be willing to sell arms to China on a case-by-case basis. While Haig was in the Far East, it was disclosed that the U.S. and the PRC were jointly operating a secret monitoring station in Xinjiang to keep track of Soviet missile tests.[1]

When Congress asked the administration for an explanation of Haig's offer to sell weapons to China, it was told that strategic considerations were the basis of the decision. John Holdridge, Assistant Secretary of State for Asian and Pacific Affairs, explained that "our China relationship is global and strategic" and based on "the premise that China is not our adversary, but a friendly, developing country with which, without being allied, we share important strategic interests."[2] That perception of China has remained throughout the Reagan administration and has served as the basis for U.S. China policy, including policies toward Taiwan and the reunification issue.

Haig's offer to sell weapons to China did not assuage Beijing on the Taiwan issue, however. Because of the new administration's well-known friendship with Taipei, speculation immediately arose that the U.S. had struck a deal with the Chinese to exchange arms sales to the

PRC for arms sales to Taiwan. To end such conjecture, the PRC Foreign Ministry said on June 10, 1981, "We would rather receive no U.S. arms than accept continuing U.S. interference in our internal affairs by selling arms to Taiwan, to which we can never agree."[3] On several occasions, the PRC accused the U.S. of selling arms to Taiwan in order to prevent China's reunification.

Taking advantage of the new administration's concern over the Soviet threat and its obvious desire to draw the PRC into a strategic relationship, the Chinese stepped up pressure by threatening to turn away from the U.S. if it continued to disregard Beijing's concerns over Taiwan. Deng Xiaoping said in August 1981:

> China hopes that Sino-American relations will further develop rather than retrogress. However, this should not be one-sided. If the United States adopts a wrong view, it will formulate a wrong policy. It is nothing serious even if the United States causes a retrogression in Sino-American relations. If worst comes to worst and the relations retrogress to those prior to 1972, China will not collapse. It did not collapse before 1972, much less will it collapse now. In the 1950s, we got some help from the Soviet Union. Later, we did not get any. But, have we not survived? The Chinese people have high aspirations. They will never bow and scrape and beg for help. . . . In the interests of the whole world and in the interests of the Chinese and the Americans, China and the United States should cooperate on an equal footing. If the United States does not play fair but forces China to act according to the will of the United States, China will not agree, nor is there any reason for China to agree.[4]

In October Chinese Foreign Minister Huang Hua warned of "storms" and "reefs" ahead in Sino-American relations and emphasized the importance of handling U.S.-PRC relations "with a strategic perspective."[5] Staking out China's bargaining position on future arms sales to Taiwan, Huang Hua told U.S. leaders that the PRC would oppose the sale of any weapons to Taiwan unless the United States made a public commitment to reduce arms sales gradually over a fixed period, with a final cutoff date around 1986.[6]

Arms sales to Taiwan became an important domestic political issue in the U.S. as well. The Reagan administration came under intense pressure, both from supporters of Taiwan who saw the FX as necessary to Taipei's defense and from those who feared that the FX sale would undermine Sino-American relations.[7] The House Subcommittee on Asian and Pacific Affairs sent a letter to President Reagan on June 18, 1981, urging him not to approve the FX on the grounds that (a) there was no PRC military threat to Taiwan, (b) Beijing was pursuing a policy of peaceful reunification, and (c) the sale of an advanced fighter would jeopardize the delicate and mutually beneficial relations between the U.S. and China.

Other members of the House Foreign Affairs Committee sent a letter to the President on November 17 asking him to approve the sale since (a) Beijing had refused to renounce the use of force against Taiwan and (b) Taiwan's fighters were obsolescent. Those favoring the sale tended to believe that China needed the U.S. more than the U.S. needed China and that, therefore, Beijing's threats to downgrade Sino-American relations were empty rhetoric. This group also believed that honoring the U.S. moral commitment to help Taiwan defend itself against communism was more important than pursuing a potential strategic alliance with China to counter the Soviet Union. A poll conducted in the Senate in June 1981 revealed that only six senators disapproved the sale of the FX to Taiwan, while 59 senators approved. The remainder were undecided or did not respond.[8]

As debate raged in Washington and the administration appeared uncertain as to what course should be followed, the PRC issued a number of extremely strong warnings in December 1981. Perhaps to test Chinese reaction or, more deviously, to provoke a Chinese reaction, the U.S. announced on December 29 that it was going to sell Taiwan $97 million in military spare parts. Although such transactions were common practice, the Chinese responded immediately.

In an important *Renmin Ribao* commentary, the PRC said that a point of crisis had been reached over the arms sales issue in Sino-American relations.[9] The article noted that the question of arms sales to Taiwan had always existed as "an obstacle on the road to the development of Sino-American relations." The commentary argued that, after extending diplomatic relations to the PRC and acknowledging "that there is only one China, that the PRC is the sole legal government of China, and that Taiwan is part of China," the U.S. had no right to sell arms "to the Taiwan authorities, who constitute a local force in China."

Despite this fact, the commentary continued, the Reagan administration had announced its intention to continue to sell arms to Taiwan and perhaps to increase the level of sales. The commentary claimed that the U.S. side had even declared that China had no right to interfere in the matter. "In this way the gravity of the problem has increased and, as a result, the problem has now reached a point where it absolutely must be solved."

The article continued: "What China requires from the United States on the Taiwan issue is that it should properly respect China's sovereignty and territorial integrity and not interfere in China's internal affairs. . . . On the issue of how to solve the problem of U.S. arms sales to

Taiwan, China both sticks to its principles and is also reasonable."
Renmin Ribao said that the Reagan administration had "tried by every
means to deny facts in an attempt to avoid being constrained" on arms
sales. The article gave the U.S. this advice: "If you want to preserve
and develop Sino-American relations, then the problem of U.S. arms
sales to Taiwan must be solved on the basis of properly respecting
China's sovereignty. There is no way this problem can be solved by
ignoring China's sovereignty."

The commentary went on to reaffirm the Chinese government's
"endeavor to solve the Taiwan issue by peaceful means." This resolution
had created a "new situation" in the Taiwan Strait which made further
U.S. arms sales to Taiwan unnecessary. The article said:

> It is precisely because the Chinese Government has made a series of
> major efforts [to promote peaceful reunification] that a new situation has
> emerged in the solution of the Taiwan issue. This has also objectively
> created the most favorable conditions for the United States to halt its
> arms sales to Taiwan, to refrain from interfering again in China's internal
> affairs, and to eliminate the obstacle that threatens relations between
> the two countries.

The commentary strongly implied that if the U.S. continued to sell
arms to Taiwan, then U.S. intentions must be to create "two Chinas."
The article concluded with a warning that Sino-American strategic
cooperation would be damaged by continued arms sales:

> The Chinese Government has always viewed and handled Sino-American
> relations from the angle of global strategy. On the issue of how to solve
> the problem of U.S. arms sales to Taiwan, the Chinese Government both
> safeguards China's sovereignty and considers the overall strategic situation.
> At present, the Chinese people . . . are watching with concern whether
> or not the U.S. Government can correctly solve the issue of arms sales
> to Taiwan. This will be a severe test of whether or not the United States
> truly treasures its relations with China and has a concept of global
> strategy.

The intensity of the Chinese protest against the spare parts sale to
Taiwan caught many in the administration by surprise. Apparently, the
PRC reaction tipped the scales in the decision-making process in favor
of denying the FX to Taiwan. There was concern that, if the Chinese
reacted so strongly to a spare parts transaction, then their response
would be much stronger if the FX were sold to Taiwan.

The FX Decision

A few days after the *Renmin Ribao* commentary, the Reagan administration announced that it was not selling Taiwan the FX. In its January 11, 1982, statement to the press, the Department of State explained:

> Concerned agencies of the U.S. Government, including the Departments of State and Defense and other national security elements, have been addressing the question of Taiwan's defense needs over a period of many months and have taken into consideration the many factors which bear on the judgments which must be made in implementing this policy.
> . . .
> A judgment has . . . been reached by the concerned agencies on the question of replacement aircraft for Taiwan. The conclusion is that no sale of advanced fighter aircraft to Taiwan is required because no military need for such aircraft exists. Taiwan's defense needs can be met as they arise, and for the foreseeable future, by replacing aging aircraft now in the Taiwan inventory with comparable aircraft and by extension of the F-5E coproduction line in Taiwan.[10]

The decision not to sell Taiwan an advanced fighter was a considerable concession to the PRC on the part of the Reagan administration. Many of the President's closest political supporters bitterly criticized the decision. Like Carter's December 15, 1978, announcement of the breaking of U.S.-ROC diplomatic relations, the FX decision was announced over the congressional Christmas recess, when Congress was unable to react strongly. When Secretary of State Haig was asked as to why he had not notified Congress prior to the FX decision, he responded:

> There was certainly no intention to avoid congressional consultation in reaching the FX decision, but events in mid-late December in Poland and China's extreme reaction to our notification of a Taiwan spare parts transaction to the Congress forced a decision earlier than we expected, before Congress returned from recess.[11]

Haig's reference to Poland is interesting, because the concession to China over the FX was made in the hope that Chinese cooperation with the U.S. on strategic issues would be forthcoming. In December 1981 the U.S. had urged Beijing to cooperate with the U.S. in opposing the imposition of martial law in Poland and in condemning the role of the Soviet Union in the crackdown on Solidarity. As it turned out, China rebuffed the U.S. appeal and signed instead an agreement with the Warsaw government increasing trade by 30 percent.[12] The fact that the Reagan administration expected Beijing to side with Washington in supporting anti-government trade unions in Poland is one of the clearest indications of U.S. mistakes in perceiving China's intentions to cooperate strategically with the U.S. Chinese officials have frequently pointed to the rise of Solidarity in Poland as an example of what they hope to avoid as China proceeds with its urban economic reforms.

A further U.S. error in perceptions was the belief that China's leaders would be satisfied with the FX decision and be willing to set aside the arms sales issue in order to proceed with strategic cooperation with the U.S. The administration dispatched Assistant Secretary of State John Holdridge to the PRC to explain the FX decision and to inform Beijing that the U.S. had also decided not to sell Taipei the Harpoon antiship missile.

Contrary to U.S. expectations, Holdridge received harsh criticism from the Chinese. Instead of praising the FX decision, the PRC lodged "a strong protest" against the extension of the F-5E coproduction line. An article in *Xinhua* stated, "The Chinese Government will never accept any unilateral decision made by the U.S. Government" on arms sales to Taiwan.[13] The PRC was signalling Washington that the arms sales issue was not resolved. It further raised its demands yet another step, insisting that Beijing be notified in advance of future sales to Taiwan.

Yet another negotiating point surfaced in a January 31, 1982, *Xinhua* commentary, when the Chinese demanded that a certain date be set for the termination of arms sales to Taiwan. The article said that while the PRC considered U.S. arms sales an "infringement" of China's sovereignty, Beijing was willing "to negotiate with the United States for an end to the sales within a time limit." The article implied that the PRC was being reasonable on this issue in the larger strategic interests of the two sides.[14]

It was during this period that negotiations between Washington and Beijing began in earnest over what eventually became the August 17, 1982, U.S.-PRC Joint Communiqué. Throughout these difficult negotiations, both sides exerted intense efforts to achieve their minimal objectives. For the U.S. these included the right to continue to sell arms to Taiwan under conditions stipulated by the Taiwan Relations Act. Beijing's objectives included limiting future U.S. arms sales to Taiwan under an agreement recognizing PRC sovereignty over Taiwan. Both sides wished to preserve friendly Sino-American relations, although the U.S. was more concerned than Beijing over strategic cooperation at this point. In hindsight this differing perception of the feasibility of a strategic relationship provided the PRC with insurmountable leverage on the U.S. In the end, both sides compromised; but, on the surface at least, the U.S. concession was significantly greater in that it set into motion trends making it more difficult for Taiwan to avoid eventual reunification with the mainland.

The August 17 Communiqué

The August 17, 1982, U.S.-PRC Joint Communiqué was important to U.S. reunification policy for several reasons. In addition to limiting future U.S. arms sales to Taiwan and thus adversely affecting Taipei's security, the communiqué contained several statements which could be interpreted as U.S. encouragement of peaceful reunification. At minimum, the provisions made it difficult for the U.S. to pursue a policy of supporting the status quo in the Taiwan Strait. The communiqué made U.S. support for Taiwan's independence virtually impossible.

PRC Increases Pressure on Arms Sales Issue

On the tenth anniversary of the February 1972 Shanghai Communiqué, *Xinhua* released a commentary linking a settlement of the Taiwan issue to continuation of the strategically important Sino-American relationship. The article said:

> Sino-U.S. relations have truly come to a critical point that will determine if relations improve or deteriorate. China has consistently held that because of the interests of global strategy, it is necessary for Sino-U.S. ties to develop. This is what China has strived to achieve. However, the United States must observe the sovereignty of China as a prerequisite for a better relationship. Unfortunately, some people in the United States always try to interfere in the internal affairs of China, flouting China's sovereignty. They seek to create "two-Chinas" by one means or another, and even regard Taiwan as an "unsinkable aircraft carrier" in the Far East for the United States. . . .
>
> In view of the fact that the Taiwan issue is inherited from history, the Chinese Government, while sticking to its principled position, has been very patient and realistic in its negotiations with Washington and has put forward many reasonable and just proposals. However, the matter has developed to such a point that China is forced into a corner without any options. If the United States insists on a long-term policy of selling arms to Taiwan, Sino-U.S. relations will retrogress.[15]

The U.S. responded to these and other warnings with assurances to China that the Reagan administration valued its strategic relationship with the PRC. President Reagan himself became involved in trying to defuse rising tensions in Sino-American relations over the arms sales issue. In early April 1982 Reagan sent personal letters to Deng Xiaoping and Zhao Ziyang expressing his desire to find a mutually acceptable solution to the Taiwan issue.[16] He also said the U.S. appreciated the lowering of tensions in the Taiwan Strait as a result of China's pursuit of peaceful reunification. In his letter to Deng, the President wrote:

> Clearly, the Taiwan issue has been a most difficult problem between our governments. Nonetheless, vision and statesmanship have enabled us in the past to reduce our differences over this issue while we have built a framework of long-term friendship and cooperation.
>
> The United States firmly adheres to the positions agreed upon in the joint communiqué on the establishment of diplomatic relations between the United States and China. There is only one China. We will not permit the unofficial relations between the American people and the people of Taiwan to weaken our commitment to this principle.
>
> I fully understand and respect the position of your government with regard to the question of arms sales to Taiwan. As you know, our position on this matter was stated in the process of normalization: The United States has an abiding interest in the peaceful resolution of the Taiwan question.
>
> We fully recognize the significance of the nine-point proposal of September 30, 1981, and the policy [of peaceful reunification] set forth by your government as early as January 1, 1979. [See Chapter 6.] The decisions and the principles conveyed on my instructions to your government on January 11, 1982, reflect our appreciation of the new situation created by these developments.
>
> In this spirit, we wish to continue our efforts to resolve our differences and to create a cooperative and enduring bilateral and strategic relationship. China and America are two great nations destined to grow stronger through cooperation, not weaker through division.

In his letter to Premier Zhao Ziyang, President Reagan reiterated his desire to preserve Sino-American relations and his appreciation of Chinese efforts to resolve the reunification issue peacefully. U.S. friendship with the people of Taiwan was rooted in history, he said, but the U.S. would not allow that friendship to undermine U.S.-PRC relations. He commented:

> The present state of relations between our two countries deeply concerns me. We believe significant deterioration in those relations would serve the interests of neither the United States of America nor the People's Republic of China.
>
> The differences between us are rooted in the longstanding friendship between the American people and the Chinese people who live on Taiwan. We will welcome and support any peaceful resolution of the

Taiwan question. In this connection, we appreciate the policies which your government has followed to provide a peaceful settlement.

As I told Vice Premier Huang [Hua] in Washington, we welcome your nine-point initiative.

As I also told the Vice Premier, we expect that in the context of progress toward a peaceful solution there would naturally be a decrease in the need for arms by Taiwan. Our positions over the past two months have reflected this view.

In May the President sent Vice President George Bush to Beijing with yet another presidential letter echoing the same general themes, this time to General Secretary Hu Yaobang.

Key administration officials continued to emphasize the importance of Sino-American relations in their public statements. On June 1 Deputy Secretary of State Walter Stoessel told the National Council on U.S.-China Trade that a "strong U.S.-China relationship is one of the highest goals of President Reagan's foreign policy." He defined China as "a friendly country with which we are not allied, but with which we share many common interests." "Strategically," he said, "we have no fundamental conflicts of interests, and we face a common challenge from the Soviet Union."

Stoessel reconfirmed the Reagan administration's acceptance of the principles underlying the normalization agreement and pointed out that the President had taken four important initiatives to demonstrate his desire to improve Sino-American relations. These were (1) the expansion of technology transfers; (2) the provision for arms transfers; (3) the removal of legislative restrictions on trade and other relations with China as a member of the communist bloc; and (4) the expansion of consular relations.

Stoessel said, "We recognize that a secure, modernizing China is important to the United States from a global and strategic perspective." He noted that arms sales to Taiwan were "the one serious issue that threaten good relations," and expressed hope that "this complex, historical issue" could be resolved by "statesmanship, vision, and good will" on the part of both the United States and China.[17]

Reaction from U.S. Supporters of Taiwan

As word leaked out that an agreement limiting future arms sales to Taiwan was forthcoming, U.S. supporters of Taiwan began to raise loud objections. Coming on the heels of the administration's refusal to sell Taiwan the FX, such an agreement was seen to be a "sell-out of old friends" on Taiwan. The administration was accused of being cowed by PRC threats, which supporters of Taiwan tended to dismiss on the grounds that China would never downgrade substantive relations with the U.S. Conservatives argued that the PRC needed the U.S. to counterbalance the Soviet Union and needed American trade, investments, and technology to succeed with the Four Modernizations. The fact that details of the negotiations were kept highly secret had the effect of fueling even greater suspicions among Taiwan's friends.

In early July 1982 the *Washington Times* reported that the State Department had prepared at least two versions of a secret communiqué limiting future arms sales to Taiwan. One version contained a U.S. pledge "to reduce gradually such sales and to eventually terminate them."[18] Senator Barry Goldwater, a leading supporter of Taiwan in the Congress, asked the State Department about the versions. He was told no such drafts had been prepared. The White House also queried the State Department and received a similar response.

But as evidence unfolded, it became apparent that the State Department had indeed secretly prepared the draft communiqués. As Goldwater commented when all of this became public: "It was clear to me and to the White House that President Reagan, Vice President Bush, and National Security Adviser William Clark had been lied to by the State Department about what they were planning."[19]

According to sources within the Congress, the withholding of information about the communiqué drafts influenced the timing of Alexander Haig's resignation as Secretary of State. When key Republican congressmen were told on June 23 of the State Department's attempt to keep the drafts from Congress and the White House, they reportedly became quite angry and demanded that something be done. The next day, President Reagan informed Haig that he would accept the Secretary's resignation.[20]

Conservatives were outraged at what they considered to be the State Department's manipulation of U.S. China policy to the detriment of Taiwan. They heavily pressured the President to make good on his promises to implement fully the arms sales provisions of the Taiwan Relations Act. During the June 23 meeting to discuss this issue, National Security Adviser William Clark told the congressmen there would be "no backing away" from Taiwan and "no time limit on the sale of arms" to Taipei.[21] On July 9 representatives from 28 conservative groups met in Washington and warned the President that he would receive an "extremely acrimonious" backlash from his supporters if he agreed to any cutoff of arms to Taiwan.[22]

Beijing ridiculed the conservatives, commenting that with "their minds crammed with the prejudices of the 1950s, they are devoid of an elementary knowledge about international affairs." *People's Daily* editorialized:"It is easily seen that the long-term and fundamental goal of these conservative die-hards is to create 'two Chinas' and keep Taiwan under the control and aegis of the United States in a vain attempt to continue the division of China indefinitely. . . . We advise these old-liners to take a dose of sobriety to sober up and return to reality."[23]

Beijing also had strong words of warning for incoming Secretary of State George Shultz. During his Senate confirmation hearings, he was asked about U.S. policy toward China and Taiwan. Shultz said he approved of the continued supply of "defensive arms" to Taiwan and pledged to carry out the provisions of the Taiwan Relations Act. Shultz also described the development of Sino-American relations as being of "great importance." He indicated that he would recommend to the President an early decision on the F-5E sale to Taiwan promised by the U.S. in its FX decision of January 11.[24] *People's Daily* warned Shultz that "Sino-U.S. relations would be sabotaged if the views held by Goldwater and his ilk prevail."[25]

Perhaps fearing the repercussions of undermining the conservative political support of his administration, Reagan decided that no further compromise to the Chinese would be made on the arms sales issue. On July 14 the administration gave several assurances to Taipei. As described in the official ROC statement on the August 17 Communiqué, Washington told Taiwan that the U.S.:

1. has not agreed to set a date for ending arms sales to the Republic of China,
2. has not agreed to hold prior consultations with the Chinese communists on arms sales to the Republic of China,
3. will not play any mediation role between Taipei and Peiping,
4. has not agreed to revise the Taiwan Relations Act,
5. has not altered its position regarding sovereignty over Taiwan,
6. will not exert pressure on the Republic of China to enter into negotiations with the Chinese communists.

The administration announced in mid-July its intention to sell Taiwan the additional F-5Es promised in place of the FX. At the same time, however, the administration proposed to China an agreement containing assurances that in the future it would not sell Taiwan weapons of higher quantity or quality than those sold in the past. On July 30 the President and his advisers told key congressional supporters that this was the final offer to the Chinese and that the F-5E sale would go forward in two weeks. Presidential aides explained that the assurances given Beijing were deliberately vague in order to give the U.S. the freedom to determine whether the flow of arms at current levels would be sufficient in the future. Implicit in the administration's explanation was the right of the U.S. to adjust its mix of arms to Taiwan to allow for inflation, technological advances, and increased threats from the mainland.[26]

Beijing twice rejected the new proposal, but when it became apparent that the U.S. would proceed with the F-5E sale regardless of whether an agreement had been signed, China accepted. Those close to the negotiations reported that, until the last moment, the PRC took an extremely tough position, warning of dire consequences should the F-5E sale go forward.

Communiqué Provisions and Interpretations

The August 17 Communiqué contained a number of provisions which were relevant to U.S. reunification policy. As a result of signing the communiqué, the U.S. moved further away from possible support of Taiwan's independence in the future, signalled U.S. approval of Beijing's policy of peaceful reunification, and made it more difficult for Taiwan to defend itself against a PRC use of force.

In the communiqué's first paragraph, the U.S. reaffirmed its acceptance of the principles of the 1979 normalization agreement. The U.S. accepted the PRC government as the sole legal government of China. It acknowledged the Chinese view that there is but one China and Taiwan is part of China. But "within that context," the U.S. will maintain "unofficial relations with the people of Taiwan."

The second paragraph pointed out that the issue of arms sales to Taiwan had never been resolved, but had been set aside in order to bring about the normalization of Sino-American relations. Paragraph three reconfirmed both sides' recognition that "respect for each other's sovereignty and territorial integrity and non-interference in each other's internal affairs constitute the fundamental principles guiding United States-China relations."

Paragraph four contained an important reference to China's "fundamental policy of striving for peaceful reunification of the Motherland." The "Message to Compatriots in Taiwan" issued on January 1, 1979, and the "Nine-Point Proposal" of Ye Jianying issued on September 30, 1981 were cited as major efforts on the part of China to promulgate this "fundamental policy."

In paragraph five the United States, after emphasizing the importance it attaches to Sino-American relations, reiterated that "it has no intention of infringing on Chinese sovereignty and territorial integrity, or interfering in China's internal affairs, or pursuing a policy of 'two Chinas' or 'one China, one Taiwan'." The U.S. said that it "understands and appreciates" China's fundamental policy of "striving for a peaceful resolution of the Taiwan question." Because of China's peaceful re-unification policy, the U.S. noted that a "new situation . . . has emerged with regard to the Taiwan question" which created an environment in which the arms sales issue might be resolved.

Paragraph six contained substantive and controversial commitments by the U.S. It stated:

> Having in mind the foregoing statements of both sides, the United States Government states that it does not seek to carry out a long-term policy of arms sales to Taiwan, that its arms sales to Taiwan will not exceed, either in qualitative or in quantitative terms, the level of those supplied in recent years since the establishment of diplomatic relations between the United States and China, and that it intends to reduce gradually its sales of arms to Taiwan, leading over a period of time to a final resolution.

In paragraph seven both sides promised to make every effort over time to resolve the arms sales issue, which is referred to as being "rooted in history." Paragraph eight stated that Sino-American relations were in the interests of both countries, as well as conducive to world peace and stability. Both governments promised, "on the principle of equality and mutual benefit," to "strengthen their ties in the economic, cultural, educational, scientific, technological and other fields."

In the final paragraph, in order to "bring about the healthy development" of Sino-American relations, the two countries reaffirmed "the principles agreed on by the two sides in the Shanghai Communiqué and the Joint Communiqué on the Establishment of Diplomatic Relations." Both sides would seek, on the basis of the above principles, to "maintain world peace and oppose aggression and expansion."

Disagreement arose immediately over the communiqué's interpretation. The reason, as noted by Senator S. I. Hayakawa, was that the "communiqué means either what you want it to mean or what you fear it means. There is enough ambiguity in the document, it seems, that no one need take offense. . . . What we have in the communiqué is a situation not uncommon in human affairs: total ambiguity."[27] Others viewed it as a highly dangerous document. Former American Institute in Taiwan (AIT) director Charles Cross warned in the *New York Times* that the communiqué took the unprecedented step of connecting the level of U.S. arms sales to Taiwan to Taipei's response to Beijing's proposals for peaceful reunification. He wrote:

> The administration . . . has now taken a step which preceding administrations carefully avoided.

By welcoming Beijing's nine-point proposal on Taiwan and establishing a negotiable connection between U.S. arms sales to Taiwan and the latter's responses to the PRC's gestures toward reunification, the President has moved us into a dangerous area. . . .

Our interest has heretofore been confined to keeping the process peaceful, without other involvement. The Chinese were never in doubt, from the beginning of normalization on January 1, 1979, that the carefully selected weapons sold to Taiwan were only for that purpose. If we slide off this simple principle in an effort to accommodate Beijing, neither we nor the Chinese will be able to finesse the Taiwan issue in the future, particularly since there is no disposition in Taiwan to change the status quo.[28]

Because of the highly politicized nature of the document, President Reagan became personally involved in its interpretation. In his official statement on the communiqué, the President said that the communiqué made possible the advancement of the "important strategic relationship" between the U.S. and China, "consistent with our obligations to the people of Taiwan." Such a relationship, the President said, "is vital to our long-term security interests and contributes to stability in East Asia."

Reagan said U.S. arms sales policy to Taiwan as contained in the communiqué "is fully consistent with the Taiwan Relations Act" and that arms sales "will continue in accordance with the Act and with the full expectation that the approach of the Chinese Government to the resolution of the Taiwan issue will continue to be peaceful." Recognizing the importance of economic stability and confidence in the future for prosperity on Taiwan, Reagan promised: "My administration, acting through appropriate channels, will continue strongly to foster that development and to contribute to a strong and healthy investment climate, thereby enhancing the well-being of the people of Taiwan."

More of the President's personal feelings and his interpretation of the August 17 Communiqué were revealed in an interview with the conservative newspaper *Human Events.* Reagan responded to criticism that he had reneged on his campaign promises to live up to the defense provisions of the TRA by saying:

Our communiqué is a very carefully worked out deal, and we did not give an inch. In that communiqué, the People's Republic has agreed that they are going to try and peacefully resolve the Taiwanese issue. We, in turn, linked our statement about weaponry to that and said that if they make progress and do, indeed, peacefully work out a solution agreeable to both sides, then, obviously, there would no longer be any need for arms. And all the reference to reducing arms is tied to progress in that. We will abide by the Taiwan Relations Act, the law of this country, which says that we will help maintain Taiwan's defensive posture and capability. . . . If the day ever comes that those two find that they can get together and become one China, in a peaceful manner, then there wouldn't be any need for arms sales to Taiwan. And that's all that was meant in the communiqué. Nothing was meant beyond that.[29]

The same interpretation was given privately to Republican congressmen on August 17, 1982. During the meeting, administration officials said the TRA would remain the guide for U.S. policy toward Taiwan. The communiqué was described as a victory for the administration because it permitted the sale of the additional F-5Es to Taipei without resulting in the downgrading of relations with the PRC. The congressmen were assured that if one day the PRC initiated hostilities toward Taiwan, the U.S. would increase arms sales to counter the threat. An important interpretation of the qualitative and quantitative limitations referred to in paragraph six of the communiqué was also given. These limitations were not intended to fix the level of arms sold to Taiwan, the congressmen were told, but rather to tie weapons transfers to the level of threat existing in the Taiwan Strait.

Assistant Secretary of State John Holdridge, who soon would be replaced by Paul Wolfowitz, appeared before the House Committee on Foreign Affairs on August 18 to explain the communiqué.[30] Holdridge said two considerations guided U.S. negotiations: the "fundamental national interests of the United States to preserve and advance its strategic relations with China" and "our historic obligations to the people of Taiwan."

Holdridge argued that because of improved relations between the U.S. and China, "Taiwan has never been more secure." He said that the TRA commits "the U.S. to sell to Taiwan arms necessary to maintain a sufficient self-defense capability," but that friendly Sino-American relations and Beijing's fundamental policy of peaceful reunification had convinced the administration that "so long as that policy continued, the threat to Taiwan would be greatly diminished." On the basis of this reasoning, Holdridge said, "We were thus able to consider a policy under which we would limit our arms sales to the levels reached in recent years and would anticipate a gradual reduction of the level of arms sales."

In an important explanation of the U.S. interpretation of the communiqué, Holdridge linked the qualitative and quantitative limitations in paragraph six with the continuation of China's peaceful approach to reunification. He explained:

Let me summarize the essence of our understanding on this point: China has announced a fundamental policy of pursuing peaceful means to resolve the long-standing dispute between Taiwan and the mainland. Having in mind this policy and the consequent reduction in the military threat to Taiwan, we have stated our intention to reduce arms sales to Taiwan gradually, and said that in quantity and quality we would not go beyond levels established since normalization. . . . While we have no reason to believe that China's policy will change, an inescapable corollary to these mutually interdependent policies is that should that happen, we will reassess ours. Our guiding principle is now and will continue to be that embodied in the Taiwan Relations Act: the maintenance of a self-defense capability sufficient to meet the military needs of Taiwan, but with the understanding that China's maintenance of a peaceful approach to the Taiwan question will permit gradual reductions in arms sales.

Holdridge defined the "new situation" referred to in paragraph five as meaning that "for the first time, China has described its peaceful policy toward Taiwan" as being "fundamental." He said the term "final resolution" in paragraph six did not have an exact meaning, but rather "a variety of different formulae that one might consider in reaching a final solution." He further emphasized that the U.S. was not operating under any specific time frame in its promise to reduce arms sales "over a period of time."

Questions immediately arose over whether the August 17 Communiqué would take legal precedence over the TRA. State Department Legal Advisor Davis Robinson explained to the Senate Judiciary Committee on September 27 that this would not be the case. He said:

[The August 17 Communiqué] is not an international agreement and thus imposes no obligations on either party under international law. Its status under domestic law is that of a statement by the President of a policy which he intends to pursue. . . . The Taiwan Relations Act is and will remain the law of the land unless amended by Congress. Nothing in the joint communiqué obligates the President to act in a manner contrary to the Act or, conversely, disables him from fulfilling his responsibilities under it.[31]

The Reagan administration attempted to minimize the damage done to Taiwan's security by the August 17 Communiqué by interpreting the agreement as lacking precedence over the TRA and by linking promises of future arms sales reductions to the continuation of China's policy of peaceful reunification. More practically, the administration sold Taiwan adequate military equipment to limit the immediate adverse effects of the communiqué. A key decision was announced in March 1983, when the State Department released figures setting ceilings for arms sales to Taiwan at $800 million for fiscal year 1983 and $760 million for fiscal year 1984.

These figures were highly important because they were the first indication that the U.S. had applied a quantitative index to the level of its arms sales to Taiwan in the post-communiqué period. The figures for 1979, 1980, and 1981—the base years referred to in the communiqué—were $598 million, $601 million, and $295 million, respectively. To reconcile the 1983 and 1984 figures with these base years, the State Department explained that an "inflationary index" had been applied. Thus, the $598 million of 1979 would be equivalent to $830 million in current, inflated dollars.[32]

After 1983 the Reagan administration reduced arms sales to Taiwan by about $20 million a year. At the same time that government-approved sales were decreasing, U.S. commercial sales of defense-related equipment to Taiwan increased.

Not surprisingly, China had a vastly different interpretation of the August 17 Communiqué. The PRC rejected any linkage between the level of arms sold to Taipei and Beijing's policy of peaceful reunification. It also attempted to use the new agreement to weaken the TRA. In its official statement on the communiqué, the Chinese Foreign Ministry noted:[33]

> U.S. arms sales to Taiwan should have been terminated altogether long ago. But considering that this is an issue left over by history, the Chinese Government, while upholding the principles, has agreed to settle it step by step. The U.S. side has committed that, as the first step, its arms sales to Taiwan will not exceed, either in qualitative or in quantitative terms, the level of those supplied in recent years since the establishment of diplomatic relations between the two countries, and that they will be gradually reduced, leading to a final resolution of this issue over a period of time.

In an important difference of interpretation with the U.S., the PRC said, "The final resolution referred to here certainly implies that the U.S. arms sales to Taiwan must be completely terminated over a period of time." The official PRC statement strongly denied any connection between the communiqué and the TRA, which was considered domestic legislation by Beijing and hence inapplicable to Sino-American relations. The Chinese said: "All interpretations designed to link the present joint communiqué to the 'Taiwan Relations Act' are in violation of the spirit and substance of this communiqué and are thus unacceptable."

An August 17 *Renmin Ribao* commentary was even more blunt in insisting that how Beijing resolved the Taiwan issue was solely China's internal affair. There was no connection, according to the commentary, between future U.S. arms sales to Taiwan and the continuation of China's peaceful reunification policy. The commentary said:

> Taiwan is China's territory and the method we choose to solve the Taiwan problem is entirely a problem of China's internal affairs. The United States has no right to demand that China undertake any obligations as to the methods it chooses in solving the Taiwan problem, nor should the United States put forth as a prerequisite condition for the cessation of arms sales to Taiwan that China commit itself to not solving the Taiwan problem by any means other than peaceful ones.[34]

Whereas the U.S. had hoped the August 17 Communiqué would placate the PRC over the Taiwan issue, the Chinese saw the agreement as one of a series of steps leading to the eventual disengagement of the U.S. from Taiwan. From Beijing's point of view, such disengagement was necessary before Taipei would agree to China's terms for reunification.

Immediately after the communiqué's announcement, China set its next marker in Sino-American negotiations over U.S. support of Taiwan. The *Renmin Ribao* commentary cited above targeted the Taiwan Relations Act as the principal obstacle yet remaining in U.S.-PRC relations. The article said, "The fundamental obstacle to the development of Sino-U.S. relations is the U.S. 'Taiwan Relations Act'. . . . If the decision-makers in Washington insist on handling the relations between the two countries in accordance with this U.S. domestic act, Sino-U.S. relations will not only come to a standstill, but will definitely face another crisis."[35]

The Chinese quickly found, however, that unlike the issue of advanced arms sales to Taiwan, where there were genuine differences of American opinion, there was strong bipartisan support for the Taiwan Relations Act in the U.S. Little sentiment could be found in the administration, Congress, or general public to repeal or even to amend the TRA. China had succeeded in limiting future arms sales to Taiwan, but it had not succeeded in removing the legal justification for such transactions.

Realism in the Post-Communiqué Period

Despite significant differences in U.S. and PRC interpretations of the August 17 Communiqué, the agreement had the effect of enabling both sides to back away from harsh rhetoric and to concentrate on more pragmatic policies. This was especially important for the U.S. After the communiqué, the U.S. assumed a more realistic assessment of Sino-American relations, particularly the limitations to strategic cooperation with the Chinese. The U.S. felt able to pursue policies which earlier were rejected on the grounds that they might seriously damage US.-PRC strategic relations.

Two days after the communiqué's release, the Reagan administration announced its intention to permit Taiwan to coproduce with Northrop an additional 30 F-5Es and 30 F-5Fs over the next two and a half years, a package worth $622 million.[36] Two additional sales were announced shortly thereafter for 500 Maverick air-to-ground missiles and $97 million worth of various armored vehicles. In February 1983 the U.S. sold Taiwan 66 F-104G fighters, previously owned by West Germany, for $31 million. And in July the administration sold Taipei $530 million in military equipment, including land- and sea-based Chaparral missiles for air defense, SM-1 Standard missiles for shipborne air defense, AIM-7F Sparrow radar-homing air-to-air missiles, conversion kits for M-4 tanks, tank-recovery vehicles, and aircraft spare parts. The Standard and Sparrow missiles had been sought by Taiwan for several years, and the sophisticated nature of these missiles indicated that the U.S. had begun to apply at least a minimal qualitative indexing to its arms sales as well. Significantly, the PRC reported these sales but did not protest too strongly.

Far more important than arms sales was the administration's decision in early 1983 to shift the centerpiece of U.S. strategy in Asia from China back to Japan, where it had rested for much of the post-World War II period. President Reagan said in Boston on February 23, 1983, that "the U.S.-Japanese relationship remains the centerpiece of our Asian policy."[37] Henceforth, the administration viewed China primarily as an important regional, but not global power. This lowered perception of China's role in international affairs tended to make administration officials less willing to compromise over Taiwan.

Paul Wolfowitz, the new Assistant Secretary of State for Asian and Pacific Affairs, told the House Committee on Foreign Affairs on February 28, 1983, that the administration wanted "to put U.S.-China relations back on a stable, realistic footing."[38] Secretary of State George Shultz said on February 18, "We're not going to turn our backs" on Taiwan, mentioning that "they fought on our side" in the Korean and Vietnam wars.[39] And in a March 5 speech in San Francisco, Shultz noted:

China's new, more constructive, though guarded, role is welcome, and a closer relationship with China will benefit the people of both our countries. However, frustrations and problems in our relationship are inevitable. They will arise not only out of differences concerning Taiwan but out of the differences between our two systems.

Progress in U.S.-China relations need not come at the expense of relations with our other friends in the region, including our close unofficial relationship with the people of Taiwan. To the contrary, it can contribute to the peace and economic progress of the entire region. The key to managing our differences over Taiwan lies in observing the commitments made in our three joint communiqués and allowing the parties themselves to resolve their differences peacefully with the passage of time.[40]

It was clear from the remarks made by administration officials following their acceptance of the August 17 Communiqué that the U.S. no longer pursued a strategic relationship with the PRC at the expense of Taiwan. China contributed to this development by publicly adopting in September 1982 an "independent" foreign policy calling for improved relations with the Soviet Union. In the absence of a strategic motivation, little need was seen to modify any further U.S. reunification policy.

In 1983 the basic policy remained one of encouraging both Chinese sides to work out their differences peacefully without direct U.S. involvement. The administration saw its arms sales policy as contributing to that process. As long as the PRC followed a policy of peaceful reunification, the U.S. was willing to reduce its arms sales to Taiwan. Given the low U.S. assessment of the PRC military threat to Taiwan and China's continued policy of peaceful reunification, there was no sense of urgency in addressing the issue of Taiwan's future.

This perception prevailed without serious challenge until the signing of the Hong Kong agreement between Beijing and London in December 1984. The Sino-British treaty over the future of Hong Kong led to a major examination of U.S. reunification policy in mid-1985. Chapter 9 will discuss that policy review and subsequent actions taken by the U.S. to assume a more active role in supporting China's peaceful reunification. Before that discussion, however, Chapters 6-8 will consider China's reunification from the points of view of both Beijing and Taipei.

Notes

1. *International Herald Tribune,* June 22, 1981, p. 1.

2. U.S. Congress, House of Representatives, Committee on Foreign Affairs, *The New Era in East Asia* (Washington, D.C.: GPO, 1981), p. 343.

3. *Xinhua,* June 10, 1981, in *FBIS-China,* June 10, 1981, p. B1.

4. *Ming Pao,* August 25, 1981, in *FBIS-China,* August 25, 1981, p. W6.

5. *Xinhua,* October 30, 1981, in *FBIS-China,* October 30, 1981, p. B1.

6. Robert G. Sutter, "China-U.S. Relations," *Issue Brief,* IB76053 (November 22, 1982), Library of Congress, Congressional Research Service, p. 18.

7. Arguments against the FX sale can be found in A. Doak Barnett, *The FX Decision: "Another Crucial Moment" in U.S.-China-Taiwan Relations* (Washington, D.C.: Brookings, 1981). Arguments in favor of advanced fighter sales to Taiwan can be found in Martin L. Lasater, *The Security of Taiwan: Unraveling the Dilemma* (Washington, D.C.: Georgetown University, CSIS, 1982).

8. American Council for Free Asia, Press Release, Washington, D.C., June 21, 1981.

9. *Renmin Ribao,* December 31, 1981, in *FBIS-China,* December 31, 1981, pp. B1ff.

10. "No Sale of Advanced Aircraft to Taiwan," *Department of State Bulletin,* February 1982, p. 39.

11. U.S. Congress, House of Representatives, Committee on Appropriations, Subcommittee on Foreign Operations, *Foreign Assistance and Related Programs, Appropriations for 1983, Part I* (Washington, D.C.: GPO, 1982), p. 131.

12. See Tad Szulc, "The Reagan Administration's Push Toward China Came from Warsaw," *Los Angeles Times,* January 17, 1982, Part IV, p. 1; and Rowland Evans and Robert Novak, "Taiwan Turnabout," *Washington Post,* January 16, 1982, p. A11.

13. *Xinhua,* January 12, 1982, in *FBIS-China,* January 12, 1982, p. B1.

14. *New York Times,* February 1, 1982, p. A3.

15. *Xinhua,* March 1, 1982, in *FBIS-China,* March 2, 1982, p. B1.

16. Texts of these letters can be found in Robert L. Downen, *To Bridge the Taiwan Strait* (Washington, D.C.: Council for Social and Economic Studies, 1984), pp. 126-128.

17. Walter J. Stoessel, "Developing Lasting U.S.-China Relations," U.S. Department of State, *Current Policy,* No. 398 (June 1, 1982).

18. *Washington Times,* July 2, 1982, p. 1.

19. Ibid. Also see *Washington Post,* July 2, 1982, p. A26.

20. Interviews by the author in Washington, D.C, June-July, 1982.

21. *Washington Post,* July 3, 1982, p. A13.

22. *Washington Post,* July 9, 1982, p. A5.

23. "'People's Daily' Refutes 'Two Chinas' Statement by U.S. Conservative Organizations," Embassy of the People's Republic of China, Press Release, No. 82/014, July 19, 1982.

24. *Washington Post,* July 14, 1982, p. A15.

25. *Washington Post,* July 19, 1982, p. A9.

26. *New York Times,* July 31, 1982, p. A2.

27. S.I. Hayakawa, "Ambiguity: The China Syndrome," *New York Times,* August 30, 1982, p. A17.

28. *New York Times,* June 3, 1982, p. A22.

29. *Human Events,* February 26, 1983, p. 19.

30. Holdridge's testimony can be found in U.S. Congress, House of Representatives, Committee on Foreign Affairs, *China-Taiwan: United States Policy* (Washington, D.C.: GPO, 1982), pp. 2-29.

31. Prepared statement of Davis R. Robinson, Legal Advisor, Department of State, given before U.S. Congress, Senate, Committee on the Judiciary, Subcommittee on Separation of Powers, September 27, 1982, pp. 1-2, ms.

32. *Washington Post,* March 22, 1983, p. A12.

33. "Chinese Foreign Ministry Spokesman on China-U.S. Joint Communiqué," Embassy of the People's Republic of China, Press Release, No. 82/017, August 17, 1982.

34. *Renmin Ribao,* August 17, 1982, in *FBIS-China,* August 17, 1982, p. B4.

35. Ibid.

36. *Washington Post,* August 20, 1982, p. A16.

37. *Washington Post,* February 23, 1983, p. A12.

38. Prepared statement of Paul Wolfowitz, "Sino-American Relations Eleven Years after the Shanghai Communiqué," given before U.S. Congress, House of Representatives, Committee on Foreign Affairs, Subcommittee on Asian and Pacific Affairs, February 28, 1983, p. 5, ms.

39. *Washington Post,* February 19, 1983, p. A5.

40. George Shultz, "The U.S. and East Asia: A Partnership for the Future," U.S. Department of State, *Current Policy,* No. 459, March 5, 1983, p. 3.

PART TWO

The Chinese Reunification Issue, 1979-1987

6

Beijing's Reunification Policy

In the negotiations leading to the signing of the August 17, 1982, U.S.-PRC Joint Communiqué, the U.S. mentioned on several occasions "the new situation" in the Taiwan Strait resulting from Beijing's "fundamental" policy of peaceful reunification. The "new situation" was the atmosphere of reduced tensions resulting from China's attempt to find a negotiated settlement to the reunification issue.

The PRC's pursuit of a peaceful resolution of the Taiwan issue was part of the normalization package suggested by President Carter and accepted by the Chinese in late 1978. Since 1979, China had set forth several proposals for peacefully reuniting the mainland and Taiwan, all of which Taipei had rejected.

Despite Taiwan's suspicions of PRC motives, Beijing's efforts significantly lowered U.S. assessments of the PRC threat to Taiwan. Moreover, as reflected in the August 17 Communiqué, the "new situation" had considerable impact on U.S. policy toward arms sales to Taiwan. This chapter will review PRC reunification proposals in the post-normalization period through 1984. Chapter 7 will examine the reasons Taiwan has rejected these proposals, and Chapter 8 will discuss increased contact between the two Chinese sides since 1985.

Three Stages of PRC Policy

According to Li Jiaquan, deputy director of Beijing's Taiwan Research Institute, China's peaceful reunification policy evolved in three stages. The first stage occurred in December 1978 at the Third Plenary Session of the 11th Party Central Committee. At that time the key decision was made to reject "armed liberation" and "peaceful liberation" as strategic policies and to adopt instead "peaceful reunification" as the fundamental policy toward Taiwan. The second stage took place in September 1981 when National People's Congress (NPC) Standing Committee Chairman Ye Jianying outlined in a *Xinhua* interview nine specific policies for the reunification of Taiwan and the mainland. The third stage was the creation of the "one country, two systems" formula designed to enable Hong Kong and Taiwan to preserve their capitalist systems but as part of one China.[1]

The December 1978 decision by the Communist Party Central Committee to adopt a "peaceful reunification" policy toward Taiwan was a highly significant change in strategy. It occurred in the context of a fundamental change in direction in other aspects of China's policies, foreign as well as domestic. At the Third Plenary Session the Central Committee decided to move ahead with the normalization of relations with the United States and to embark on a pragmatic course of economic modernization. The latter included an open door to trade, investment, and contact with the West, and the decentralization and privatization of certain sectors of the Chinese economy.

Since the policy of peaceful reunification with Taiwan was required in order to normalize relations with the U.S., and normalized Sino-American relations were essential to China's new open door policy to the West—itself an integral part of the PRC economic modernization—Beijing's peaceful reunification policy must be seen in the context of a pragmatic policy "package" introduced by the reformers to achieve the Four Modernizations.[2] This point is relevant to this study, since it raises the as yet unanswerable question of whether changes in other aspects of the reform policy package might affect Beijing's reunification policy.

Prior to the 1978 Third Plenary Session, the PRC's basic approach to reunification was one of "liberation," although there were periods in which liberation was to be achieved militarily and periods in which liberation was to be pursued by peaceful means. A noticeable change in rhetoric began to emerge on December 16, 1978, the day after President Jimmy Carter announced the normalization of Sino-American relations. Avoiding talk of "liberation" altogether, Hua Guofeng said: "It is the common desire of the people of China, our Taiwan compatriots included, that Taiwan should return to the embrace of motherland and the country be reunited."[3]

The new policy of peaceful reunification was first declared in the New Year's Day Message of January 1, 1979, from the Standing Committee of the National People's Congress. The message to "Taiwan Compatriots" read in part:

> It is our fervent hope that Taiwan returns to the embrace of the motherland at an early date so that we can work together for the great cause of national development. . . . The responsibility for reunifying the motherland rests with each of us. We hope the Taiwan authorities will place national

interests paramount and make valuable contributions to the reunification of the motherland.[4]

The NPC committee suggested that Taiwan and the mainland arrange for mutual visits and tours, establish postal and transportation services, set up various academic and cultural exchanges, and open up trade. On the same day of the message's release, Beijing announced that it was ceasing the shelling of Kinmen on alternate days for the convenience of "civilians and armymen on Taiwan, Penghu, Jinmen and Mazu islands who wish to visit their relatives and friends and make tours on the mainland and to facilitate shipping and production activities in the Taiwan Straits."[5]

The Nine-Point Proposal

The second stage of China's peaceful reunification policy was launched with Ye Jianying's Nine-Point Proposal of September 30, 1981. Ye's nine points were as follows:

(1) In order to bring an end to the unfortunate separation of the Chinese nation as early as possible, we propose that talks be held between the Communist Party of China and the Kuomintang of China on a reciprocal basis so that the two parties will cooperate for the third time to accomplish the great cause of national reunification. The two sides may first send people to meet for an exhaustive exchange of views.

(2) It is the urgent desire of the people of all nationalities on both sides of the Straits to communicate with each other, reunite with their relatives, develop trade and increase mutual understanding. We propose that the two sides make arrangements to facilitate the exchange of mails, trade, air and shipping services, and visits by relatives and tourists as well as academic, cultural and sports exchanges, and reach an agreement thereupon.

(3) After the country is reunited, Taiwan can enjoy a high degree of autonomy as a special administrative region and it can retain its armed forces. The Central Government will not interfere with local affairs on Taiwan.

(4) Taiwan's current socio-economic system will remain unchanged, so will its way of life and its economic and cultural relations with foreign countries. There will be no encroachment on the proprietary rights and lawful right of inheritance over private property, houses, land and enterprises, or on foreign investments.

(5) People in authority and representative personages of various circles in Taiwan may take up posts of leadership in national political bodies and participate in running the state.

(6) When Taiwan's local finance is in difficulty, the Central Government may subsidize it as is fit for the circumstances.

(7) For people of all nationalities and public figures of various circles in Taiwan who wish to come and settle on the mainland, it is guaranteed that proper arrangements will be made for them, that there will be no discrimination against them, and that they will have the freedom of entry and exit.

(8) Industrialists and businessmen in Taiwan are welcome to invest and engage in various economic undertakings on the mainland, and their legal rights, interests and profits are guaranteed.

(9) The reunification of the motherland is the responsibility of all Chinese. We sincerely welcome people of all nationalities, public figures of all circles and mass organizations in Taiwan to make proposals and suggestions regarding affairs of state through various channels and in various ways. . . . China's reunification and prosperity is in the vital interest of the Chinese people of all nationalities—not only those on the mainland, but those in Taiwan as well. . . . We hope that the Kuomintang authorities will stick to their one-China position and their opposition to "two Chinas" and that they will put national interests above everything else, forget previous ill will and join hands with us in accomplishing the great cause of national reunification and the great goal of making China prosperous and strong.[6]

PRC leaders made it clear that Ye's statement was considered the most comprehensive and important proposal on reunification to date. Deng Xiaoping called the proposal "a fair and reasonable principle and policy concerning the return of Taiwan to the motherland and the realization of China's peaceful reunification that we have put forward in the light of the actual situation."[7] Ye's nine points were referenced in the August 17 Communiqué by both China and the U.S. as an example of Beijing's efforts to achieve reunification through peaceful means.

But when Taipei rejected the nine points (see Chapter 7), the PRC refined its reunification policy even further. In early December 1982 the new PRC constitution was promulgated, with provisions for "special administrative regions" written into Article 31. Veteran CPC leader Peng Zhen said the article was designed specifically with Taiwan, Hong Kong, and Macao in mind. Peng said the article demonstrated the fact that China was unequivocal on the principle of safeguarding its sovereignty, unity and territorial integrity, but highly flexible with regard to specific policies and measures.[8]

Unable to talk directly to Taiwan's leaders, the PRC during 1983 routinely used visits by Overseas Chinese to convey its reunification policies to Taiwan and the U.S. In May, for example, Hu Yaobang told

Pennsylvania State University professor Parris Chang that the reunification of China would be achieved before 1991 and that Taiwan would become a special administrative region of China.[9] In June Deng Xiaoping went to considerable length to describe the generosity of China's reunification policies to Seton Hall professor Winston Yang.[10]

Dr. Yang quoted Deng as saying, "The CPC sincerely wants to cooperate with Taiwan and has no intention to weaken and isolate Taiwan." Deng went on to say: "Our many practices are not directed at Taiwan but at the 'two Chinas' policy of the United States." Deng's detailed scheme for China's reunification was summarized by Professor Yang in this way:

1. After reunification, Beijing will not dispatch its army to Taiwan, nor will it send officials to take over, to take part in, or to oversee Taiwan's "internal affairs." Beijing will not concern itself with the personnel affairs in Taiwan's administrative structure and will not bother about the troop movements in Taiwan. . . . Taiwan can maintain its economic system, its way of living, and its party, government, army, and intelligence agency. The mainland and Taiwan will coexist peacefully. He said: "We will never harm even a single blade of grass or a tree on Taiwan." He also said that this arrangement should remain unchanged for at least 100 years. If disputes occur in the course of implementing the reunification terms, both sides can seek solutions through consultation. The most important thing is that neither side will conduct anything causing harm to the other side in its own territory. Taiwan's army will have the right to buy weapons from other countries to consolidate its self-defensive ability.
2. After reunification, Taiwan will enjoy independent legislative rights and can basically maintain its existing laws. On the principle of not violating the Constitution, Taiwan's legislature has the right to enact its own laws which act as the foundation for Taiwan's administration.
3. After reunification, Taiwan will have its independent jurisdiction and judicial organs. The laws and acts on the mainland will not be applied to Taiwan. The court of last instance for Taiwan should be set in Taiwan rather than in Beijing.
4. After reunification, Taiwan will maintain certain rights to handle foreign affairs. It can handle its foreign economic relations independently. The Taiwan authorities can issue special passports to Taiwan people and grant entrance visas to foreigners. It can even have the right to sign some agreements directly with other countries.
5. After reunification, Taiwan can still use its special flag and use the title of "China, Taiwan."

The official *Xinhua* version of the interview added several important points. The newspaper said "seats in the central government will be reserved for Taiwan." It stressed that Deng was proposing talks between two political parties—the KMT and CPC—not negotiations between central and local authorities. At the same time, however, the *Xinhua* version made it clear that Taiwan's freedom would not be unlimited. Deng was quoted as saying, "Complete autonomy is simply out of the question. . . . Only the PRC is entitled to represent China in the international arena." He further maintained that Taiwan's government would be a local government only; that Taiwan's armed forces must "not constitute a threat to the mainland"; that Taiwan's exclusive rights must "not impair the interests of the unified state"; and that "foreign interference absolutely will not be permitted."

Throughout the 1979-1984 period, the PRC did not ask the U.S. to change its reunification policy. No effort was made to draw the U.S. in as a mediator between the two Chinese sides. In October 1983, for example, Chinese Foreign Minister Wu Xueqian said: "We do not ask for U.S. assistance in achieving the reunification of Taiwan with the mainland, but we ask the United States to refrain from obstructing in our effort."[11] Following the development of the "one country, two systems" formula and its application to Hong Kong in the 1984 Sino-British agreement over the future of the crown colony, however, the PRC began to ask the U.S. to help in China's reunification. (The U.S. response will be discussed in Chapter 9.)

"One Country, Two Systems" Formula

The third and most elaborate step taken by the PRC in proposing a solution to the Taiwan question was the "one country, two systems" formula designed for Hong Kong and Taiwan. In May 1984 a high-ranking but unnamed Chinese official said, "China's policy toward the Taiwan and Hong Kong issues is that in a period to come, there will be two systems within one China." The official stated that the practice of capitalism in Taiwan and Hong Kong will not hamper their reunification with the socialist mainland. He noted that both Taiwan and Hong Kong will become special administrative regions in the future, retaining their current systems and ways of life and enjoying a high degree of autonomy.[12]

In his report to the National People's Congress on May 15, 1984, Zhao Ziyang repeated the "one country, two systems" formula for Hong Kong and Taiwan. Regarding the Taiwan issue, Zhao said: "We hold that provided the Kuomintang and the Communist Party of China share a common language on peaceful reunification, everything else can be negotiated. It is better to solve the Taiwan question sooner than later."[13] In June Premier Zhao told newsmen in Copenhagen that China intended

to resolve the Taiwan question before 1997, the year of Hong Kong's
return to Chinese sovereignty.[14]

Later that month Deng Xiaoping told a group of leading businessmen
from Hong Kong that China had "discussed the policy of two systems
in one country for several years. It is now approved by the NPC."
Deng said the policy will not change unless experience shows it to
be wrong. The Chinese leader explained that the "one country, two
systems" concept had been designed to take into consideration the
actual conditions existing in China, Hong Kong, and Taiwan. Regarding
the problem of Taiwan's reunification, Deng asked:

> What is the solution to this problem? Is it for socialism to swallow up
> Taiwan, or for the "Three Principles of the People" preached by Taiwan
> to swallow up the mainland? The answer is that neither can swallow up
> the other. If the problem cannot be solved peacefully then it must be
> solved by force. This would do neither side any good. Reunification of
> the country is the aspiration of the whole nation. If it cannot be reunified
> in 100 years, then it will be reunified in 1,000 years. In my opinion, the
> only solution to this problem is to practice two systems in one country.[15]

Deng expanded upon this theme somewhat in an October 1984
meeting with another Hong Kong delegation.[16] The Chinese leader
said: "There are two ways to settle the issue: peaceful and non-peaceful.
The non-peaceful way, or the way to settle the issue by force, was
deemed inappropriate." Deng explained that this decision was based
on a realistic assessment of "the history and present conditions of
Hong Kong and Taiwan." He then said regarding Taiwan:

> Our proposal for reunifying the mainland and Taiwan is reasonable. After
> reunification is realized, Taiwan can still practice capitalism while the
> mainland maintains socialism. Both of them are part of a united China.
> This is what we mean by "one country, two systems" which also applies
> to Hong Kong. . . . China's present socialist system cannot be changed
> and will remain in the future. But, if the capitalist system in Hong Kong
> and Taiwan is not guaranteed, stability and prosperity there cannot be
> maintained and peaceful settlement will become impossible.

Deng concluded:

> We must always decide whether we are going to solve an international
> issue in a peaceful or a non-peaceful way. We must find a way to break
> deadlock. When we worked out the idea, we also took into consideration
> what methods should be used to resolve international disputes. . . . If
> both refuse to budge, in the long run hostilities will break out, and

even armed conflicts may break out, and war may be used to resolve them. So, if stability is desired, instead of fighting, the only way to settle problems is by the method we have advanced. Using this method we can justify ourselves to the people, stabilize the situation, and neither side is hurt.

The first real test of the "one country, two systems" formula for China's reunification came in December 1984, when the Chinese and British agreed to use the formula to govern Hong Kong after 1997. (July 1, 1997, is the date the 99-year British lease on Hong Kong's New Territories ends.) The PRC negotiating style with the British suggests how Beijing might approach Taipei on the question of Taiwan's reunification.[17]

The Hong Kong Agreement

From the moment the issue of Hong Kong's future was formally joined in September 1982, the PRC insisted on the principle of the restoration of Chinese sovereignty in 1997 and rejected any British administrative role after that date. Once those basic positions were accepted by London, however, China demonstrated great patience and flexibility in attempting, first, to understand how Hong Kong functioned as a mecca for capitalism and free trade and, second, to write sufficient guarantees into the agreement to ensure Hong Kong's continued prosperity and way of life.

The wide range of PRC assurances written into the 1984 Sino-British Agreement provide useful insight into the type of guarantees Taipei might expect from Beijing should it accept the "one country, two systems" formula for its own reunification with the mainland.

In the Hong Kong Agreement the PRC promised that its "one country, two systems" policies would be enshrined in a "Basic Law of the Hong Kong Special Administrative Region of the People's Republic of China." The Basic Law will stipulate that after 1997 "the socialist system and socialist policies shall not be practiced in the Hong Kong Special Administrative Region and that Hong Kong's previous capitalist system and life-style shall remain unchanged for 50 years."

Some of the more important provisions laid out in the agreement were as follows:[18]

- A high degree of autonomy shall exist, except in foreign and defense affairs, which will be the responsibility of Beijing.
- An executive, legislative, and independent judicial power shall be established with the current laws remaining basically unchanged.

- An executive shall be appointed by Beijing on the basis of local elections or consultations, and held "accountable to the legislature."
- A legislature shall be constituted by elections, which "may on its own authority enact laws in accordance with the provisions of the Basic Law and legal procedures, and report them to the Standing Committee of the National People's Congress for the record."
- The laws of the Hong Kong Special Administrative Region (SAR) shall be from three sources: the Basic Law, the laws previously in force in Hong Kong, and laws enacted by the Hong Kong SAR legislature.
- Judicial power in Hong Kong shall be vested in its own courts. "The courts shall exercise judicial power independently and free from any interference. . . . The power of final judgement . . . shall be vested in the court of final appeals in the Hong Kong SAR."
- "The Hong Kong Special Administrative Region shall maintain the capitalist economic and trade systems previously practiced in Hong Kong." Hong Kong "shall retain the status of a free port and continue a free trade policy, including the free movement of goods and capital." Hong Kong "may on its own maintain and develop economic and trade relations with all states and regions."
- "The current social and economic systems in Hong Kong will remain unchanged, and so will the life-style. Rights and freedoms, including those of the person, of speech, of the press, of assembly, of association, of travel, of movement, of correspondence, of strike, of choice of occupation, of academic research and of religious belief will be ensured by law. . . . Private property, ownership of enterprises, legitimate right of inheritance and foreign investment will be protected by law."
- Hong Kong will remain a separate customs territory. It will remain an international financial center, and its markets for foreign exchange, gold, securities and futures will continue. There will be free flow of capital.
- The Hong Kong dollar will continue to circulate and remain freely convertible. Hong Kong will have independent finances and Beijing will not levy taxes on Hong Kong.
- "Mutually beneficial economic relations" may be established with the United Kingdom "and other countries, whose economic interests in Hong Kong will be given due regard."
- Under the name "Hong Kong, China," the Special Administrative Region "may on its own maintain and develop economic and cultural relations and conclude relevant agreements with states, regions and relevant international organizations."

- Hong Kong may issue its own travel documents and maintain its own public security forces.
- "Apart from displaying the national flag and national emblem of the People's Republic of China," Hong Kong "may use a regional flag and emblem of its own."
- "The Hong Kong Special Administrative Region shall maintain the educational system previously practiced in Hong Kong."

Although written promises are no guarantee that Beijing will honor its commitments, there is considerable evidence that the PRC's own interests would be served by continued prosperity and stability in Hong Kong. The crown colony generates an estimated 40% of China's foreign-exchange earnings and is an important source of Western technology, investment funds, and managerial skills. Under Beijing's policy of opening the Chinese economy to the outside, China has become firmly enmeshed in Hong Kong's financial system. Hong Kong trade statistics reflect this growing interdependence with the PRC. The value of domestic exports to China (in Hong Kong dollars) rose from $1.6 billion in 1980 to $27.9 billion in 1987. During the same period, re-exports to China increased from $4.6 billion to $60.2 billion, and imports rose from $21.9 billion to $117.4 billion.[19] The volume of contact between China and Hong Kong is such that many top Hong Kong government officials freely speculate that by the year 2000 much of southern Guangdong Province will be integrated economically with Hong Kong.[20]

Why Taiwan Should Negotiate: Beijing's View

PRC analysts, such as Li Jiaquan of Beijing's Taiwan Research Institute, have set forth elaborate arguments as to why the proper conditions now exist for a peaceful settlement of the Taiwan issue. In his *Beijing Review* article of February 3, 1986, Li listed several common grounds existing between the mainland and Taiwan:[21]

- The Communist Party of China and the Kuomintang, as well as the people on both sides of the Taiwan Straits, agree that there is only one China.
- Both the CPC and the KMT oppose Taiwan independence.
- Both the mainland and Taiwan have given priority to economic development. A close relationship between the mainland and Taiwan will benefit both economically.
- Historically, the mainland and Taiwan have close ties and "the two shared a common destiny."

• More than 98 percent of Taiwan's residents are originally from the mainland and are Chinese. In addition to speaking a common language, the people on both sides of the Taiwan Strait have inherited the same culture and way of life.

According to Li, various international conditions also make reunification possible. The most important of these is the gradual weakening of U.S. support for Taiwan. As Taiwan becomes more of a burden for the U.S., Li speculated, the American government will adopt a more flexible Taiwan policy.

Li noted that four basic formulas for Taiwan's unification with the mainland have been proposed: "the Taiwan pattern," "the federal state pattern," the "Singapore pattern," and the special administrative region under "one country, two systems."

In considering each of these alternatives, Li said the Taiwan pattern, by which is meant "reunifying China with the Three People's Principles," was impractical because the KMT will never return victoriously to the mainland. The federal state pattern was unsuitable because it would create equal entities called China, Hong Kong, and Taiwan. In effect, this formula would create "two Chinas" or even "three Chinas," which the PRC has rejected. The Singapore pattern implies that Taiwan is Chinese culturally but not necessarily part of China politically. This was unacceptable because "unlike Singapore, Taiwan is an inseparable part of China." To adopt this formula would establish in fact an independent Taiwan, something the PRC cannot tolerate. According to Li, the special administrative region under "one country, two systems" was the most suitable pattern because it provided for one China, but allowed Hong Kong and Taiwan to retain their separate ways of life.

Despite efforts on the part of the PRC to convince Taipei that its interests would best be served by joining the mainland in an early, peaceful reunification, Taiwan consistently has rejected China's proposals. The next chapter discusses Taipei's reasons for maintaining the status quo in the Taiwan Strait, but also examines ROC proposals for a reunited China under a democratic system.

Notes

1. Li Jiaquan, "Formula for China's Reunification," *Beijing Review,* February 3, 1986, p. 19.

2. For a Chinese discussion of the various elements of the reform "package," see Deng Xiaoping, "Emancipate the Mind, Seek Truth from Facts and Unite as One in Looking to the Future," *Selected Works of Deng Xiaoping (1975-1982)* (Beijing: Foreign Languages Press, 1984), pp. 151-165.

3. New China News Agency (NCNA), December 16, 1978, in *FBIS-China,* December 18, 1978, p. A5.

4. NCNA, December 31, 1978, in *FBIS-China,* January 2, 1979, p. E1.

5. NCNA, December 31, 1978, in *FBIS-China,* January 2, 1979, p. E8.

6. *Xinhua,* September 30, 1981, in *FBIS-China,* September 30, 1981, p. U1.

7. *Xinhua,* October 2, 1981, in *FBIS-China,* October 5, 1981, p. G2.

8. *Xhongguo Xinwen She,* November 28, 1982, in *FBIS-China,* November 30, 1982, p. K19.

9. *Hsia Pao,* June 28, 1983, in *FBIS-China,* June 28, 1983, p. W1. 10. The official version of the conversation was reported in *Xinhua,* July 29, 1983, in *FBIS-China,* August 1, 1983, pp. U1-U2. Winston Yang's somewhat different version can be found in his article, "Deng Xiaoping's Latest Concept on Peaceful Reunification," *Chishih Nientai,* August 1, 1983, in *FBIS-China,* August 4, 1983, pp. W1-W6.

11. *Xinhua,* October 15, 1983, in *FBIS-China,* October 17, 1983, p. B1.

12. *Wen Wei Po,* May 1, 1984, in *FBIS-China,* May 1, 1984, pp. W5-W6.

13. *Xinhua,* May 31, 1984, in *FBIS-China,* June 1, 1984, p. K20.

14. *Japan Times,* June 10, 1984, p. 4.

15. *Xinhua,* June 30, 1984, in *FBIS-China,* July 2, 1984, pp. E1-E2.

16. A summary of Deng's remarks can be found in *Beijing Review,* February 3, 1986, pp. 25-26.

17. For a concise history of Sino-British negotiations, see Frank Ching, *Hong Kong and China: For Better or For Worse* (New York, NY: China Council of The Asia Society and the Foreign Policy Association, 1985).

18. The text of the Hong Kong Agreement can be found in *A Draft Agreement between the Government of the United Kingdom of Great Britain and Northern Ireland and the Government of the People's Republic of China on the Future of Hong Kong* (London: Her Majesty's Government, September 26, 1984).

19. Hong Kong Government, Census and Statistics Department, "Hong Kong in Figures: 1986" and "Hong Kong in Figures: 1988" (Hong Kong: Government Printer, February 1986 and February 1988).

20. Author's interviews in Hong Kong, September 1986.

21. *Beijing Review,* February 3, 1986, pp. 21-22.

7

Taipei's Reunification Policy

The PRC has proposed several plans for China's peaceful reunification since 1978, but Taipei has refused to accept these proposals or even to enter into negotiations with Beijing. Instead, the ROC has set forth its own ideas for reunification. Both Chinese governments maintain there is but one China and Taiwan is part of China. The basic disagreement is over whether China should be communist or non-communist. In practice, this translates into whether the central government of China should be ruled by the Communist Party of China or the Kuomintang.

Taiwan's attitude toward reunification is important to the reunification policy of the U.S., because since June 1950 U.S. policy has been to support Taipei in its resistance against Beijing's forceful attempts to bring Taiwan under mainland control. U.S. support of Taiwan has become more complicated since 1979, when Washington recognized the PRC as the sole legal government of China and Beijing initiated its policy of peaceful reunification. Since a fundamental objective of U.S. reunification policy has been a peaceful resolution of the Taiwan issue, Taiwan has been put in the awkward position of opposing "peaceful reunification" while the PRC has become its most active proponent.

An understanding of the reasons why Taipei rejects the PRC proposals for peaceful reunification, as well as knowledge of Taiwan's own reunification proposals, will help clarify certain aspects of U.S. policy—such as continued arms sales—and also help explain why the U.S. since 1987 has become more supportive of unofficial contacts between the two Chinese sides.

The "Three-No" Policy

The fundamental policy of the Republic of China in regards to reunification is to reject all proposals requiring Taiwan to be a local government under the national government of the People's Republic of China. After all, the KMT and CPC have engaged in a power struggle for sixty years. Why should the KMT give in unless and until it has to? The ROC policy of rejecting reunification under the PRC has become crystallized in the so-called "three-no" policy: "no negotiations, no compromise, and no contact" with the Beijing regime.[1]

There are several reasons why Taipei has adopted the "three-no" policy. Perhaps the most important psychological barrier to reunification is the widespread belief on Taiwan that Beijing eventually will attempt to impose a socialist system on the island—despite whatever assurances might be given beforehand. There are indications that this might well be the case. In February 1979, for example, Liao Chengzhi, head of the PRC Office of Overseas Chinese, told a meeting of the National Association of Overseas Chinese:

> After China has achieved peaceful unification the long-term road for Taiwan will be the socialist road. Under the leadership of a single, proletarian political party, there is no reason why one segment should have a socialist system while the other follows the capitalist road. However, the main problem at present is how can we first realize the peaceful unification of China and end the state of disunity that has endured for thirty years. Party Central has spelled out that our task with regard to Taiwan under the present situation is to achieve the goal of peaceful unification through negotiation.[2]

Although it is true that Liao's comments were before the introduction of the "one country, two systems" formula, Taiwan remains suspicious of PRC motives. Taipei points out that the very principles on which the PRC bases its legitimacy demand the supremacy of socialism in China. These principles are "keeping to the socialist road and upholding the people's democratic dictatorship, leadership by the communist party, and Marxism-Leninism and Mao Zedong thought." They are embodied in the PRC's 1982 Constitution and exhaustively repeated in official Chinese statements. Zhao Ziyang in his address to the 13th CPC National Congress in October 1987, referred to these four cardinal principles as "the foundation underlying all our efforts to build the country."[3]

The people on Taiwan fear reunification with the mainland because it might mean the end of their lifestyle. In 1987 Taiwan's 19 million residents produced a gross national product (GNP) of $98 billion and a per capita GNP of $5,000—the fourth highest in Asia.[4] Average annual growth rates range between 7-10%, one of the world's highest. Taiwan was the world's twelfth largest trading nation in 1987, with a surplus of nearly $19 billion out of a total trade of $88 billion. Taipei's foreign exchange reserves of more than $70 billion were the world's second largest. Taiwan also had one of the most equitable distributions of national income in the world. Unemployment was around 2%; the non-agricultural population was 83%; and the literacy rate was 92%. Life expectancy was 71 years for males and 76 for females. Many other statistics could be cited to demonstrate that Taiwan's "economic miracle" is a reality which its citizens do not want to risk giving up to achieve reunification with the mainland.

As powerful as these psychological barriers are to reunification, there are other considerations which make it difficult for the KMT to change its "three-no" policy and to contemplate political contact with the CPC.

Political Barriers
to Negotiations with the Mainland

One important reason why Taipei cannot easily discuss reunification with the PRC is the complicated political situation on Taiwan. Since the ROC assumed control over the island from the Japanese following World War II, Chinese from the mainland have dominated Taiwan's political life at the central government level. After the Nationalist defeat on the mainland, the ROC government was transferred to Taipei. According to the KMT, Taipei became the temporary capital of all of China, including Taiwan.

The ROC government on Taiwan retained the various ministries and bureaucrats responsible for mainland Chinese affairs, although over time the practical functions of the government focused almost exclusively on matters concerning territory under de facto control of Taipei. Native-born Taiwanese did not play a significant role in ROC national politics until very recently. They did, however, play a dominate role in local and provincial (Taiwan province with its provincial capital near Tai-chung) politics.

Because of the bitter anti-Japanese sentiment on the part of China and the fact that Taiwan had been occupied by the Japanese for 50 years prior to 1945, Nationalists soldiers behaved like occupying forces when they first arrived on Taiwan in 1945. The island's infrastructure was ruined by U.S. bombing during the war, food was scarce, and ROC army discipline was poor. As a result, there were numerous incidents of Nationalist abuse of Taiwanese.

The worst incidents occurred in February and March 1947, when Nationalist soldiers and security forces killed several thousand Taiwanese during riots around the island. Order was restored by force, and numerous

Taiwanese leaders were arrested and executed. The unfortunate February 27 incident left a legacy of hatred for the mainlanders on the part of many Taiwanese which surfaces in certain radical elements of anti-KMT political movement today. Some Taiwanese believe the mainlanders deliberately killed or imprisoned Taiwan's intellectual and leadership elite, thus depriving the Taiwanese of an opportunity to play a significant political role.

President Chiang Kai-shek, who was on the mainland at the time of the 1947 incident directing the civil war against the communists, attempted to heal the schisms between the Taiwanese and the mainlanders after 1949. This effort became increasingly important during the 1950s, when it became apparent that the Nationalists would be unable to return "victoriously" to the mainland in the foreseeable future. The mainlanders and Taiwanese would have to coexist indefinitely on the island, and the cooperation of the Taiwanese was essential if Taiwan was to be made into a model province for all of China. An important tactical decision was made to allow the Taiwanese to benefit most from the economic growth of Taiwan, whereas the political processes at the national ROC level would remain in the hands of the mainlanders. Local level politics were left in the hands of the Taiwanese.

What evolved was a process of democratization from the grass roots upward. Local Taiwan elections were first held in 1950 and have been held regularly ever since. Voter turnout has rarely fallen below 70% of the registered voters, and Taiwanese win virtually every seat.[5] National ROC elections, however, posed a dilemma for the Nationalist government. Since the ROC maintained that it represented all of China, its elected officials (members of the National Assembly, Legislative Yuan, and Control Yuan) had to reflect this official view.

The Temporary Provisions Effective During the Period of Communist Rebellion (called martial law in the West), enacted on the mainland in April 1948 and subsequently amended on Taiwan until repealed in 1987, permitted those representatives elected on the mainland in 1947 to continue to hold their offices without reelection on Taiwan. This solution worked well enough until the late 1970s and 1980s, when large numbers of the mainland-elected representatives became too infirm to carry out their responsibilities.

To increase the vitality of the legislative bodies, as well as to reflect the reality of the ROC maintaining de facto control only over the islands of Taiwan, Penghu, Matsu, and Kinmen, supplementary elections have been held on Taiwan for the ROC national elected bodies. The first was held in 1969 and subsequent supplementary elections were held in 1972, 1975, 1980, 1983, and 1986. Those elected were predominately Taiwanese, but even in the 1986 elections newly elected members represented only a small portion of the total number of members in the Legislative Yuan (one-third) and National Assembly (one-tenth). The other members were elected on the mainland and had served without challenge for 40 years.

Beginning in 1977 a new factor was introduced into Taiwan politics: legitimate competition between KMT and non-KMT candidates. Prior to that time, virtually everyone running for office was a member of the ruling Kuomintang or the two officially sanctioned but ineffective competitive parties, the Chinese Youth Party and the Democratic Socialist Party. Under martial law the formation of new political parties was not permitted.

Since 1977 opposition to KMT policies has come through non-partisan or non-KMT members, the so-called *tang-wai* or independents. *Tang-wai* candidates generally receive 25-30% of the votes and win 15-20% of the contested seats. In 1986 another key step was taken toward the democratization of Taiwan's politics: the decision to lift martial law and to permit the formation of new political parties.[6] The *tang-wai* took advantage of the liberalized political atmosphere on Taiwan to announce the formation on September 28, 1986, of the Democratic Progressive Party (DPP).

The appearance of the DPP on the political scene in Taiwan introduced a new, somewhat unpredictable element in the reunification issue. One DPP policy recommendation was that all residents of Taiwan should determine the island's future. The DPP opposed any talks between the KMT and the CPC on the grounds that negotiations would violate the principle of self-determination by the Taiwan people. A second policy recommendation called for the cessation of the confrontation between the two sides of the Taiwan Strait. The DPP suggested that both sides compete with each other on an equal footing to preserve peace in the region. Thus, the DPP, whose membership is almost exclusively Taiwanese, advocated the right of the people of Taiwan to become an independent nation and proposed direct contact with the mainland. Both suggestions ran counter to official ROC policy.

Because of the appearance of the DPP and its advocacy for policies diametrically opposed to traditional KMT positions on Taiwan independence and contact with the PRC, the December 6, 1986, elections were considered important indicators for the future of Taiwan. The elections were held for seats in the National Assembly and Legislative Yuan.

In an internationally acclaimed fair election, KMT candidates received 69% of the votes and won 80% of the contested seats. DPP candidates received 21% of the votes and 15% of the seats. The DPP increased its seats in the Legislative Yuan from six to twelve and in the National

Assembly from four to eleven seats. The KMT won 59 and 68 seats respectively. The remainder of the votes and seats went to independents and the Young China Party and China Democratic Social Party.

Although DPP representatives in the legislature consist of a small group, they are exceptionally active and vocal. Realizing that their popular appeal depends to a great extent on their ability to challenge KMT policies, the DPP representatives have adopted a confrontational style that antagonizes many. Despite occasional disruptive tactics, DPP representatives are becoming more sophisticated in their parliamentary behavior and are having an impact on legislation. Some of their concerns are over waste within the defense budget, environmental issues, labor grievances, direct election for the President and Vice President, re-election of the entire legislature, and policy toward the mainland.

In addition to KMT-*tang-wai* differences, Taiwan's political system is further fragmented into generational, provincial, and socioeconomic factions.[7] Whereas the KMT enjoys the support of the majority of each of these factions, the DPP and other newly formed opposition political parties find strong support among the younger generation, Taiwanese of Fujian (as opposed to Hakka) ancestry, and the middle and labor classes. Since the lifting of travel restrictions to the mainland by President Chiang Ching-kuo in late 1987, these groups have engaged in a vigorous debate over Taiwan's policy toward China. This debate intensified still further following Chiang's passing in January 1988 and the coming to power of President Lee Teng-hui, a Taiwanese who served as Chiang's Vice President.

All the various politically active groups recognize that the character of Taiwan's politics is changing dramatically. In the past the KMT mainlanders dominated central government politics. Since the mid-1970s a gradual Taiwanization of the political system has taken place. The President is Taiwanese, and he is chairman of the KMT. More than 50% of the ROC cabinet and the KMT Central Standing Committee are Taiwanese. Taiwanese, who make up some 85% of the total population of Taiwan, comprise over 70% of the KMT's membership and are actively being recruited on an affirmative action basis into the government and party. Almost all candidates endorsed by the KMT for local, provincial, and supplementary elections are Taiwanese.

The Taiwanization of the political process means that decision making will soon be in the hands of those Chinese on Taiwan least emotionally committed to the principle of "one China." Their concerns focus on how best to serve Taiwan's interests, including the preservation of the lifestyle of the island's residents. Although Taiwanese generally share mainlander perceptions of the PRC as being a serious threat to Taiwan, they frequently are willing to deal with China as a trading partner.

Taiwanese, it will be recalled, dominate Taiwan's economy. As international competition for Taiwan's exports increases, many Taiwan businessmen look to the mainland for lucrative potential markets.

The first generation KMT members who served in the ROC government and military on the mainland are relatively few in number, but remain very influential because of their age, experience, and personal ties to ROC ruling circles. This group sees Taiwan as a province of China. Having experienced firsthand the war against the communists, most insist on having no official contact whatsoever with Beijing. Nonetheless, their personal ties to the mainland are the strongest among all segments of Taiwan society, and in a Chinese cultural context this can be significant. To a great extent it was their pressure to visit their homes before becoming too infirm which led President Chiang to relax travel restrictions to the mainland.

Taiwan politics are thus rather complex. All politically active groups distrust the PRC, however, and want to see Taiwan develop economically and politically. All support a strong national defense (now consuming roughly 40% of central government expenditures). A move toward government by consensus is seen as inevitable, as is an increasingly strong role played by native-born Taiwanese—most of whom are members of the KMT. Each group supports Taipei's policy of "no negotiations, no compromise" with Beijing, although a strong movement is underway to drop the "no contacts" portion of the "three no" policy. Most people on Taiwan now seem to support nongovernmental contacts with China, but without political reunification.

It would be difficult for Taiwan's leaders to accept Beijing's invitation to discuss reunification without tearing the political fabric of Taiwan apart. No consensus exists as yet on Taiwan for the future of the island, and a move toward talks with the PRC could lead to major social instability. The source of instability could come from several sources, including hardliners within the KMT, military leaders concerned over ROC security, or Taiwanese worried that the KMT and CPC might enter into an agreement at their expense.

Other Barriers to Reunification Talks

In addition to the powerful political incentives to avoid reunification talks, there are important economic, social, and foreign policy barriers to Taiwan's reunification with China. Together, these form a variety of pragmatic reasons why Taipei does not find it in its interests to reunify with the mainland at this time.

Economically, most Taiwan scholars believe that reunification talks with Beijing might undermine the ROC economy. It is feared that negotiations would raise questions about Taiwan's future in the eyes of both trading partners and domestic and foreign investors. Trade is vital to Taiwan's economy. The island's 90% trade/GNP ratio is one of the highest in the world. Taipei fears that if foreign and local businessmen saw movement toward ROC-PRC negotiations, the uncertainty of the outcome of the talks would adversely affect trading agreements.

Similarly, there are concerns that talks would undermine domestic and foreign investor confidence. Although foreign investment remained strong through 1987, domestic investment has fallen seriously. In the 1979-1980 period, gross domestic capital formation averaged nearly 34%; by 1986 that percentage had dropped below 16%. In contrast, the 1986 saving rate was around 38%, a gap of 22% between gross saving and domestic investment. To a large extent, this reflects Taiwan business uncertainty about the future of the island. Analysts believe that Taipei's entering into negotiations with Beijing might worsen this trend and adversely affect foreign investments as well.

A related problem which would likely occur once negotiations started with the PRC would be an exodus from Taiwan of talented managers, scientists, technicians, entrepreneurs, and other personnel essential to Taiwan's industry and science. A similar "brain drain" has been seen in the case of Hong Kong following the 1984 London-Beijing agreement returning Hong Kong to Chinese sovereignty in 1997. A great many Taiwan families have relatives residing in the United States or other countries as an escape hatch in case communist rule appears likely. Negotiations might well precipitate a rapid emigration from Taiwan and further weaken the economic and social fabric of the island.

Socially, there is great difficulty about entering into talks with the PRC. The perception of the communist threat has been so firmly crystallized in people's minds on Taiwan that reunification talks might touch off serious problems. Confidence in the future would erode; mainlander-Taiwanese tensions would heighten; criticism of the government would mount; radical elements on both the right and the left would find more sympathy for their views; and people would become susceptible to rumors and wild speculations. These conditions would tend to undermine social stability and make it very difficult for the government to maintain order. In all likelihood, the government would find itself threatened not only by a growing Taiwanese movement toward independence, but also by hardline elements within the KMT and military who would refuse to support the government in reunification talks with Beijing.

In terms of international relations, it is virtually certain that Taipei would not benefit from negotiations with Beijing. The ROC is recognized by only 22 governments of the world, most of them in Latin America.

If Taipei agreed to discuss reunification with the mainland, many of these small countries (and perhaps even larger ones such as South Korea and Saudi Arabia) would feel their interests best served by quickly normalizing relations with Beijing. Hence, joining reunification talks is likely to further isolate Taiwan in the international community.

Taiwan's overall security situation would probably worsen as well. Domestically, the possibility of civil disturbance would increase. The principal arms suppliers of Taiwan, particularly the United States, would probably feel justified in limiting the amount of weapons sold to Taipei so as not to jeopardize negotiations. This, in turn, would adversely affect Taiwan's morale and the effectiveness of its armed forces.

The conclusion that must be reached after examining the wide range of political, economic, social, international, and security factors bearing on Taiwan's reunification policy is that the official policy of no negotiations with Beijing is difficult to change. Further, if the ROC does elect to negotiate, public knowledge of these talks might result in a significant weakening of Taiwan's bargaining position. This would make it more difficult for Taipei to arrive at a satisfactory arrangement. Hence, if there eventually is to be discussion of reunification, pragmatic considerations might dictate that these talks remain out of the public's eye—something difficult to do in today's media-conscious world.

Taiwan's Proposal
for a United, Democratic China

With these factors in mind, Taipei's cautious reaction to PRC reunification proposals is understandable. The ROC position is not simply a negative one, however. Taipei offers its own reunification proposals based upon the scenario of a non-communist China in the future. Insight into ROC thinking on reunification can be gained by reviewing the point-by-point rebuttal of Ye Jianying's Nine-Point Proposal offered on September 30, 1981 (Chapter 6). As summarized from an official publication, Taipei rejected the proposal on these grounds:

1. The problem is not talks but two different ways of life. The ROC wants China to be united under a system which is free, democratic and in the interests of the people. Unification under communism is forever unacceptable. Peaceful unification under conditions of freedom is the common will of the Chinese people everywhere. Moreover, previous talks between the KMT and CPC have resulted in communist treachery; the communists seek to gain through negotiations what they cannot gain on the battlefield.

2. Beijing is proposing the free exchange of mail, trade, visits, and services when these do not exist on the mainland. How can they offer Taiwan—which already enjoys these things—what the communists deny their own people? In essence, there is little that Taiwan would gain from these arrangements.

3. Not only are the communists refusing to acknowledge the legitimacy of the Republic of China, they are proposing that Taiwan retain "a high degree of autonomy as a special administrative region." As shown in the case of Tibet, where Beijing offered similar promises but later brutally imposed communism, the autonomy offered by the PRC is worthless. Besides, Taiwan currently enjoys freedom and has its own armed forces. The proposal gives the ROC nothing but takes away what it already has.

4. A similar argument is made here. Why should Taiwan take the chance that its social-economic structure will be left intact under the communists? To think that Beijing would not eventually impose socialism on the island is naive. When that occurs, the high standard of living enjoyed by the people on Taiwan will be lost. It is far better that Taiwan prosper to demonstrate valid methods of modernization which one day can be applied to development on the mainland.

5. It is unrealistic to expect that leaders of a democratic system such as that which exists on Taiwan could effectively function in a communist state where policy is dominated by those following Marxism-Leninism. Any posts given to current ROC leaders would be ceremonial at best.

6. Taiwan doesn't need Beijing's economic assistance. In truth, the communist leaders would like to share in Taiwan's economic prosperity.

7. Again, it is unrealistic to expect that Beijing will offer the people of Taiwan rights and privileges which are not enjoyed by the people on the mainland. Freedom of movement would have catastrophic results within the system of control on the mainland; it cannot be tolerated, nor promised with true intent.

8. Although it is true that Taiwan's businessmen are similar to fellow tradesmen around the world in looking for investment potential, the fact is that foreign and Overseas Chinese investments on the mainland have not proven to be very profitable. Far more money is to be gained from investments on Taiwan.

9. It is hard to take the communist proposal seriously when the freedom to make suggestions for the direction of government on the mainland is strictly forbidden. Any criticism of communist policy or suggestion for change in leadership is punishable. These

inconsistencies lead one to conclude that Ye's proposals were not meant seriously to be considered by Taipei; rather, they were intended to influence opinion in the U.S. and elsewhere in order to further increase pressure on the ROC to accommodate Beijing.[8]

Many friends of the ROC have advised Taipei that Taiwan was losing the international propaganda war with the PRC because of Taipei's consistently negative policy regarding contacts, while Beijing offered reasonable sounding proposals for peaceful reunification. Perhaps in response to these suggestions, the ROC publicly advanced its own proposal for China's unification in June 1982. The focus of Taipei's proposal, however, was quite different from that of Beijing. Whereas the PRC sought to find a way to incorporate Taiwan and its government into a provincial relationship with the PRC, Taiwan concentrated on the form of government a reunited China should have in the future.

The best known statement of Taiwan's reunification policy was given by Premier Sun Yun-suan before the Eleventh Sino-American Conference in Taipei on June 10, 1982. Sun noted that the future of China, not Taiwan, was the real issue.[9] He said, "We should leave the problem of China's future to the decision of the Chinese people as a whole." Sun went on to explain Taiwan's perspective on the reunification issue:

> Regarding "Chinese reunification," the two sides have advanced different views. Free China calls for Chinese reunification under the Three Principles of the People, whereas the Chinese Communist regime has advanced through . . . Yeh Chien-ying a nine-point proposal for so-called peaceful reunification which is actually intended to communize free China.
>
> We believe that Chinese reunification should be based on the free will of the Chinese people as a whole. . . . The Chinese Communists . . . should give up the "four fundamental principles" as quickly as possible and take steps to change their way of life.

The ROC Premier then presented the heart of the ROC proposal, which held out the prospects for reunification if the mainland's economic and political reforms sufficiently liberalized conditions in China. Sun said: "If the political, economic, social and cultural gaps between the Chinese mainland and free China continue to narrow, the conditions for peaceful reunification can gradually mature. The obstacles to reunification will be reduced naturally with the passage of time."

A July 1983 commentary from Taipei's international wire service reiterated this basic position:

> The Republic of China does not reject national reunification, nor does Taipei insist that the Kuomintang must be in control of a reunited China.

The fact is that the government of the Republic of China on Taiwan has been persistently working toward China's national reunification. The difference is that Taipei aims at achieving a reunited China under a democratic system.

To the Chinese Communist leadership, however, reunification with Taiwan means subjugation of the island province's 18 million people under communism. . . . It is not a question of a quarrel between two political parties. At stake is the future of China, a question of whether Chinese people will have democratic government or remain slaves under a totalitarian regime forever.[10]

In May 1983 President Chiang Ching-kuo explained to *Der Spiegel* why his government refused to negotiate directly with Beijing. He said the Republic of China "had held several peace talks with the Chinese Communists and learned a bitter lesson. Therefore, since 1949, we have made up our minds not to talk with them again." Chiang said:

The ultimate aim of the Chinese communists in proposing "peace talks" is to communize Taiwan, Penghu, Kinmen and Matsu. This is not only unacceptable to the 18 million people in free China but is also detested by the Chinese abroad and on the Chinese mainland. Free China's success in implementing democracy and in pursuing economic development has enabled the people as a whole to enjoy the blessings of freedom, progress and prosperity in Taiwan. All Chinese have therefore pinned their hopes on free China.[11]

One of the most eloquent explanations of the ROC position on reunification was delivered by President Chiang in March 1986 before the Third Plenary Session of the Twelfth Central Committee of the KMT.[12] Chiang placed the reunification issue in an historical context, noting that a strong, united China was the goal of Sun Yat-sen and his successor, President Chiang Kai-shek. To achieve reunification remains the goal of the KMT, Chiang noted, but its realization should be based upon the lessons of history. The first of these was that the Three Principles of the People as implemented on Taiwan have proven their superiority over the communist system on the mainland.[13] The second was that "freedom cannot co-exist with slavery, nor can democracy with totalitarianism." Chiang further elaborated on this theme:

Accordingly, we declare we will never compromise with the Chinese communists. We are firm in this stance because this party is responsible for the fate of our country, for the security of this bastion of national revival, and for fulfilling the aspirations of all the Chinese people.

. . . China must be reunified, but only under the Three Principles of the People. This position will never change!

Chiang expressed the view that, in the opinion of the KMT, the CPC faced an inescapable dilemma on the mainland: "If the communist regime does not fundamentally reform itself, it is doomed to growing chaos. However, if the communist regime does make fundamental reform, it is bound for self-destruction." The ROC President then explained his government's view of the international situation and the way in which the KMT's reunification policy served world peace:

Many people believe that as far as international relations are concerned, pluralism has now replaced polarized rivalry. They contend that divisions within the communist camp, conflicts of interest in the democratic community, the rise of the so-called "Third World" countries, and impasse in the nuclear arms race have completely transformed the global strategic situation.

The consensus of members of our party, on the other hand, is that although the world situation today appears complex, the underlying conflicts of democracy versus dictatorship and freedom verses slavery remain unchanged. The distinction in essence is so profound and so incompatible that they leave no room for compromise and appeasement. To defend democracy and freedom, therefore, one has to be staunchly anti-communist.

If we allow communist forces to expand, we in fact allow freedom and democracy to shrink. This is why the Republic of China has not only identified fully with the democratic community, but insisted on an anti-communist national policy.

Chiang went on to reaffirm, "Yes, there is only one China. It is a China that must be reunified, but only under a system in clear accord with the Three Principles of the People." He then spelled out the KMT's "guidelines for governing a united country":

- Politically . . . we will implement the ROC Constitution on the Chinese mainland. That means the institution of constitutional democracy, elimination of totalitarianism and class struggles, the responsiveness of government policy and programs to the will of the people, equality of political power for all Chinese citizens, and assurances of equal rights for all before the law.
- Economically, we uphold the principles of free enterprise, protection of private property, and freedom of employment and private economic activities. Meanwhile, we believe that producers should be able to earn according to their individual efforts, thereby raising standards of living and fostering harmonious development of the national economy. . . .

- Socially, we support equal opportunity for all, and actively plan for the abolition of the privileged class of the communist system, of forced labor, and of all restraints on human thought and person. . . .
- In culture and education, we regard the cultivation of national consciousness as a fundamental requirement, and welcome different opinions and the spirit of innovation. We believe in the freedom of academic research, in the desirability of absorbing the essentials of world civilization, and also in the promotion of traditional Chinese ethics and morals, thus ensuring the continued vigor of the Chinese culture.
- Regarding foreign relations, we will carry out our international responsibilities and welcome international cooperation on the basis of equality and mutual benefit. We will endeavor to maintain world peace and foster global development on the basis of respect for sovereignty so that the communist policy of "exporting revolution" will be left behind in the ash heap of history.

President Chiang's last will and testament, made public on the occasion of his passing in January 1988, contained an appeal that "the people of the entire country, military and civilian alike, must unite and struggle with the utmost dedication for an early recovery of the mainland, the completion of the great task of reunifying China under the Three Principles of the People."[14]

Chiang's successor, President Lee Teng-hui, promised in his inaugural address to strive for this goal, saying he said would "devote my utmost efforts, together with all our compatriots, to accomplish the great task of reunifying China under the Three Principles of the People."[15] Nonetheless, in his first press conference Lee hinted that he would be open-minded in ways to achieve this goal. He said: "I sincerely hope that the issue concerning relations between both sides of the Straits can be handled by new concepts."[16]

Lee's willingness to apply new approaches to the problem of China's reunification reflected a more pragmatic, flexible outlook in Taiwan which became apparent following the signing of the Hong Kong Agreement between London and Beijing in December 1984.

Taiwan's Reaction to the Hong Kong Agreement

The forthcoming transfer of Hong Kong to Chinese sovereignty in 1997 poses a series of problems and opportunities for Taiwan. On the one hand, Taipei refuses to accept the agreement as legally binding since it claims the PRC had no right to negotiate Hong Kong's fate on behalf of China. On the other hand, the ROC supports the return of Hong Kong to Chinese sovereignty since it opposes all unequal treaties signed by China in the 19th century.

On September 26, 1984, ROC Premier Yu Kuo-hwa declared that while his government would not recognize the agreement, it would aid the people of Hong Kong in several ways, including "assisting those who want to remain in Hong Kong and struggle for freedom," "helping those from Hong Kong who wish to settle in Taiwan," and "assisting those who want to invest in Taiwan or who wish to trade with or deposit their money in Taiwan."[17]

One question which arose for Taipei in the wake of the Hong Kong Agreement was whether the "one country, two systems" formula could work for Taiwan's reunification with the mainland as well. Taiwan scholars quickly pointed out that the formula would not work for several reasons, including the fact that "Taiwan under the rule of the Republic of China presents a completely different case from that of Hong Kong under British colonial rule. The Republic of China is an international judicial person. It has an independent government with sovereign rights and a sufficient defense capability."[18]

In May 1985 the ROC Government Information Office (GIO) released a position paper on the "one country, two systems" model.[19] According to the study, Beijing had four objectives in propagating the "one country, two systems" formula. First, the PRC wanted to "highlight the 'Taiwan issue' in the international community along with their assertion that Peking enjoys sovereignty over Taiwan." Thus, the PRC hoped to "mislead foreign nations into believing that the status of Hong Kong and that of Taiwan are identical." Second, China wanted to "erode the anti-communist sentiments of the Overseas Chinese and reduce their antipathy toward communist ideology, its system, and its way of life, through exploitation of nationalism and patriotism." Third, the PRC hoped to "lessen our people's alertness against Chinese communism, and use it to predetermine the future political environment and structure of the Republic of China as well as her position in the international community." And fourth, Beijing wanted to "defuse the crisis arising from 'leftist' tendencies with the Chinese communist hierarchy."

But again, behind the rhetoric there were practical considerations as to why Taipei was unwilling to discuss reunification with the PRC under the Hong Kong formula. ROC scholar Shaw Yu-ming published an article in the summer 1985 issue of *Foreign Affairs* in which he explained:

> The ROC . . . cannot afford to enter into any official negotiations with the PRC. Internal politics in Taiwan are delicate and confrontational, and any move by the government to negotiate with the PRC regarding Taiwan's future would immediately trigger mass opposition. Although the people of Taiwan welcome a united China, this must come about on their terms

and not under those imposed by the PRC. It would be suicidal for the Nationalist government to be a party to any negotiations with the PRC so long as the PRC remains an essentially communist state.[20]

A similar opinion was expressed by Professor Wu An-chia. He said Taiwan would be faced with four immediate crises if it should agree to negotiate, including crises over "its legally constituted authority," "possible instability in Taiwan," "a possible military adventure by the Chinese communists," and an economic crisis wherein "a large amount of capital invested in Taiwan would be moved to other countries, and foreign businessmen would hesitate to come to Taiwan." Above all, Wu argued, the people of Taiwan have "grave doubts as to whether the Chinese communists will keep their promise."[21]

Nonetheless, not all ROC observers saw the Hong Kong Agreement as detrimental to Taiwan's interests. Some scholars saw Hong Kong as "the most important point of contact between mainland China and Taiwan," enabling Taiwan to flood the mainland with "ideas of democracy and freedom, the capitalist system, and even the new Confucianism" which would "have the effect of negating Marxist-Leninist-Stalinist and Mao Tse-tung Thought." As one leading ROC scholar predicted: "We therefore conclude that the Hong Kong issue of today provides the Republic of China with a turning point in its struggle to bring freedom and democracy to the entire Chinese mainland and to move another step toward the eventual unification of China."[22]

A complicating factor is the importance of Hong Kong as Taiwan's third largest trading partner, after the U.S. and Japan. Most trade through Hong Kong is in fact trade with China. Indirect trade with the mainland through Hong Kong, estimated to be between $1.5 and $2 billion in 1987, is important to Taiwan businessmen as an alternative market and source of cheap raw materials. That importance may grow in the future as Taiwan faces protectionism in the U.S. and Western Europe and rising costs of raw materials from the Third World. But Taiwan's government rejects direct trade with China for political reasons. To reconcile the various sets of conflicting interests involved in trade with Hong Kong, Taipei set forth its policy in May 1987:

> To maintain the normal trade with Hong Kong and to ease the concerns of local businessmen, the government has announced three basic principles for ROC businessmen to do business with their Hong Kong partners:
>
> • No trading with the Chinese communists is the basic policy of the government;
> • ROC's traders are not allowed to contact, negotiate with, sign contracts with or make any business dealings with the Chinese communists or

personnel of the Chinese communist offices stationed in any other countries or areas. Violators will be punished according to law;
• Once the ROC-made products are exported to a foreign country or area, the ROC Government is not concerned about whether the goods will be re-exported by foreign traders to another place.

In the meantime, the government strictly enforces its ban on imports of Chinese communist goods in order to strengthen its economic warfare with the Chinese communists.[23]

As can be seen in the government's policy statement, Taipei is attempting both to uphold its "three-no" principles in dealing with China, but also to maintain those indirect or unofficial contacts of benefit to itself or its citizens. The next chapter examines the increased contact between China and Taiwan since 1985. It is this trend toward pragmatic intercourse across the Taiwan Strait that led to a reexamination of U.S. reunification policy in 1985 and 1986 and a subsequent change in the orientation of that policy toward support for increased contact in 1987.

Notes

1. China News Agency (CNA), January 27, 1983, in *FBIS-China,* January 27, 1983, p. V1.

2. Liao's speech was translated in *Inside China Mainland* (Taipei), May 1982.

3. Zhao Ziyang, "Advance Along the Road of Socialism with Chinese Characteristics," *13th National Congress of the Communist Party of China* (Beijing: Beijing Review Publications, 1987), p. VI.

4. See Charles Chung-lih Wu, "Economic Developments in the Republic of China," paper presented for a conference sponsored by the American Enterprise Institute, Washington, D.C., May 18, 1988.

5. For a discussion of the evolution of Taiwan's political process, see the testimony of Martin L. Lasater in U.S. Congress, House of Representatives, Committee on Foreign Affairs, Subcommittee on Asian and Pacific Affairs, *Political Developments in Taiwan* (Washington, D.C.: GPO, 1985), pp. 63-98. For a more detailed examination, see John F. Copper and George P. Chen, *Taiwan's Elections: Political Development and Democratization in the Republic of China* (Baltimore, MD: University of Maryland School of Law, 1984).

6. For a discussion of the significance of the 1986 steps to expand political participation on Taiwan, see Martin L. Lasater, ed., "Democracy in China, Part 2: Taipei Style," *Heritage Lecture No. 106* (February 12, 1987).

7. See Tin-yu Ting, "Socioeconomic Development and Party Competition in Taiwan: The Case of the Kuomintang and the Democratic Progressive Party in the 1986 Supplementary Legislative Yuan Election," paper presented for a

conference sponsored by the American Enterprise Institute, Washington, D.C., May 18, 1988.

8. Paraphrased from "China's Reunification: Is the 'Nine-Point Proposal' a Yesable Solution" (Taipei: China Mainland Research Center, May 1982).

9. The text of Premier Sun's speech can be found in "The China Issue and China's Reunification" (Taipei: Government Information Office, 1982).

10. Taipei International Service, July 27, 1983, in *FBIS-China,* July 29, 1983, pp. V1-V2.

11. "President Chiang Ching-kuo's Interview with an Editor of *Der Spiegel,* May 16, 1983" (Taipei: Government Information Office, June 1983), pp. 8-9.

12. See Chiang Ching-kuo, "China's Reunification and World Peace," *Free China Review,* May 1986, pp. 61-68.

13. This point seems to be the basis of most ROC objections to reunification with the mainland under terms thus far advanced by Beijing. See, for example, Chang King-yuh, *A Framework for China's Unification* (Taipei: Kwang Hwa Publishing Co., October 1986).

14. "In Memory of a Beloved Leader," *Free China Review,* February 1988, p. 76.

15. *Free China Journal,* January 18, 1988, p. 1.

16. *Washington Post,* February 23, 1988, p. A17. 17. *Chung-yang jih-pao,* September 27, 1984, p. 1.

18. Shaw Yu-ming, "An ROC View of the Hong Kong Issue," *Issues and Studies,* 22, 6 (June 1986), pp. 29-30. The entire issue of *Issue and Studies* was devoted to the Hong Kong problem.

19. "A Republic of China Study of Peking's 'One Country, Two Systems' Concept," (Taipei: Government Information Office, May 29, 1985).

20. See Shaw Yu-ming, "Taiwan: A View from Taipei," *Foreign Affairs,* 63, 5 (Summer 1985), pp. 1050-1063.

21. See Wu An-chia, "'One Country, Two Systems': A Model for Taiwan?" *Issues and Studies,* 21, 7 (July 1985), pp. 33-59.

22. Shaw Yu-ming, "An ROC View of the Hong Kong Issue," p. 30.

23. CNA, May 18, 1987, in *FBIS-China,* May 19, 1987, p. V1.

8

Contact Across the
Taiwan Strait

The large volume of indirect trade between Taiwan and China through Hong Kong demonstrates the necessity of both sides to work out pragmatic solutions to the economic and cultural affinities shared by the two Chinese societies. These affinities have become much more pronounced since reforms were introduced into China in 1978. Moreover, if Taiwan and China are to participate in the dynamic growth of the Pacific Basin, then some interaction between the two sides is inevitable. Largely as a result of these trends, Taipei from about 1985 has gradually relaxed its restrictions on unofficial contact with the mainland.

Fundamental political differences still exist, however, between the CPC and KMT. The two governments are evolving policies designed to accommodate demands for increased interaction yet preserve their respective political positions. The problem for Beijing is how to use the growing contacts with Taiwan to draw Taipei under PRC sovereignty, while avoiding social unrest caused by the unfavorable comparison of the standards of living on Taiwan and the mainland. The problem for Taipei is how to interact profitably with China but avoid being "swallowed" by its larger, more powerful neighbor. Some on Taiwan want to use increased contacts with the mainland to undermine the Chinese people's confidence in the CPC.

At the end of 1987, relations between the two Chinese sides remained in a state of evolution. But it appeared that a major hurdle had been passed in that Beijing realized that it could not isolate Taiwan, even as Taipei failed earlier in its efforts to isolate the PRC. Although both sides retained their goals of eventually "taking over" the other, a great deal of effort was being expended to find those areas of cooperation in which both Taiwan and China could benefit. It was for the purpose of encouraging this cooperative process that the U.S. in 1987 began to support increased unofficial contact between the two Chinese societies.

Contact across the Taiwan Strait began slowly in 1985-1986 and increased sharply in 1987. This chapter examines these developments.

Beijing-Taipei Relations, 1985-1986

During 1985 and 1986 there were somewhat contradictory trends that appeared in the policies of Beijing and Taipei. The PRC renewed its threats of military action against Taiwan (see Chapter 4), but at the same time offered additional concessions to Taipei under the "one country, two systems" formula. In Taiwan there was reaffirmation of the "three-no" policy, but relaxation on rules governing unofficial contact with China. Overall, one could perceive a trend toward gradually increased contact between the two sides.

PRC Elaboration of "One Country, Two Systems"

Following the signing of the Hong Kong Agreement in December 1984, the PRC issued several statements on how the "one country, two systems" formula would be flexibly applied to Taiwan. These statements made it clear that Taiwan was being promised more favorable treatment than Hong Kong. It was evident that Beijing hoped the momentum gained in settling the Hong Kong, and later the Macao, reunification issues would provide the necessary pressure on Taipei to move positively toward some kind of arrangement with the mainland in the near future. The PRC said the most important symbolic first steps in that direction were Taiwan's acceptance of trade, mail, and air and shipping services between Taiwan and China.

The PRC adopted this more flexible approach for at least three reasons. First, it was evident that Taiwan's situation differed from Hong Kong's and that additional incentives were necessary to draw Taipei into reunification. Second, despite Taiwan's persistent refusal to change its "three-no" policy, PRC assessments of trends on Taiwan predicted the KMT would find it increasingly difficult to adhere to that policy. Third, the resolution of the Taiwan issue assumed a higher national priority for the PRC once the Hong Kong and Macao issues had been satisfactorily resolved.

In January 1985 *Zhongguo Xinwen She* listed five factors said to be causing Taiwan to become more passive in implementing its policy of no contact, no compromise, and no negotiations with the mainland:[1]

- Taiwan authorities were unable to enforce their ban against Taiwan residents visiting the mainland for family visits or sightseeing. Further, some magazines and individuals on Taiwan were openly criticizing government policy in this regard.

- The KMT government was being criticized at home and abroad for closing down newspapers and magazines which published unauthorized information about the Hong Kong settlement, China's outstanding performance in the Los Angeles Olympic Games, and the murder of anti-KMT journalist Henry Liu by Taiwan agents in California.
- The KMT government was being criticized on Taiwan for refusing to apply the so-called Olympic formula to more than international sports events. The formula was one whereby the PRC would not object to Taiwan's participation if it did so under the name "China-Taipei."
- Taipei was under a great deal of pressure as a result of the Hong Kong settlement under the "one country, two systems" model. Taiwan could not avoid the assumption that the model might be appropriate for Taiwan's reunification with the mainland as well.
- The Taiwan government was also under pressure because the successful implementation of economic reform on the mainland meant that Taiwan was not the sole model for China's prosperity in the future.

Another indicator of increased unofficial contact between the two sides pointed out by PRC analysts, despite Taipei's continued adherence to its "three-no" policy, was the level of indirect trade between the two sides through Hong Kong. Beijing cited the growth of indirect trade to argue that Taiwan's economy was in bad shape. The reluctance of Taiwanese to invest in the island and major fraud cases involving leading financial institutions were pointed to as proof that economic cooperation with the mainland was Taipei's only recourse.[2]

In July 1985 Deng Xiaoping said that Taiwan would receive more favorable treatment than Hong Kong, if it elected to pursue reunification through peaceful as opposed to nonpeaceful means. The key difference pointed out by Deng and other PRC spokesmen was that, unlike Hong Kong, China would not send troops to Taiwan and Taiwan could keep its armed forces intact. Deng said: "We have always insisted on settling the Taiwan issue by peaceful means. We offer Taiwan more generous terms than those offered to Hong Kong. We are going to station troops in Hong Kong. However, we are not going to station troops in Taiwan."[3] Later that month in Los Angeles, PRC State Councillor Ji Pengfei reiterated that China's "policy toward Taiwan is more lenient than that toward Hong Kong. Taiwan can keep its troops, but Hong Kong cannot."[4]

China justified more favorable conditions being offered Taiwan on the grounds that the Taiwan issue was not a question of sovereignty, as was the case with British rule in Hong Kong. At the same time, the PRC assured foreign countries—meaning principally the U.S.—that the "one country, two systems" model would not adversely affect their interests in Taiwan. PRC Vice President Ulanhu said in October 1985:

> The question of Taiwan differs from the question of Hong Kong. It is not a question of recovering sovereignty, but a question of peaceful reunification of the motherland. It is China's internal affair. However, it can also be solved through the concept of "one country, two systems." At the same time, the conditions may be even more flexible. This policy of peaceful reunification of ours completely conforms with the interests of the people and authorities in Taiwan. In the meantime, it also takes into consideration the legitimate interests of relevant countries in Taiwan.[5]

Toward the end of 1985, several major articles appeared in the PRC press outlining the basic conditions for Taiwan's reunification with the mainland under the "one country, two systems" approach. *Ban Yue Tan* summarized the PRC Central Committee's policy as containing the following four points:[6]

- There is only one China and Taiwan is an inseparable part of China. A special administrative region can be set up in Taiwan "to implement a high degree of autonomy and maintain some unique powers that no other province has ever had, including some powers concerning foreign economic and cultural exchanges, but not including diplomatic powers. There will be only one name for the country, namely the People's Republic of China."
- Although the PRC "cannot promise to give up nonpeaceful means," the "adoption of peaceful means [of reunification] is a policy decision that has been made out of the consideration of the interests of the Taiwan people and Taiwan authorities and the needs for a peaceful environment for the construction of the mainland and that has been made to meet the international situation."
- "The method for realizing reunification is to hold talks on an equal footing between the KMT and the CPC and to conduct a third round of cooperation between these two parties. These will be talks carried out on an equal footing and will not be talks between central and local governments."
- Beijing hopes that the Taiwan authorities and Taiwan people will help realize China's peaceful reunification. "Fundamentally, peaceful reunification conforms to the basic interests of the people of all nationalities in Taiwan."

A more forceful series of articles appeared in the September 16, 1985, *Liaowang* overseas edition. The two articles reflected a carrot-and-stick approach to the Taiwan issue characteristic of PRC policy during 1985-1986. One article praised both Chiang Kai-shek and Chiang Ching-kuo for insisting upon "one China" and opposing "two Chinas" and "Taiwan independence." According to the article, this provided "some common language between us."[7] The other September article warned, "There have always been two different ways with regard to the reunification of China—a nonpeaceful way and a peaceful way."[8] The article said:

> There is not just one way to China's reunification. If the Taiwan KMT leaders consistently refuse to negotiate, if foreign military intervention occurs and hampers China's reunification, and if the island of Taiwan "floats away" from the mainland due to a change in Taiwan's situation— under these three conditions—the PRC Government would have no choice but to reunify the country in a nonpeaceful way. And after the reunification of the country, the system in Taiwan will be determined by respecting history, Taiwan's actual conditions, and the desires of the Taiwan people. But those who are opposed to the reunification of the country will be punished by history. It is impermissible to delay China's reunification.

The second September article introduced some interesting clarifications of Taiwan's potential status as a special autonomous region. It said: "Among the conditions of the CPC's proposing negotiations with the KMT is that the CPC agrees with maintaining Taiwan's capitalist society, economic system, and lifestyle." Taiwan "will be in charge of its own party, government, and Army." Furthermore, the "problem of 'democratization' is Taiwan's own affair."

As to what steps the PRC wanted to see in the near future to advance peaceful reunification, the article said: "We are expecting the formal opening of postal communications, navigation, and air traffic, and the formal establishment of trade relations between the mainland and Taiwan. We are looking forward to formal economic, cultural, and scientific exchanges between them."

The mainland's peaceful reunification efforts during the 1985-1986 period were perhaps best symbolized by the February 3, 1986, issue of *Beijing Review*. On the cover was a heart, encompassing both the mainland and Taiwan, but with Taiwan's portion broken off to signify the pain of separation. The description of the cover was "Taiwan and the Mainland: Longing for an End to Division."[9]

Yet another significant step in increasing the credibility of the "one country, two systems" approach to national reunification was taken in

June 1986, when the PRC and Portugal opened talks on the return of
Macao to Chinese sovereignty. The nine-month negotiations were mostly
amicable, in sharp contrast to the sometimes acrimonious two years
of talks between Beijing and London over the future of Hong Kong.
The final agreement, providing for the return of the colony to China
on December 20, 1999, was initialled on March 26 and signed on April
4, 1987. Based on the "one country, two systems" formula, most of
the agreement's provisions were similar to those contained in the
Beijing-London accord.[10]

In a September 1986 interview with Mike Wallace on CBS "60
Minutes," Deng Xiaoping answered the question, "Why is it necessary
for Taiwan to be reunified with the mainland?" Deng replied:

> First of all, it is a national question, a question of national sentiments.
> All the descendants of the Yan and Huang emperors want to see China
> reunified. The present state of division runs counter to our national will.
> So long as Taiwan is not reunified with the mainland, Taiwan's status as
> part of Chinese territory will remain uncertain. No one knows when
> Taiwan will be taken away again. Furthermore, we have adopted the
> formula of "one country, two systems" for resolving the reunification
> issue. . . . This will neither bring changes to Taiwan and the lifestyle
> of the people there nor cause them losses. . . . I believe the mainland
> will not fall behind Taiwan in the speed of development in the years
> to come. The reason is very simple, for Taiwan has scarce resources
> while resources on the mainland are plentiful. If we say Taiwan has
> already brought into play its potential, the mainland's potential is yet
> untapped, but will surely be brought into play soon. The mainland is
> now much stronger than Taiwan in its overall strength. It is insufficient
> to measure the strength of the two sides solely by Taiwan's current higher
> average per-capita income.[11]

A summary of PRC policy toward the peaceful reunification of Taiwan
and the mainland was given by PLA military leader Yang Shangkun
during his May 1987 trip to the U.S. In a Los Angeles speech Yang
said that Taiwan's reunification with the mainland under the formula
of "one country, two systems" was a national priority of China to be
carried out through the end of this century.[12] He detailed what the
"one country, two systems" formula would mean for Taiwan:

> To settle the Taiwan question according to the concept of "one country,
> two systems" will do Taiwan only good and no harm. As a special
> administrative region of the People's Republic of China, Taiwan will
> enjoy a high degree of autonomy. It may retain its own administrative
> system, its own troops and its independent judicial power. The mainland

will not send personnel to Taiwan, neither troops nor administrative staff. The Taiwan authorities and representatives of various circles may join China's national political bodies for discussion of state affairs and decision-making. In economic affairs, Taiwan as a special administrative region may have its own budget and will be under no financial obligation to the mainland. It may continue its foreign trade as usual and maintain its economic and trade relations with foreign countries. All the economic rights and interests of foreign investors in Taiwan will also remain intact. Taiwan is quite strong technologically and experienced in foreign trade while the mainland has rich resources, a huge market and a rapidly developing economy. Consequently, if the mainland and Taiwan carry out exchange and cooperation to make up for each other's deficiencies, it will surely contribute to the prosperity and economic development on both sides of the Taiwan Straits.

As the first step toward eventual unification, Yang said that China wanted to establish the "three exchanges" for humanitarian purposes. He said:

We also maintain that before the ultimate peaceful reunification of China, there should be exchanges of trade, mails, air and shipping services between the mainland and Taiwan. Since people on both sides of the Taiwan Straits are Chinese, why can't they do business and have contacts with each other freely? Such exchanges should be conducted even if it is out of pure humanitarian consideration of enabling numerous separated families on both sides of the Taiwan Straits to get reunited. We will make our utmost efforts to this end in the belief that the people in Taiwan will make corresponding efforts.

The PRC, therefore, following the announcement of the settlement of the Hong Kong issue, pursued two parallel tracks to set in motion eventual reunification with Taiwan: a clear message that force might be used to settle the issue if Taipei did not respond positively to Beijing's offers of a peaceful settlement, combined with ever more generous terms to Taiwan. The minimum level of contact Beijing sought during this period was the establishment of postal, transport, and trade links.

Taiwan also pursued two tracks in its reunification policy during this period. First, Taipei reaffirmed on numerous occasions its determination to adhere to its fundamental "three-no" policy of no contacts, no negotiations, and no compromise with the PRC. But second, Taiwan demonstrated a willingness to deal with China on unofficial levels when prudence so dictated. The actual definition of when such unofficial contacts were necessary fluctuated, however. On the whole, a trend toward increased pragmatism and flexibility could be seen emerging in Taipei's policy. The principal reason for Taiwan's flexibility was the need to find maneuvering room in an increasingly hostile international environment in which the PRC held significant advantages.

Principle and Flexibility in Taipei's Policy

That Taipei did not change its official "three-no" policy can be seen in ROC government and academic statements. For example, in October 1985 President Chiang Ching-kuo said: "Our policy of not negotiating with the Chinese communists will never change."[13] Premier Yu Kuo-hwa told domestic and foreign reporters in February 1986: "The Republic of China will never change, under any situation, its basic stand of 'no compromise, no contacts and no talks' with the Chinese communists."[14] And in November 1986 the ROC Executive Yuan reaffirmed the "three-no" policy in answer to an interpellation from the Legislative Yuan: "The Republic of China established its 'no contact, no negotiations, no compromise' policy against the Chinese communists after learning a bloody historical lesson. And the Government will stick firmly to the 'three-no' policy until the Peiping regime abandons Marxism, gives up its tyrannical control, assumes a free economic system, and acknowledges the Three Principles of the People."[15]

Despite Taipei's adherence to its "three-no" policy, there were significant signs of increased flexibility and pragmatism on the part of Taiwan in dealing with the PRC during 1985-1986. In early May 1985 representatives of Taiwan's Dinghai Shipping Company and Fujian's Shima Fishing Company met in Xiamen Port to settle an accident involving a collision between fishing vessels.[16] And in June a Taiwan fishing boat, the *Yongfeng 3,* called at the port of Shanghai to undergo repairs and left routinely in late July.[17]

In March 1986 a major debate arose in Taipei over whether Taiwan should continue to participate in the Asian Development Bank (ADB) under a name other than the official name of the country, the "Republic of China." The ROC was a founding member of the 1966 organization, and one of the Bank's 17 lending countries. On March 10, 1986, the PRC was formally admitted to membership in the ADB, but only after the ADB's Board of Directors agreed with Beijing that Taiwan's participation as the "Republic of China" would be unacceptable. A compromise was worked out whereby the PRC accepted Taiwan's full participation in the ADB under the name "Taipei, China," a formula similar to that used by the international Olympic Committee and other world bodies to enable both the PRC and Taiwan to be members of international organizations.

When the PRC was admitted as the legal representative of China in the past, the ROC had withdrawn from participation in international governmental organizations. Concerned that Taipei had been eliminated from all but ten international governmental organizations because of this policy, many in Taiwan urged the government to accept the "Taipei, China" designation for the ADB. The ROC government, however, argued that to accept the name change would signify in an official organization, as distinct from an unofficial sporting event, that Taiwan was part of the PRC. As a compromise, the government finally announced that it would neither withdraw from the ADB nor participate in it under the name "Taipei, China."[18]

This awkward situation ended in April 1988, when Taiwan attended the 21st annual ADB conference in Manila under the designation "Taipei, China." This was the first occasion since 1949 where government officials from both the PRC and ROC sat around a conference table. In a gesture of reconciliation to Taipei, the PRC and other ADB members allowed Taiwan's delegation to use "Republic of China" in private, unofficial contexts. Taiwan demonstrated that it would attempt to play a more prominent role in ADB affairs in the future by donating $1 billion to the Asian Development Fund, thereby securing more voting rights in the organization.[19]

One of the first major nongovernmental exchanges between the PRC and ROC took place in May 1986 in the form of talks between Taipei's China Airlines and Beijing's Civil Aviation Administration of China over the return of a 747 diverted to Guangzhou by the Taiwan pilot. The pilot of the plane, Wang Hsi-chuen (a highly decorated Nationalist U-2 spy plane pilot), flew to Canton from Bangkok, reportedly in order to be reunited with his 82-year old father in Sichuan province. After several days of talks in Hong Kong between representatives of the two airlines, the plane and two other crew members, who did not wish to remain in China, were delivered back to Taiwan authorities in Hong Kong.

The talks drew worldwide attention because this was the first time in 37 years that representatives of the two sides met. The meetings were held in Hong Kong, thought symbolically important because of its pending return to Chinese sovereignty in 1997. Because of the intense publicity surrounding the talks between the two sides, Taipei insisted that its decision to talk was based solely on humanitarian grounds and that it had no intention of changing its "three-no" policy.[20]

In September 1986 the ROC announced a new policy of separating politics from sports and academic events: "On the condition of not violating the nation's anti-communist stand, the government will allow domestic scholars and athletes to take part in international conferences or games in communist nations on a case-by-case basis. . . . the government will try to be as flexible as possible in handling these cases."[21] A few days earlier, the PRC had said it would welcome the participation of Taiwan's athletes in the 1990 Asian Games in Beijing as long as they would participate under the designation "Chinese-Taipei."[22]

It was an interesting coincidence that the increase in contacts between Taiwan and China occurred simultaneously with political liberalization on Taiwan. One of the results of the lifting of martial law in the ROC was the appearance of politically active groups calling for the "self-determination" of the Taiwan people—a euphemism for possible Taiwan independence. Both the ROC and PRC governments strongly denounced this tendency.

President Chiang Ching-kuo stated on October 6, 1986, that new political parties could be formed on Taiwan, but only if they adhered to three principles: abiding by the ROC Constitution, remaining anti-communist, and steering clear of the Taiwan independence movement.[23] In making this statement, Chiang was reiterating longstanding KMT policy that separatism of any form on Taiwan would not be tolerated.

The PRC has often stated similar policies. In October 1985 *Zhongguo Xinwen She* called the idea of self-determination of Taiwan "extremely absurd" and warned that to pursue this path would mean "the future of Taiwan will embark on a dangerous road."[24] *Liaowang* warned in December 1985: "Making use of the slogans of 'democracy,' 'self-determination,' and so on, the 'Taiwan independence' elements attempt to cut Taiwan off from the embrace of the motherland. Saying that they are concerned about the future of Taiwan, in fact they are throwing obstacles in the way of Taiwan's future, and will eventually plunge Taiwan into an extremely unfavorable, isolated, and helpless position."[25] *Renmin Ribao* stated in May 1986: "The CPC does not support the 'Taiwan Independence Movement.' It has always resolutely opposed the idea of 'two Chinas,' the 'Taiwan Independence Movement,' and splittism, and has done its utmost to strive for the reunification of the motherland."[26] And in December 1986, when Taiwan dissident Hsu Hsin-liang attempted to return to Taipei from the United States to take part in the December 6 elections, the PRC Foreign Ministry stated that it did not support Hsu's efforts to return to Taiwan. The Foreign Ministry said: "China will strongly oppose any move which helps lead to the independence and self-determination of Taiwan."[27]

Hence, during the 1985-1986 period there were a growing number of instances in which Taiwan and China were contacting each other unofficially or pursuing somewhat parallel policies. Rather than proving to be an aberration, these contacts increased dramatically in 1987.

Increased Contacts in 1987

There is an element of the KMT-CPC competition for the future of China which is highly personalized and sometimes baffling to the Western observer. For example, when the PRC became aware of the possible involvement of a member of President Chiang Ching-kuo's family in the murder of Henry Liu in October 1984 in California, Beijing eased up on its propaganda about the case. According to PRC diplomats, this was intended to signal to President Chiang that Chinese leaders understood the situation and would do nothing to exacerbate mainlander-Taiwanese tensions. ROC sources close to President Chiang indicated that the message had been received.[28]

People-to-people contact between Taiwan and China has been fairly frequent since 1978. Joint participation in international scholarly conferences is common; Overseas Chinese freely visit both sides; and unofficial meetings between officials from both sides occasionally occur in third nations. In 1985 about 20,000 Taiwan citizens visited the PRC after transits through intermediate destinations like Hong Kong.[29] Beijing often uses these occasions to signal its "peaceful" intentions and to convey variations of its reunification proposals. Taipei, on the other hand, sometimes uses these unofficial contacts to signal that the ROC government remains dedicated to the one-China principle and also to raise its objections to PRC proposals.

From 1978 to 1986 the PRC was far more active than Taiwan in promoting contact between Beijing and Taipei. Even though some indirect contact was allowed, Taiwan appeared rigid in its application of its "three-no" policy. During 1987, however, Taiwan made a dramatic change in its tactics and began to allow greatly increased unofficial contact across the Strait—but still within the framework of adhering in principle to its "three-no" policy. In relaxing its rules governing people-to-people contact, Taiwan received much international acclaim and strengthened its image as a creative, forward-looking society.

By far, the most important of the ROC decisions was the October 1987 announcement that Taiwan residents would be allowed to visit their relatives on the mainland for "humanitarian purposes." Although such visits had been taking place for some time and public pressure was strong on the government to relax its travel ban, the formal announcement of the new visitation policy on October 16 was seen as heralding a major shift in Taiwan's policy toward the mainland.

The new policy permitted all ROC citizens, except for government employees and military servicemen on active duty, to make one family visit to the mainland each year for a period not to exceed three months. (The ban on civil servants, except those in confidential and sensitive positions, was lifted a month later.) Those wishing to travel to the mainland would be assisted by the ROC Red Cross.[30] Within a month, over 100,000 people had inquired into the program,[31] and by May 1988 some 100,000 Taiwan residents had visited China.[32]

At the time of the announcement, Premier Yu Kuo-hwa emphasized that the visitation policy was adopted on "humanitarian grounds" and that it would "in no way affect the government's policy toward the Chinese communists."[33] From statements made by ROC officials, it was clear that Taiwan was hoping the policy would cast Taipei in a more favorable international light and perhaps discredit Beijing. Premier Yu, for example, said that Taipei was launching an "offensive [of] ideas," which would "offer the people of the mainland an alternative more viable and attractive than the communist system that currently rules them, namely freedom, democracy, the prosperity of free enterprise, and stability and security under the rule of law."[34]

Despite some misgivings that the CPC might appear unfavorable in comparison between China and Taiwan in the eyes of Taiwan visitors, the PRC welcomed Taipei's new visitation policy as a positive step toward eventual reunification. The PRC State Council issued a circular on how visitors from Taiwan were to be received. "Taiwan compatriots" were sincerely welcomed and guaranteed their "freedom to come and go." They were given "lenient treatment" at customs, allowed to visit places "in the same way as their mainland compatriots," and allowed to bring in and exchange any amount of foreign currency.[35]

But by 1987 the KMT-CPC competition had become more complex. The opposition to the KMT on Taiwan, symbolized by the formation of the Democratic Progressive Party (DPP) and at least four other new political parties, also had a voice in determining the future relationship of Taiwan and the mainland. In this instance, however, most opposition groups were in favor of dropping the ban on travel to China.

A short time before the October 16 announcement, a leading spokesman for the DPP moderate faction, Legislative Yuan member Kang Ning-hsiang, said that the DPP principle of "self-determination" might mean the people of Taiwan will choose reunification instead of independence. He envisioned three stages for reunification, occurring over a six to seven year period: (1) mutual visits and communication to dispel suspicions and doubts on both sides, (2) normalization of trade and investment ties, and (3) "consultations could take place [and] a formula for reunification could be thrashed out." He insisted, however, that the DPP must be consulted in any KMT-CPC talks over the future of Taiwan.[36]

Thus, by the end of 1987 the three principal Chinese parties to a possible reunification of China—KMT, CPC, and DDP—were in agreement that their mutual interests were served by increased contacts between Taiwan and China. This consensus created a new atmosphere in Taiwan-China relations which was cautious, but more exploratory and conciliatory than in the past.

Since the new atmosphere further reduced tensions in the Taiwan Strait and held out the possibility of an eventual peaceful solution to the Taiwan issue, the U.S. saw these developments as consistent with U.S. interests. They were also seen as justification for at least verbal U.S. support of the process of increased contacts across the Taiwan Strait.

The next section (Chapters 9-11) examines the evolution of U.S. reunification policy from the Hong Kong Agreement to the end of 1987. Chapter 9 examines the initial review of U.S. reunification policy in early 1985 as a result of the London-Beijing agreement over the future of Hong Kong. Chapter 10 reviews the strategic calculations behind U.S. reunification policy in light of Gorbachev's new policies in Asia. And Chapter 11 explains why the U.S. determined in late 1986 and early 1987 to more actively support contacts between Taipei and Beijing.

Notes

1. *Zhongguo Xinwen She,* January 4, 1985, in *FBIS-China,* January 9, 1985, pp. U1-U2.

2. *Zhongguo Xinwen She,* March 5, 1985, in *FBIS-China,* March 8, 1985, pp. U1-U2.

3. *Zhongguo Xinwen She,* July 21, 1985, in *FBIS-China,* July 22, 1985, p. D2.

4. *Zhongguo Xinwen She,* July 30, 1985, in *FBIS-China,* August 2, 1985, p. U1.

5. *Xinhua,* October 25, 1985, in *FBIS-China,* October 29, 1985, p. U3.

6. *Ban Yue Tan,* September 25, 1985, in *FBIS-China,* October 18, 1985, p. U2.

7. *Liaowang,* September 16, 1985, in *FBIS-China,* December 5, 1985, p. U2.

8. *Liaowang,* September 16, 1985, in *FBIS-China,* December 5, 1985, pp. U3-U5.

9. *Beijing Review,* February 3, 1986, p. 3.

10. For the text of the Joint Declaration of the Government of the People's Republic of China and the Government of the Republic of Portugal on the Question of Macao and Annexes, see *China Daily,* March 27, 1987.

11. *Xinhua,* September 6, 1986, in *FBIS-China,* September 8, 1986, p. B3.

12. See "Speech by Vice Chairman Yang Shangkun at Welcoming Dinner Hosted by World Affairs Council in Los Angeles," May 26, 1987, pp. 7-10, ms.

13. From Chiang Ching-kuo's message on the ROC National Day on October 10, 1985, in *China Post,* October 10, 1985, p. 1.

14. China News Agency (CNA), February 4, 1986, in *FBIS-China,* February 4, 1986, p. V1.

15. CNA, November 24, 1986, in *FBIS-China,* November 25, 1986, p. V1.

16. *Xinhua,* May 1, 1985, in *FBIS-China,* May 3, 1985, p. U1.

17. *China Daily,* July 27, 1985, p. 3.

18. For a record of the debate, see CNA, March 4, 1986, in *FBIS-China,* March 5, 1986, p. V1; CNA, March 15, 1986, in *FBIS-China,* March 17, 1986, p. V1; *Jingji Ribao,* April 4, 1986, in *FBIS-China,* April 10, 1986, pp. A2-A3; and *Xinhua,* May 2, 1986, in *FBIS-China,* May 2, 1986, pp. E1-E6.

19. *Free China Journal,* May 2, 1988, p. 1.

20. For comments on this unprecedented meeting, see "Hints of Flexibility," *Time,* June 2, 1986, pp. 24-25.; *New York Times,* May 20, 1986, p. A3; *Wall Street Journal,* May 21, 1986, p. 36; *Washington Post,* May 14, 1986, p. A25; and CNA, May 24, 1986, in *FBIS-China,* May 27, 1986, pp. V1-V5.

21. CNA, September 29, 1986, in *FBIS-China,* September 30, 1986, p. V3.

22. AFP, September 17, 1986, in *FBIS-China,* September 17, 1986, p. V1. 23. *Tzu Li Wan Pao,* October 11, 1986, in *FBIS-China,* October 20, 1986, p. V3.

24. *Zhongguo Xinwen She,* October 23, 1985, in *FBIS-China,* October 25, 1985, p. U1.

25. *Liaowang,* December 2, 1985, in *FBIS-China,* December 16, 1985, p. U3.

26. *Renmin Ribao,* May 27, 1986, in *FBIS-China,* June 3, 1986, p. U1.

27. *Kyodo,* December 3, 1986, in *FBIS-China,* December 3, 1986, p. A2.

28. Interviews by the author in Taipei in June 1986 and in Washington, D.C., in July 1986.

29. *Wall Street Journal,* June 18, 1986, p. 30.

30. CNA, October 16, 1987, in *FBIS-China,* October 16, 1987, p. 36.

31. Taipei International Service, November 12, 1987, in *FBIS-China,* November 13, 1987, pp. 58-59.

32. *Free China Journal,* April 25, 1988, p. 3.

33. CNA, October 15, 1987, in *FBIS-China,* October 16, 1987, p. 36.

34. *Hong Kong Standard,* October 16, 1987, p. 8.

35. *Xinhua,* October 16, 1987, in *FBIS-China,* October 16, 1987, p. 35.

36. *Asiaweek,* September 6, 1987, p. 26.

PART THREE

Evolution of
U.S. Reunification Policy,
1984-1987

9

The Impact of
the Hong Kong Settlement

Prior to the signing of the Joint Declaration on the future of Hong Kong between London and Beijing in December 1984, there was little thought in the United States about playing a role in China's reunification. Taipei was firmly against U.S. involvement; Beijing's focus was on stopping U.S. interference through the repeal or revision of the Taiwan Relations Act and curtailing arms sales to Taiwan; and Washington could see no advantage or moral justification in nudging Taipei into closer contact with the PRC.

But the signing of the Hong Kong Agreement introduced a new element in policy debates in the U.S. regarding the wisdom of non-involvement in China's reunification. By first making it clear that the Hong Kong settlement was intended to be a model for Taiwan and then by demonstrating an arguably sincere effort to preserve Hong Kong's way of life after 1997, the PRC strengthened its image of flexibility and pragmatism on the Taiwan issue in the eyes of many U.S. policymakers.

When China approached the U.S. in early 1985 to ask for its assistance to resolve the Taiwan issue, there was a willingness to examine U.S. policy to see if indeed something could be done to help remove this long-term problem in U.S.-PRC relations. The results of that examination form the basis of this chapter.

U.S. View of the Hong Kong Agreement

Although it did not play a role in the London-Beijing talks over the future of Hong Kong, Washington did signal its interests in a peaceful and satisfactory resolution of the issue that would (1) preserve Hong Kong's unique status as a financial and trading center (Hong Kong was the tenth largest trading partner of the U.S. in 1985) and (2) preserve the way of life of the people of Hong Kong. The U.S. also hinted that the manner in which Hong Kong's future would be handled could greatly influence the future prospects for reunification with Taiwan. The U.S. further indicated that it would support Hong Kong's separate participation in the GATT (General Agreement on Tariffs and Trade) and other multilateral organizations.[1]

When the terms of the Hong Kong Agreement were announced in September 1984, the U.S. reaction was favorable. The State Department said:

> The U.S. Government welcomes the successful conclusion of two years of negotiations between the United Kingdom and the People's Republic of China over the future of Hong Kong. The United States has a strong interest in the continued stability and prosperity of Hong Kong and believes the agreement will provide a solid foundation for Hong Kong's enduring future progress. In this regard, we have noted statements by both sides indicating that Hong Kong's way of life will be guaranteed for 50 years from 1997 and that systems existing in Hong Kong will continue in the special administrative region. We expect the American business communities, both in the United States and Hong Kong, will see in this agreement good reason for sustained confidence in the future of Hong Kong as an attractive and thriving commercial center. The United States will provide any assistance it can, in close cooperation with the United Kingdom and the People's Republic of China, to maintain Hong Kong's appropriate participation in international bodies.[2]

Because of its overall positive assessment of the Hong Kong Agreement and interest in Beijing's "one country, two systems" formula, the Reagan administration carefully considered Deng Xiaoping's message, relayed through British Prime Minister Margaret Thatcher, that the U.S. should "do something" to assist China's reunification. Thatcher conveyed Deng's message during a stopover in Washington following the signing of the Hong Kong Joint Declaration in Beijing in December 1984.

As it turned out, the administration, after extensive consideration of Deng's request, determined that its existing policy of noninvolvement best served U.S. interests. The U.S. sent this message to Beijing via several channels, the most formal of which was conveyed by Vice President George Bush during his trip to China in October 1985.

Nonetheless, the arguments supporting increased U.S. involvement in China's reunification and those supporting the existing policy of noninvolvement were important indications of the pragmatism with which the administration approached its China policy. Although the Reagan administration was committed ideologically to the support of Taiwan, the FX decision and the August 17 Communiqué had shown that the administration was willing to compromise Taiwan's interests to some extent when necessary to preserve Sino-American relations.

Arguments in Favor of U.S. Involvement

Arguments supporting U.S. involvement in the reunification issue stressed the timeliness of reunification, the peaceful intentions of the PRC, and U.S. interests allegedly served by assisting China to reunify under existing favorable circumstances.[3]

The timeliness factor was important, because ageing leaders on both sides—particularly Deng Xiaoping and Chiang Ching-kuo—were thought to share a vision of one China and to possess the necessary political power to make the difficult concessions required to achieve a peaceful, workable reunification. Also, in the case of the mainland, the PRC had embarked on a path of pragmatic economic modernization which made Beijing more flexible in working out reunification arrangements with Taipei. In the case of Taiwan, the emergence of a native-Taiwanese political force on the island made a settlement of the reunification issue more urgent. Mainlanders on Taiwan believed in "one China," but the possibility existed of a Taiwanese-dominated government deciding to pursue independence ("self-determination") at some time in the future. Moreover, East Asia was peaceful at the time, both Chinas were stable politically, and the PRC and ROC economies were strong. All of these factors contributed to the perception that the time might now be appropriate for the U.S. to assume a more active role in promoting China's peaceful reunification.

Another reason advanced for assisting in China's reunification was the belief that PRC leaders were sincere in desiring reunification through peaceful means. China's need for a peaceful international environment and friendly relations with the U.S. in order to modernize necessitated a peaceful approach to Taiwan's reunification. Moreover, for the foreseeable future the PRC lacked the military capability to achieve reunification by force at an acceptable level of cost. Signals of Beijing's peaceful intentions had been seen since 1979 in statements by PRC leaders, several different proposals for peaceful reunification, a reduction of PLA forces opposite Taiwan, and the avoidance of major clashes with the Nationalists in the Taiwan Strait. China's intention to find an equitable solution to the Taiwan issue could also be seen in the extent of PRC promises to preserve Hong Kong's way of life as found in the London-Beijing accord. A common perception in Washington was that the PRC would do almost anything to solve the issue if only Taiwan would accept the PRC's sovereignty and fly the PRC flag.

Given the supposed timeliness of peaceful reunification and the sincerity of the PRC, it was felt by some in the U.S. that a unique opportunity was presenting itself for Washington to help resolve the Taiwan issue in such a way as to improve relations with China without sacrificing ties to Taiwan. U.S. interests would be served thereby, because the strategically important Sino-American relationship would be strengthened, while at the same time the lifestyle and well-being of the people of Taiwan would be preserved. The U.S. would be able to continue its trade and other nongovernmental relations with Taiwan, even if the island reverted to PRC sovereignty. Since reunification would take place peacefully, the image of the U.S. would not be damaged in the eyes of Asian allies.

Among the steps the U.S. could take to help achieve peaceful reunification, the following might have been considered. The U.S. could:

- urge Taipei through private channels to consider increasing contacts with the mainland
- publicly note that U.S. interests would be served by a peaceful resolution of the Taiwan issue and encourage more frequent contact between the two sides
- show reluctance to sell Taiwan advanced military technology or equipment on the grounds that it was interfering in the peaceful reunification process
- publicly endorse a proposal for peaceful reunification advanced by Beijing or some other source
- demonstrate a willingness to help Beijing and Taipei work out their differences and perhaps to provide an international guarantee for any agreement reached between the two sides.

Arguments Against U.S. Involvement

Despite the logic of the arguments in favor of the U.S. becoming involved in some way in the reunification of China, there were significant reasons for the U.S. to retain its existing policy of noninvolvement.

First, the timeliness of reunification was subject to some debate. Although Beijing had indicated a desire to reunify Taiwan with the mainland in the near future, Taipei had on no occasion signalled its willingness even to discuss reunification. Whereas the PRC had requested the U.S. to become involved, Taiwan had asked the U.S. to stay out of the issue. The only way Taipei would go to the negotiating table would be for the U.S. to apply pressure. There was little U.S. sentiment to force Taipei to talk to Beijing. Also, the political support enjoyed by Taiwan in the U.S. would make it difficult for the administration to push Taipei into negotiations without damaging the administration's domestic political base.

In addition, no one knew for certain whether the reform policies initiated by Deng Xiaoping would continue beyond his tenure as power broker in the PRC. China's peaceful reunification policy was part of the reformists' policy package introduced at the Third Plenary Session of the 11th Central Committee in December 1978. If that package became unraveled either by failure or attack by orthodox Marxists in the future, then the policy of peaceful reunification might be changed as well. Even the implementation of the Hong Kong Agreement rests in the final analysis on the good will of the PRC. A new leadership might well rescind important parts of the Agreement. It made little sense to pressure Taiwan into reunification before a reasonable period passed to see how Beijing upheld its part of the Hong Kong Agreement.

Also, the economic and political evolution underway on Taiwan militated against American involvement in the reunification issue. U.S. interests have been served by a peaceful, stable, and prosperous Taiwan. Those conditions have been heavily influenced by continued support and assistance from the U.S. A move by the U.S. to nudge Taiwan into reunification could undermine Taiwanese confidence in their own future and result in social, political, or economic instability. This possibility was particularly serious in an era of political liberalization on the island, when Taiwanese were becoming more politically active and the ability of the KMT to dominate political activities was weakening. Further, the PRC on several occasions had indicated that it would use force against Taiwan if the island became unstable. Beijing felt it necessary to issue such a warning because of the latent potential of Taiwan to move toward national independence. Thus, a U.S. move to help Beijing achieve peaceful reunification might in fact result in Taiwan's political instability and PRC intervention by force.

A second reason advanced as to why the U.S. should retain its existing policy of noninvolvement centered on U.S. domestic political considerations. Conservative supporters of the Reagan administration were not altogether happy with friendly U.S. relations with Beijing. However, the strategic importance of Sino-American relations was recognized. As long as the U.S. continued to support Taiwan and to reject PRC appeals to play a role in China's reunification, the Reagan administration could claim that its China policy was "balanced" and thus deserving of conservative support.

On the other hand, if the administration became involved in China's reunification, conservatives would object because of their deep distrust of Beijing and their moral commitment to the ROC. Moreover, American liberals would object to U.S. involvement in reunification because of their strong support for the right of the people of Taiwan to determine their own future. Opposition leaders from Taiwan and representatives of the Formosan Association for Public Affairs (FAPA) had lobbied Congress for years about alleged exploitation of the Taiwanese people by the mainlander KMT. The concept of self-determination of the Taiwanese people was popular among many congressmen. A sizeable number of congressmen feared that the Taiwanese would be treated even worse by the communist mainland. Thus, any U.S. involvement in China's reunification ran the risk of alienating both conservatives and liberals and of undermining the broad consensus supporting current U.S. China policy.

A third and very important reason not to become involved was the deep suspicion that even if the Taiwan issue were resolved to China's satisfaction, it would make very little substantive difference in Sino-American relations. China would continue to pursue its independent foreign policy, to maintain friendly ties with the U.S. while rejecting a strategic alliance, and to improve relations with the Soviet Union. Beijing would neither renounce socialism, nor expand its economic and political reforms. U.S.-China trade would not increase dramatically, because of the PRC's shortage of foreign exchange and the low quality of most Chinese exports. The tone of Sino-American relations might improve somewhat, but the outstanding issues would remain: levels of technology and arms sold to Beijing; textile and other trade quotas; human rights violations and political defections; access to information by American scholars and journalists in China; and appropriate U.S. contact with Taiwan. Friendly Sino-American relations existed already, despite the issue of Taiwan, because fundamental U.S. and PRC interests were involved. In reality, reunification would have little substantive impact on those relations.

A fourth reason offered not to become involved was the fact that most Asian allies of the U.S. supported Washington's existing reunification policy. They approved of the dual-track U.S. China policy of pursuing friendly official relations with Beijing and friendly unofficial ties with Taiwan. Most of China's neighbors were not anxious to see China unified because of the increased national power that the PRC would then acquire. A stronger China would be one better able, even if not necessarily more willing, to intervene in the affairs of its neighbors. From the point of view of non-Chinese Asians, there was no reason why Taiwan should be reunited with the mainland in the near future.

For these and other reasons, including President Reagan's friendly feelings for the people of Taiwan, the U.S. decided in the spring of 1985 to turn down Deng's request to help expedite China's reunification.

In spite of this decision, however, the widespread discussion of a possible role of the U.S. sensitized American policymakers to the evolving relationship between the two sides of the Taiwan Strait. U.S. policy remained consistent with noninvolvement, save for expressions of a desire to see a settlement reached peacefully by both sides. But closer attention began to be paid to the postures adopted by Beijing and Taipei as they wrestled with their historic problem.

Yet another examination of U.S. reunification policy took place in the fall of 1986 to determine whether Washington should become more directly involved. The critical question asked in this instance was whether the increased Soviet presence in East Asia and improved Sino-Soviet relations required the U.S. to take some initiative on the Taiwan issue to ensure that Washington's strategically valuable relationship with Beijing was maintained. As discussed in the next chapter, Soviet leader Mikhail Gorbachev's speech in Vladivostok in July 1986 precipitated this major review of U.S. China policy.

Notes

1. For an excellent discussion of the U.S. position on the future of Hong Kong, see Hungdah Chiu, "The Hong Kong Agreement and American Foreign Policy," *Issues and Studies,* 22, 6 (June 1986), pp. 76-91.

2. "U.K. and China Reach Agreement on Hong Kong," *Department of State Bulletin,* November 1984, p. 56.

3. The arguments expressed are summarized from extensive interviews conducted by the author in Washington, D.C., during the period December 1984-February 1985.

10

The Soviet Factor

There has long been a close interconnection between U.S. reunification policy and the overall American strategic posture in East Asia. This is because the PRC identifies reunification as the key aspect of the Taiwan question. The Taiwan question, in turn, has generally been the major disruptive issue in Sino-American relations. And Sino-American relations have been of fundamental concern to the U.S. because of its global competition with the USSR.

From the outset of normalization of relations with the PRC, the U.S. has wanted to use friendly Sino-American relations as a strategic counterweight to the growing Soviet military and political presence in Asia. Similarly, Beijing has used friendly ties with Washington to counterbalance the Soviet threat around China's borders.

During the early normalization period, particularly 1978-1980, the PRC was interested in pursuing a strategic alliance with the U.S. because Chinese perceptions of the Soviet threat were quite high. But by late 1982 Beijing had reassessed its security environment, downgraded the immediate Soviet threat, and determined that its interests would best be served by an "independent" foreign policy of nonalignment with either superpower but friendly relations with both. Even with an independent foreign policy, however, Chinese leaders recognized that the major threat to the PRC would remain for the foreseeable future the Soviet Union, not the U.S. Hence, China continued to "lean" in the direction of Washington even while seeking improved relations with the USSR.

China's independent foreign policy posed a difficult problem for the U.S. At what level would improved Sino-Soviet relations adversely affect U.S. interests? True, Sino-Soviet relations remained strained over the "three obstacles," and Chinese nationalism effectively ruled out a 1950s style Sino-Soviet alliance; but as relations between China and the Soviet Union improved from about 1982, both countries somewhat reduced their short-term assessments of the other's threat. American analysts were concerned that this reassessment might result in fewer Soviet and Chinese divisions "tied down" along their common border. What would the Soviet Union do with these divisions? Some might be demobilized in an effort to put more money into the civilian sector. But some Soviet forces might be redeployed against U.S. forces and bases in East Asia, the Middle East, or Europe. Depending upon the circumstances, the redeployments might weaken the U.S. position in these regions.

Hence, even a gradual improvement of Sino-Soviet relations contained certain risks for the U.S. Understandably, what became foremost in the minds of some American strategists was what steps the U.S. could take either to slow down or limit improving Sino-Soviet relations. Since the key problem area in Sino-American relations was the Taiwan issue, there was a natural inclination to examine U.S. ties with Taiwan to see if compromise with the PRC on this issue could contribute to the seemingly larger objective of restraining Soviet expansion in Asia. The 1982 decisions not to sell Taiwan the FX and to approve the August 17 Communiqué were examples of the link seen by the administration between the Taiwan issue and Sino-American strategic relations.[1]

Sino-American Strategic Relations After 1982

Although the Reagan administration lagged somewhat behind in its assessment of the implications of China's "independent" foreign policy, by 1983 most American policymakers had downgraded the possibility of Sino-American strategic cooperation and had decided to pursue a more traditional American strategy based on a string of alliances along the rimland of Asia, anchored in Japan, the Philippines, and Australia. Nonetheless, the logic of having a quasi-strategic or some kind of military relationship with the PRC appealed to many planners in the Pentagon.

With the State Department and National Security Council acting as a restraining influence, the Department of Defense after the signing of the August 17 Communiqué moved gradually to expand military links with the People's Liberation Army (PLA) under the overall umbrella of friendly Sino-American relations. Essentially, these links followed the guidelines established in January 1980 by Secretary of Defense Harold Brown. As reiterated by James Kelly of the Pentagon's International Security Affairs (ISA) in June 1984, these were:

1. "a strategic dialogue between senior defense leaders to promote understanding of each other's policies and interests so that parallel actions could be taken when interests were seen to coincide"

156 The Soviet Factor

2. "reciprocal visits between . . . defense establishments in various mutually agreed functional areas, such as military education and training, logistics, and military medicine . . . to identify areas where limited cooperation might be mutually beneficial"
3. "the willingness of the United States to cooperate with China in selected areas of defense technological development."

Kelly said the goal of the Reagan administration was "to have an enduring defense relationship which will move in measured steps."[2]

A fuller explanation of the U.S.-PRC military relationship was given by Edward Ross of ISA in January 1986 at a conference in Washington, D.C.[3] Ross cited as important events in the developing relationship the liberalization of U.S. guidelines for the sale of "dual-use" items to the PRC in August 1983 and the visit to China of Defense Secretary Caspar Weinberger in September 1983. Weinberger's trip was especially important because it reinvigorated the military relationship between the two countries, which had been held somewhat in abeyance during the first two years of the Reagan administration because of the Taiwan issue.

Weinberger's trip initiated a series of high level military exchange visits between Chinese and American defense officials and identified several military mission areas where the U.S. and the PRC could cooperate. These included anti-tank, artillery, air defense, and surface-ship antisubmarine warfare. Subsequently, the U.S. offered to Beijing sales of equipment and technologies in each of these areas. These included the coproduction of Improved-TOW anti-tank guided missiles; the sale of technical data packages, plant layout designs, and technical assistance for large caliber artillery fuse and detonator plants; the sale of an advanced avionics modernization package for China's F-8-II high altitude interceptor; and the coproduction of the Mark 46, Mod-2 antisubmarine torpedo.

Ross explained that the administration desired closer military relations with the PRC because of a shared concern with the Soviet threat. The U.S. hoped through its military ties to the PLA to help make China a stronger force for regional peace and stability. Ross said:

The willingness of the United States to develop a military relationship with the PRC is founded on the assessment that the United States and the PRC share important parallel interests, both globally and regionally. Foremost among these is a common security concern—the growing threat posed by the Soviet Union. Thus, an objective of U.S. policy is to build an enduring military relationship with the PRC which would support China's national development and maintain China as a force for peace and stability in the Asia-Pacific region and the world. We believe a more secure, modernizing, and friendly China—with an independent foreign policy and economic system more compatible with the West—can make a significant contribution to peace and stability. One of our aims in strengthening our relationship is to support these healthy trends.

In this context, our goal is to play a positive role in China's military modernization—a role which not only serves our mutual interests, but which also takes into account the concerns and interests of our friends and allies in the region. Such a role also must take into consideration China's legitimate defense requirements and its own modernization objectives. . . . As in the case of its economic modernization, the acquisition of U.S. and Western technology is fundamental to Beijing's strategy for military modernization.[4]

As of early 1986, therefore, the administration had lowered its expectations of formal strategic cooperation with China but had in place a promising informal military relationship with the PLA, based on certain overlapping national interests. In those areas where national objectives coincided, both sides pursued parallel and loosely coordinated policies. To encourage this process, the U.S. was willing to provide the PLA with access to much needed advanced technology, training, and some military hardware.

The July 1986 Vladivostok Speech

In the context of these lower-level military relations, concessions over Taiwan by the U.S. would serve no useful purpose for Washington. However, the question of possible concessions arose again in mid-1986 when Soviet General Secretary Mikhail Gorbachev delivered a major speech at Vladivostok declaring Soviet intentions to assume a larger political, economic, and security role in the Far East and the Pacific.[5]

In this address Gorbachev made several sweeping pronouncements and proposals. He announced that the Soviet Far East would become export-oriented, and open to foreign investment and joint enterprises. He proposed to limit the arms race in Asia and promised to improve bilateral relations with all regional countries. He also suggested that the Soviet Union and the U.S. reach an understanding over the future of the Pacific, one that would include the Soviet Union in any future Pacific economic community. Additionally, he reiterated the old Soviet plan to establish an Asian regional cooperative security system. He called for the normalization of Sino-Vietnamese relations and the establishment of closer ties between the countries of Indochina and the Association of Southeast Asian Nations (ASEAN). He proposed limiting nuclear weapons in the region, reducing U.S. and Soviet naval fleets, and cutting back regional conventional forces, including those along the Sino-Soviet border.

The scope of Gorbachev's speech was dramatic. But perhaps the most important of his initiatives were proposals for improved Sino-Soviet relations. The Soviet leader addressed the three obstacles raised by the PRC concerning normalization of relations. In the case of the Vietnamese occupation of Cambodia, the most critical issue from the point of view of China, Gorbachev said only that "much . . . depends on the normalization of Chinese-Vietnamese relations." He added, however, that Soviet interests would be served by the restoration of good relations between Beijing and Hanoi. On Afghanistan, Gorbachev announced the withdrawal of six Soviet regiments, including three anti-aircraft units.

Gorbachev's proposals concerning the withdrawal of Soviet forces along the Chinese border were more substantive. He disclosed that "the question of withdrawing a considerable number of Soviet troops from Mongolia is being examined." This was symbolically important, because the PRC had long viewed these forces as a threat due to their proximity to Beijing. The Soviet leader also held out the prospects for major troop reductions along the Sino-Soviet border, saying that, "the USSR is prepared to discuss with the PRC specific steps aimed at a balanced reduction in the level of land forces."

In addition to his references to the three obstacles, Gorbachev held out several additional carrots to the PRC:

- Gorbachev made statements to the effect that the Soviet Union and China were neighbors and "predestined . . . to live side by side from this day forward and for all time."
- He praised "the noticeable improvement" in Sino-Soviet relations in recent years and hoped for improved relations in the future. Gorbachev said: "I want to confirm that the Soviet Union is ready at any time and at any level in the most serious way to discuss with China matters concerning supplementary measures to create an atmosphere of good-neighborliness."
- He called for cooperation in economic development and an increase in trade.
- Gorbachev said the Soviets accepted the Chinese position on the location of the Sino-Soviet border along the main channel of the Amur and Ussuri Rivers—a longstanding territorial dispute between the two communist governments.
- He proposed Sino-Soviet cooperation in building a railway linking China's Xinjiang Uygur Autonomous Region and the USSR's Kazakhstan.

- He also extended offers for mutual cooperation in space, including the training of Chinese cosmonauts.

Following Gorbachev's speech, the Soviets stepped up high-level contact with the Chinese. Vice-premier Ivan Arkhipov, who was in Beijing at the time of Gorbachev's speech to receive "acupuncture treatment," discussed the new Soviet initiatives with several PRC vice-premiers including Wan Li, Yao Yilin, and Li Peng. Nikolay Maslennikov, head of a Kremlin budget control committee, led a Soviet team to the first inter-parliamentary talks between Beijing and Moscow in late August.[6]

Early in September Nikolay Talyzin, chairman of the Soviet State Planning Commission and alternate Politburo member, visited the PRC. *Izvestiya* described his visit as a "detailed, constructive discussion with the PRC leaders of the prospects for Soviet-Chinese ties." From the Soviet point of view, "A number of new agreements and documents were signed and real steps were outlined for cooperation in the area of planning activity and the quest for new, up-to-date forms of foreign economic ties, and also for additional growth in traditional trade."[7] Also in September, Chinese Foreign Minister Wu Xueqian and Soviet Foreign Minister Eduard Shevardnadze met in New York during the U.N. General Assembly session and jointly announced that Sino-Soviet border talks would be resumed. The talks had been suspended by the Chinese since 1978.

In yet another signal of Soviet intentions to improve relations with China, Deputy Foreign Minister Igor Rogachev was appointed as the chief Soviet negotiator in the ninth round of Sino-Soviet talks held in October 1986 in Beijing. Rogachev, who had previously been the head of the Soviet Foreign Ministry's Asian Affairs Department, was one of the chief architects of Gorbachev's Asia policy. Following the talks, Rogachev announced that an accord had been achieved on resuming talks on border issues starting in February 1987. He told *Izvestiya*:

It is hard to exaggerate the significance of Soviet-Chinese relations for the future of the world. . . . At the ninth round of consultations, which took place in a businesslike, frank atmosphere, the sides continued the discussion of questions of the normalization of Soviet-Chinese relations, and reaffirmed their sincere desire to further improve and develop them. . . . In particular, we put forward certain practical considerations regarding ways of implementing ideas and proposals for the future development of USSR-PRC relations which were set forth in the speech of M.S. Gorbachev . . . on 28 July 1986.[8]

PRC Reaction to Gorbachev's Initiative

Beijing took Gorbachev's proposals and the stepped-up diplomatic efforts of Moscow seriously since they indicated a possible shift in at least short-term Soviet strategy toward the PRC. Nonetheless, the Chinese were cautious in their response. Little of actual substance had been forthcoming from the Soviets. The Chinese perceived Gorbachev as having limited ability to implement reform within the Soviet system. Moreover, the Soviet threat remained along China's borders.[9]

Statements by PRC leaders reflected this caution. Deng Xiaoping told a visiting Japanese delegation in early August 1986: "It is premature to believe that Soviet foreign policy has been determined by that [speech]. However, a positive stance was also hammered out and thus it is important to see through to the real substance with caution."[10] PRC Foreign Minister Wu Xueqian said: "We cannot determine now whether the Soviet Union is still seeking hegemonism or has changed its strategy for world hegemony," but added that Gorbachev's speech "indeed says, among other things, something that has not been said before."[11] A PRC Foreign Ministry spokesman said the PRC had "taken notice" of Gorbachev's proposal to withdraw troops from Mongolia and that the Chinese government was studying the speech.[12]

Always aware that China's security is tied intrinsically to Beijing's relations with the superpowers, the PRC attempted to use the new atmosphere in Sino-Soviet relations to advance its own interests. It sought to demonstrate to Moscow through various channels a sincere desire to improve relations, while at the same time pressing for meaningful Soviet concessions on the "three obstacles" as threats to PRC security. It also sought to convince Washington that Sino-Soviet rapprochement would not harm U.S. interests and that the U.S. should continue supporting the Four Modernizations, while also stressing the need for change in U.S. policy toward Taiwan. At the time, China's focus was on the reunification aspects of that policy.

These objectives became clear in Deng Xiaoping's September interview on the CBS TV program, "60 Minutes." Regarding relations with the Soviet Union, Deng stated: "If Gorbachev takes a solid step towards the removal of the three major obstacles in Sino-Soviet relations, particularly urging Vietnam to end its aggression in Kampuchea and withdraw its troops from there, I myself will be ready to meet him."

As for the U.S., Deng said: "There is one obstacle in Sino-U.S. relations. That is the Taiwan question, or the question of China's reunification of the two sides of the Taiwan Straits. . . . I hope that President Reagan will, during his term in office, bring about further progress in Sino-U.S. relations, including some effort in respect of

China's reunification. I believe that the United States, President Reagan in particular, can accomplish something with regard to this question."[13]

Review of U.S. Policy Toward Asia and China

The U.S. carefully analyzed the Soviet proposals and Chinese responses to determine whether some adjustment in U.S. policy in Asia was required. Three factors weighed heavily in the analysis: the Soviet military buildup in the Asia-Pacific region; the implications of a more sophisticated Soviet political approach to Asia; and the strategic implications of more rapidly improving Sino-Soviet relations.

In terms of Moscow's military expansion into Asia, the administration noted with alarm that since 1978 the Soviet Union had increased dramatically its power projection capabilities in the region.[14] By 1986 over one-third of the Soviet mobile SS-20 missile force was deployed in the Far East. More than 50 Soviet Army divisions were in the region, and their mobility and firepower had been enhanced by helicopters and modern self-propelled weapons systems. Some 1,700 tactical jet fighters were deployed in the region, including the most modern Soviet interceptors and ground-attack fighters. The introduction of at least 85 Backfire bombers into the Soviet Air Force and Pacific Ocean Fleet Air Force had dramatically increased USSR strategic and maritime strike capabilities. The Soviet Pacific Fleet, composed of some 840 vessels, had been transformed from a homeland defense force into an offensive "blue water" fleet capable of threatening shipping lanes throughout the Pacific and Indian Oceans. Soviet air and naval units were forward based at Cam Ranh Bay, enabling them to operate throughout Southeast Asia and the Indian Ocean. The Soviet Union's right to use North Korean airspace and ports increased Soviet flexibility and created an additional threat to the PRC, South Korea, and Japan. Furthermore, the Soviet Union had invaded Afghanistan with more than 120,000 Soviet troops, thereby threatening not only Afghan sovereignty but also Pakistan, Iran and the oil fields of the Middle East. Moscow had even stationed advanced fighters and troops on the Soviet-occupied Japanese island of Etorofu, threatening northern Hokkaido.

Although the rapid Soviet military buildup alienated much of Asia, the Soviet Union had begun to leverage its growing military might into political advantage in various ways. Beijing had felt it necessary to improve relations with Moscow to reduce the immediate Soviet threat. Moscow could claim greater influence in Pyongyang, a close military alliance with Vietnam, stronger ties with India, and expanding economic and political links with South Pacific island nations such as Kiribati and Vanuatu. And there were other regional developments which potentially could serve Soviet political-military objectives, including the Philippine insurgency, Vietnam's occupation of Laos and Cambodia, the anti-nuclear movement in the South Pacific, and the withdrawal of New Zealand from its ANZUS treaty obligations.

On a great many of these issues, the U.S. and China shared security interests. This was particularly true of the need to limit the overall Soviet military presence in Asia and political influence in Afghanistan, Indochina, Korea, and India. The possibility of improving Sino-Soviet relations, therefore, was troublesome to American policymakers. Although the official U.S. position was that "neither Beijing or Washington seeks strategic partnership,"[15] in reality the Reagan administration had repeatedly stressed the strategic importance of China to the United States. The administration was inclined to view the U.S.-PRC-USSR triangle in strategic terms. To the Department of Defense, "even a slight improvement in bilateral [Sino-Soviet] relations is interpreted by Moscow as a loss for the U.S. on the global balance sheet and an enhancement of Moscow's image."[16]

In the months following Gorbachev's speech, major studies were undertaken in the U.S government to determine the impact of the Soviet initiative on U.S. interests in Asia and whether U.S. counteractions were necessary. Fundamentally, the question was being asked: Is the U.S. too complacent in its policy toward Asia? Implicit in the question was whether some initiative should be taken to improve Sino-American relations or to forestall improving Sino-Soviet relations. And of the initiatives the U.S. could take, none would be better received in Beijing than some U.S. effort to help China resolve the reunification issue.[17]

After extensive review of Soviet and American capabilities in Asia, the administration concluded that while the Gorbachev speech indicated a more active role for the Soviet Union in Asia, the U.S. should not overreact. The U.S. enjoyed a strong position in the Asia-Pacific region and could set its own policy agenda without being forced into action by Moscow. U.S. bilateral ties with Japan, China, South Korea, the ASEAN states, Australia and (to a lesser extent) New Zealand, and the South Pacific island states were essentially sound. Furthermore, administration policies toward Indochina and the Philippines enjoyed considerable regional support. The one area recognized as needing additional attention was the South Pacific, where the USSR had established limited political and economic inroads. Nonetheless, Soviet advances in this area were due not to Moscow's inherent strength in the region, but rather to American neglect. The administration's conclusion was that Gorbachev's initiatives in Asia were not much of an additional threat to U.S. interests, save under those circumstances where American policy mistakes led to Soviet targets of opportunity.

U.S. assessments of the prospects for improving Sino-Soviet relations were mixed. Some within the administration were apprehensive that the Soviets might be able to take advantage of the Taiwan issue in Sino-American relations and China's problems with the influx of unwanted Western "decadence" to drive a wedge between Washington and Beijing. Most policymakers, however, adopted a less pessimistic interpretation of Moscow's ability to achieve a strategic realignment with Beijing. These officials concluded that, despite some steps Gorbachev could make toward improving relations with China, the security threat posed by the Soviets to the PRC would not be removed. The maintenance of troops along the Sino-Soviet border, the occupation of Afghanistan, and Soviet alliances with Vietnam, North Korea, and India were too important to Moscow's perception of itself as a superpower in worldwide competition with the U.S. Hence, although some movement toward improved Sino-Soviet relations could be expected, those relations would not improve to the point where significant damage would occur to U.S. interests. In fact, limited Sino-Soviet rapprochement could be in U.S. interests insofar as regional tensions might be reduced.

These assessments minimizing the Soviet challenge to U.S. interests in Asia in general and in China in particular led to the conclusion that U.S. policy toward Asia and China should remain essentially the same. The preservation of the status quo remained in U.S. interests, although more attention should be paid to the Soviet role in Asia and Sino-Soviet relations should be monitored more closely. In regards to the U.S. policy towards China's reunification, no compelling strategic reasons could be seen to change existing policy during 1986.

As discussed in the next chapter, however, signs of increased contact between the two Chinese sides during this period eventually led the administration to adopt a new emphasis in its reunification policy. Beginning in early 1987, the U.S. signalled its support of these contacts between Taiwan and China. This new emphasis was not brought about by PRC pressure or requests, nor by a reassessment of the strategic balance in Asia, but rather—as seen in Chapter 8—by signs that Taipei had decided to adopt a more flexible approach in its relations with China. Although the U.S. was not willing to play a leading role in helping to resolve the Chinese reunification issue, it also was not willing to try to keep the two Chinese sides apart. Given Taipei's increased flexibility, the U.S. had no choice but to support the trends toward increased contact across the Taiwan Strait.

Notes

1. For a discussion of the relationship between the Taiwan issue and U.S. strategic concerns in Asia, see Martin L. Lasater, *The Taiwan Issue in Sino-American Strategic Relations* (Boulder, CO: Westview Press, 1984).

2. Testimony of James A. Kelly, "Defense Relations with the People's Republic of China," given to U.S. Congress, House of Representatives, Committee on Foreign Affairs, Subcommittee on Asian and Pacific Affairs, June 5, 1984, pp. 1-2, ms.

3. See remarks of Edward Ross in Martin L. Lasater, ed., *The Two Chinas: A Contemporary View* (Washington, D.C.: Heritage Foundation, 1986), pp. 83-95.

4. Ibid., pp. 85-86.

5. Gorbachev's July 28 speech may be found in *FBIS-Soviet Union,* July 29, 1986, pp. R1-R20.

6. *Asiaweek,* August 31, 1986, p. 17.

7. *Izvestiya,* October 24, 1986, in *FBIS-Soviet Union,* October 24, 1986, p. B2.

8. *Izvestiya,* October 24, 1986, in *FBIS-Soviet Union,* October 24, 1986, p. B3.

9. Based upon interviews by the author in the PRC in September 1986.

10. *Mainichi Shimbun,* August 6, 1986, p. 7.

11. *Yomiuri Shimbun,* August 5, 1986, p. 5.

12. *Xinhua,* August 6, 1986, in *FBIS-China,* August 6, 1986, p. A1.

13. Embassy of the People's Republic of China, "Deng Xiaoping on Sino-U.S. Relations" and "Deng Xiaoping on Sino-Soviet Relations," Press Release, September 6, 1986, pp. 1-3.

14. See Captain Jack Roome (USN), "Soviet Military Expansion in the Pacific," paper presented at a conference on U.S.-ASEAN Relations, March 31-April 2, 1986, Kuala Lumpur, Malaysia, sponsored by Georgetown University's Center for Strategic and International Studies and Malaysia's Institute for Strategic and International Studies.

15. Edward Ross, in *The Two Chinas,* p. 85.

16. U.S. Department of Defense, *Soviet Military Power: 1986* (Washington, D.C.: GPO, March 1986), p. 140.

17. Interviews with U.S. government officials by the author in Washington, D.C., September-November 1986.

11

Expanding the U.S. Role:
Support for Increased Contacts

The period 1985-1987 saw a gradual shift in U.S. reunification policy. At the beginning of the period, there was no inclination on the part of the Reagan administration to assist or encourage China's reunification in any way. U.S. policy was that the Taiwan issue had to be settled by the Chinese themselves, without U.S. involvement other than its insistence that the issue be resolved peacefully. U.S. arms sales to Taiwan were designed to help Taipei field an adequate defense, so that Beijing's military option would not be a viable one. The administration's policy of developing an enduring friendly relationship with China contributed to this strategy, since the U.S. believed that the closer U.S.-PRC relations became, the less likely Beijing was to harm those relations by attacking Taiwan.

U.S. reunification policy remained consistent through 1985-1986, despite two major reviews following the Hong Kong Agreement and Gorbachev's speech in Vladivostok. There is a strong possibility that U.S. policy would have remained static had it not been for indications that Taipei itself wished to change its relations with Beijing. As increased indirect contact occurred between the two Chinese sides, the U.S. determined that its interests were served by encouraging this process, rather than by discouraging these trends or remaining indifferent. But the level of encouragement under the Reagan administration was carefully restricted to a few public statements in 1987. No changes were made in U.S. arms sales policy to Taiwan, nor did the administration in any way apply pressure on Taipei.

Nonetheless, the U.S. efforts to "clarify" its reunification policy in 1987 may prove to be a dangerous precedent. It further committed the U.S. in the direction of eventual reunification, thereby increasing pressure on Taipei to work out suitable arrangements with the PRC. If Taiwan moves too slowly in this direction or determines that it wants to curtail contacts with the mainland, the U.S. may be placed in an awkward position of appearing to be in opposition to Taipei on the issue of Taiwan's future status. This and other possible scenarios are discussed in Chapter 12.

This chapter briefly reviews the statements made by U.S. officials on the Taiwan issue during 1985-1987. These statements demonstrate the gradual evolution of U.S. policy under the Reagan administration toward more active support of the "process" of peaceful reunification.

U.S. Policy, 1985-1986

When PRC President Li Xiannian visited the U.S. in July 1985, he called the Taiwan question "a major obstacle to be surmounted" in improving Sino-American relations and asked the U.S. to help resolve the issue. President Reagan, echoing a message he delivered to the Chinese while in the PRC the previous year, said the U.S. wants the Chinese to solve the Taiwan question themselves without American involvement.[1] This message was repeated by Vice President George Bush just prior to his departure for China in October 1985. Bush emphasized that the U.S. would not play the role of an intermediator in the reunification of Taiwan and the mainland.[2]

Nonetheless, during Bush's visit the Chinese on several occasions called upon the U.S. to assume a more positive role in China's re-unification. Peng Zhen, for example, told Bush: "We hope that the U.S. Congress and government will adopt a more positive attitude on the question of peaceful reunification of Taiwan with China's mainland." Such an attitude, Peng promised, would help promote relations between China and the U.S.[3]

During Bush's trip to China a very strongly worded article appeared in *Beijing Review* criticizing the U.S. on its reunification policy.[4] Entitled "Opportunities and Potential Crisis" in order to emphasize to the U.S. the benefits of friendly relations with the mainland and the costs of maintaining close ties to Taiwan, the article noted that "unprecedented opportunities have emerged for co-operation between China and the United States." The article warned, however, that "despite all these promising opportunities, all is not roses on the road to the development of Sino-U.S. relations."

The article stated that the fundamental issue between the U.S. and China is the U.S. attitude towards China's reunification:

Whenever the United States is asked to exercise some positive influence on the peaceful reunification of China, Americans hurry to say that the U.S. position is that this is a question to be settled among Chinese on both sides of the Taiwan Strait, with which the United States has nothing to do. If it were really so, then the Taiwan issue would have long ceased to be an outstanding issue in Sino-U.S. relations. However, the fact remains that the United States has already involved itself deeply in the question and until now it has not taken its hands off.

The authors then issued a stern warning that "a sense of urgency" was being brought to the reunification issue because of political developments on Taiwan, especially the growing role of Taiwanese in the political process and the uncertain outcome of the pending leadership succession change on Taiwan following the departure of President Chiang Ching-kuo. The article warned that the PRC might be forced to use nonpeaceful means to resolve the Taiwan issue under certain conditions:

> If, by relying on the support of the United States, the Taiwan authorities should stick to a diehard position, if the appearance of "two Chinas" on the international arena should become a real danger and if, because of succession crises or other factors, an unsolvable chaotic situation should arise on the island including, *in extremis,* the seizing of the power by a few "Taiwan independence" elements and the declaration of the independence of Taiwan, the PRC government is bound to do something. Should this happen, the United States will find itself in a real dilemma and, with one misstep, its relations with China will meet with serious and potentially critical setbacks.

The Chinese were not altogether amiss in pressuring the U.S. to play some role in China's reunification. As seen in Chapter 9, there was some sentiment among American analysts for the U.S. to become involved following the Hong Kong Agreement. Moreover, some analysts believed that Taipei and Beijing would eventually establish more contact and that U.S. policy should assist that process. One such view was expressed in October 1985 by Mark Pratt, the principal official in the State Department responsible for Taiwan affairs. In an interview he said that the U.S. did not think Taiwan would become independent, because Beijing would intervene in the matter and neither the U.S. nor Japan would recognize Taiwan's independence. He further stated that in spite of the differences between the KMT and CPC, they agreed on some things. Both sides, he said, hold that Taiwan is one of the provinces of China and an inseparable part of Chinese territory; both sides oppose the idea of letting Taiwan become independent; and both sides accept that there is only one China. Pratt expressed the opinion that after a few years of commercial transactions, peace talks might be expected between the two sides.[5]

These views, described by Pratt as being strictly personal, were reiterated in a speech he gave at St. John's University later in October.[6] In that speech, Pratt noted that "positing a single possibility for Taiwan's future does not seem to me to fit with the facts." Further, he said that the U.S. does not seek to influence the outcome of a particular future for Taiwan. He remarked, "It is clearly U.S. official policy that Taiwan's future is not a matter of concern for the U.S., whose only interest is that any resolution of the Taiwan issue be arrived at peacefully. . . . Some may claim that one future or another will affect U.S. interests favorably or unfavorably, but such concerns are not part of the U.S. policy which is to emphasize the importance of peaceful means and not the end result."

Pratt was confident that Taiwan and the mainland would expand their contacts. He acknowledged that while "the formal positions of the two sides are incompatible, and it is doubtful that they will be converging in the near-term," there are "other factors such as economic, political, cultural and social developments [which] may increase the possibility of some convergence as each side evolves." He went on to say: "Increasing contact between Taiwan and the PRC will help create a mutual interest in evolving their relationship. Taiwan's possible future role in influencing and assisting China's economic modernization could further enhance Beijing's stake in maintaining peace in the area."

In terms of U.S. policy toward China's reunification, Pratt stated:

> The U.S. role in the area will continue to be questioned, particularly from the PRC side. However, as time goes on and the U.S. policy and intentions are more clearly understood, there should be greater acceptance in Beijing of the fact, that this policy is not directed against the PRC but is in the interest of all the Chinese people. The U.S. is not attempting to separate Taiwan from China in order to have an unsinkable aircraft carrier. If the U.S. maintains a principled position which is in accord not only with U.S. policy but with the U.S. character, then we may be able to reduce suspicions and reassure both Taipei and Beijing of the benevolence and beneficence of our policy.

Although there was some speculation by Pratt and other government officials that the two Chinese sides might eventually work out their differences, the U.S. remained committed to its policy of noninvolvement. This policy was reaffirmed once again in May 1986 by U.S. Ambassador to China Winston Lord:

> The United States is not at the center of differences between the PRC and Taiwan. The core of the problem is historical mistrust between

Chinese on both sides of the Straits. We are determined to make new friends [referring to the PRC], but we cannot abandon old ones [referring to Taiwan]. We will adhere fully to the three communiqués signed with the People's Republic of China while meeting our obligations under the Taiwan Relations Act. We will seek neither to mediate nor to obstruct reconciliation between China and Taiwan. The United States believes this question should be solved by the parties themselves. We have only one interest—that the process be peaceful.[7]

The PRC continued its appeals for U.S. involvement, however. One example was Deng Xiaoping's September 1986 appearance on "60 Minutes" in which he said: "There has been talk in the United States to the effect that the United States has taken an attitude of 'non-involvement' on the question of China's reunification. . . . That is not true. The fact is that the United States has all along been involved." Deng expressed the hope that President Reagan will make some effort in respect of China's reunification. Specifically, Deng said the U.S. "can encourage and persuade Taiwan first to have 'three exchanges' with us, namely, the exchange of mails, trade, and air and shipping services." Deng said: "Contacts of this kind can help enhance mutual understanding between the two sides of the Taiwan Straits, thus creating conditions for them to proceed to discuss the question of reunification and ways to achieve it."[8]

As 1986 drew to a close, the U.S. once again issued a formal restatement of its reunification policy, refusing to become involved in helping to resolve differences between the two Chinese sides. On December 11 Assistant Secretary of State Gaston Sigur said in San Francisco:

Some have urged the U.S. government to become involved in efforts to promote peaceful resolution of the differences between Beijing and Taipei. However, there is a real danger that American involvement would be counterproductive. For at least two decades, we have viewed this issue as an internal matter for the PRC and Taiwan to resolve themselves. We will not serve as an intermediary or pressure Taiwan on the matter. We leave it up to both sides to settle their differences; our predominant interest is that the settlement be a peaceful one.[9]

But then in a statement implying close U.S. observation of the steps taken by the two Chinese sides to work out their differences, Sigur said: "Earlier this year, a Taiwan cargo plane was hijacked and flown to China. The authorities on Taiwan authorized airline-to-airline talks to gain the return of the plane and some members of its crew. The success of these talks demonstrates the virtue of letting the Chinese work things out for themselves."

Thus, at the close of 1986 the U.S. had not changed its reunification policy, although greater attention was being paid to Taipei-Beijing relations, which were clearly in a state of evolution. A U.S. acknowledgement of the importance of this evolution in the Taiwan Strait came in early 1987.

"Clarification" of U.S. Reunification Policy

Indication that U.S. reunification policy might assume a slightly more active direction appeared in the banquet speech of Secretary of State George Shultz in Shanghai on March 5, 1987. In remarks the Secretary said "were chosen with great care,"[10] he reaffirmed that the U.S. would adhere to the principles contained in the Shanghai Communiqué of February 28, 1972, the Joint Communiqué on the Establishment of Diplomatic Relations on January 1, 1979, and the August 17, 1982, Communiqué.[11] Shultz noted that the U.S. "made clear that our policy is based on the principle that there is but one China. We have no intention of pursuing a policy of 'two Chinas' or 'one China, one Taiwan'." He further stated: "We understand and appreciate that striving for a peaceful resolution of the Taiwan question is also a fundamental policy of the Chinese government."

In remarks which he later described "as an effort to clarify our consistent policy of the past fifteen years which supports developments that reduce tensions in the Strait,"[12] Secretary Shultz said:

> These principles of one China and a peaceful resolution of the Taiwan question remain at the core of our China policy. While our policy has been constant, the situation itself has not and cannot remain static. We support a continuing evolutionary process toward a peaceful resolution of the Taiwan issue. The pace, however, will be determined by the Chinese on either side of the Taiwan Strait, free of outside pressure.
>
> For our part, we have welcomed developments, including indirect trade and increasing human interchange, which have contributed to a relaxation of tensions in the Taiwan Strait. Our steadfast policy seeks to foster an environment within which such developments can continue to take place.

Some amplification of the Secretary's remarks were given by Assistant Secretary of State Gaston Sigur before the Brookings Institution on April 22, 1987.[13] Sigur noted that the three communiqués had "established a framework . . . for dealing with the problem of Taiwan," but that the U.S. and the PRC "still differ at times over how these principles are applied." In terms of U.S.-China relations, the "chief priority" of the U.S. "is to continue building a friendly and cooperative relationship with China that will be a stabilizing factor in East Asia and the world." Sigur noted that the Reagan administration was fortunate to have established a domestic consensus on its China policy. One central belief of this consensus was "that Taiwan's future should be determined by the Chinese on both sides of the Strait." "Our sole interest," he said, "is that the issue be resolved peacefully." Sigur listed several specific political objectives of the Reagan administration in its China policy. "Regarding Taiwan," he said, the U.S. seeks to "facilitate an environment in which an evolutionary process toward a peaceful solution, worked out by the parties themselves, can occur."

When questioned, U.S. officials denied that the statements of Secretary Shultz or Assistant Secretary Sigur represented a change in U.S. re-unification policy.[14] Yet, from an historical perspective, it was the first time the U.S. had expressed its reunification policy in terms of "fa-cilitating an environment" in which the future of Taiwan could be peacefully worked out. While it is true that the statements may be a dangerous precedent in that they may justify greater U.S. involvement in China's reunification in the future, there is no indication that this was the intention of the Reagan administration.

Although the U.S. claimed no change had occurred in its policy, Chinese officials on the mainland and Taiwan felt that the U.S. statements signalled a subtle but important new emphasis in U.S. reunification policy. Both Chinese sides felt that by supporting exchanges across the Strait, the U.S. was moving toward the more active posture urged by Beijing since 1985. Assuming that more exchanges would contribute to rather than hinder eventual reunification, PRC sources were elated at Shultz's remarks. ROC commentators were deeply concerned, although privately some top-ranking officials expressed "understanding and ap-preciation" of the U.S. restatement of its policy. Given the degree of U.S. influence over Taiwan, both Chinese sides felt that the U.S. position would make it more difficult for Taipei to adhere strictly to its "three-no" policy in the future.[15]

The two Chinese governments may have been oversensitive to Shultz's new formulation of U.S. reunification policy because of political de-velopments in Beijing and Taipei. The PRC faced political difficulties following the January 1987 resignation of Deng's heir-apparent Hu Yaobang and the resurgence of central planners urging a slowdown of the political, social, and economic reforms introduced in China since 1979. And in Taiwan the democratization of the political process had unleased a latent tendency toward Taiwan independence which troubled both the KMT and CPC.

Complicating the reunification issue was the support given the call of the Democratic Progressive Party (DPP) for "self-determination" by ranking U.S. Senators such as Claiborne Pell (D-Rhode Island), Edward Kennedy (D-Massachusetts), and Carl Levin (D-Michigan). Pell, Chairman of the influential Senate Foreign Relations Committee, told the Washington-based Formosan Association for Public Affairs on February 23, 1987:

> The position of the DPP is clear. It does not call for separation; it calls for self-determination. It does not say that Taiwan should declare its independence from the mainland; it says the people of Taiwan must be free to determine their own future. It says, if the Taiwanese people freely vote for independence, the world should respect their judgement.
>
> I fully support that position. . . . America was built on the principle that the American people should determine their own destiny. We cannot and should not expect the Taiwanese people to settle for anything less.[16]

Perhaps because of this heightened sensitivity over the nuances of American policy towards China's reunification, the May 1987 visit to the U.S. of Yang Shangkun, Vice Chairman of the powerful PRC Central Military Commission, was viewed carefully. PRC officials said the high status of Yang was meant to convey to Washington the importance China places on friendly Sino-American relations.[17] While in the U.S., Yang raised the Taiwan issue on several occasions and expressed China's desire to see the U.S. "do something" to help achieve peaceful re-unification. In a speech in Los Angeles, Yang said: "We are convinced that peaceful settlement of the Taiwan question will further enhance Sino-U.S. friendship and cooperation by eliminating the only obstacle in the way of Sino-U.S. relations and turning negative elements into positive ones. In this sense, both China and the United States will benefit from the peaceful settlement of the Taiwan question."[18]

Despite Yang's arguments to promote China's reunification, the Reagan administration reaffirmed its policy of noninvolvement in the issue. Secretary of State Shultz told Yang that U.S. policy toward the Taiwan question was based on two principles. The first, he said, is that "there is but one China." The "second fundamental principle" of U.S. policy, according to Shultz, was that "the issue of Taiwan should be resolved peacefully between the parties themselves."[19] President Reagan reaffirmed this message in his talks with Yang, saying that the Taiwan issue is a problem "for the Chinese to resolve among themselves." According to a White House spokesman, Reagan's comment reflected a position always taken by the U.S., and that "our position is nothing new."[20]

U.S. Arms Sales and
Technology Transfers to Taiwan

There were other indications that the administration had not changed the substance of its reunification policy, even though its statements had changed somewhat in recognition of the evolution underway in the Taiwan Strait. In the critical area of arms sales to Taiwan, the administration continued to ensure that Taipei fielded an adequate deterrence against a PRC use of force. This was most dramatically demonstrated during 1985-1987, when the U.S. began to supply Taiwan with advanced defense technology.

In early July 1985 the U.S. sold Taiwan 262 Chaparral ground-to-air missiles for $94 million to replace obsolete M42 anti-aircraft guns. This sale, plus the previous year's sale of 12 C-130 transport aircraft to replace obsolete Taiwan planes, raised the critical issue of whether the August 17 Communiqué permitted the U.S. to sell Taiwan new types of equipment to replace outmoded models. Because of the difficulty in finding operational equipment of old vintage, the U.S. concluded that limited upgraded sales could be made within the framework of the communiqué. The PRC protested these sales, but little attention was paid in Washington since finding identical models for replacement was impossible.

In 1986 the U.S. began to sell Taiwan advanced technology enabling Taiwan to upgrade its armed forces. The best example was the help American companies were giving Taiwan to develop an indigenous fighter, the IDF. Unable to purchase the FX from the U.S. or another replacement fighter for its ageing inventory, Taipei decided in 1982 to build the IDF. On a strictly commercial basis, several American aerospace companies helped Taiwan design the aircraft and plan its avionics and weapons systems.

When information about the U.S. commercial role became known, Hu Yaobang warned that the U.S. could be violating the terms of the August 17 Communiqué by supplying Taiwan with advanced technology it did not already possess. Hu argued that the "transfer of technology sounds better, but it is the same thing as arms sales." Hu warned: "If it is a fact that the U.S. is using technology transfers to circumvent the limits on quantitative and qualitative increases, it would constitute bad faith. China would take a stern position and would give serious consideration to the proper measures of response."[21]

As a result of this and other technology transfers, China attempted to persuade the U.S. to redefine the August 17 Communiqué to include limitations on the sale of advanced technology to Taiwan. To sound the Americans out on this possibility and to emphasize the importance China attached to the matter, Vice Foreign Minister Zhu Qizhen—who had been directly involved in negotiations over the August 17 Communiqué—came to Washington to protest the technology sale as a violation of the Communiqué. Zhu was told that U.S. government-licensed transfers of technology to Taipei were permitted under the August 17 agreement, since the communiqué did not explicitly limit technology transfers but only arms sales.[22]

Many within the administration were irritated at the level of the Chinese protests, especially since the U.S. government had just gone through a bruising bureaucratic battle to offer the PRC $550 million of advanced avionics to upgrade its F-8 interceptor to all-weather, day-night capabilities. Implying that the U.S. was tired of Chinese protests and that sentiment existed in the U.S. government to sell Taiwan even more sophisticated weapons if the communiqué's restrictions were not in place, one administration official said privately: "If Zhu wants to declare the 17 August Communiqué dead, Reagan would like nothing better."[23]

In August 1986 the U.S. announced another arms sale to Taiwan, a $260 million avionics package to modernize thirty S-2 maritime-surveillance and ASW aircraft. The PRC protested: "The sale is an act of defiance of China's consistent stand against the U.S. sales of weapons to Taiwan."[24] Perhaps to clarify its policy on arms sales to Taiwan once and for all, the U.S. sent a note to Beijing in mid-August stating that the August 17 Communiqué stood on its own and there was no need to reinterpret or renegotiate it. The Reagan administration had gone through a very difficult period of internal debate leading up to the signing of the communiqué and did not want to reopen old wounds. As one administration source said: "We don't want to reopen negotiations with the Chinese on this score. The text is very clear. It talks of arms sales and not technology."[25]

Yet another significant transfer of technology took place in mid-1987, when the U.S. quietly sold Taiwan blueprints and data packages necessary to build FFG-7 Oliver Hazard Perry-class frigates, similar to the USS Stark attacked in the Persian Gulf in May. The warships, to be built in Taiwan, were intended to replace the World War II destroyers and frigates comprising the backbone of Taipei's antisubmarine warfare fleet. Six of the frigates were to be built initially, with a possible option of six more. Administration sources justified the reported $40 million sale on the grounds that it was for defensive purposes only and that the technology transfer involved did not violate the August 17 Communiqué.[26]

These arms sales, particularly the high technology sold to Taiwan in 1986-1987, made it clear that even if some flexibility had appeared in U.S. policy in the direction of contributing to the "process" of peaceful reunification or to the creation of a "peaceful environment" in the Taiwan Strait, in the main, the Reagan administration's reunification policy was consistent with the principles introduced in embryonic form in the Shanghai Communiqué. The reunification issue remained one for the Chinese themselves to work out, with the U.S. acting to protect its interests in a peaceful settlement of the issue. As long as adequate arms and defense technology are sold to Taiwan, there is little possibility of the U.S. pressuring Taipei into reaching an accommodation with Beijing.

The principal reason the U.S. adheres so closely to its policy of noninvolvement in the reunification issue is that the existing policy serves so many interests. The policy enables Washington to pursue a dual-track China policy finely tuned to maintain friendly, cooperative relations with the PRC and close, nondiplomatic ties with Taiwan. The policy allows American businessmen to profit in both China and Taiwan; it maintains the usefulness of the PRC as a strategic counterweight to the Soviet Union in Asia; it reduces China's threat to U.S. interests in Asia; and it contributes to regional peace and stability by reducing tensions in the Taiwan Strait. Furthermore, U.S. reunification policy increases U.S. credibility and prestige in Asia since most American friends in the region want the U.S. to maintain close ties with both Beijing and Taipei. U.S. allies in the region do not want Washington to strengthen PRC national power by promoting China's reunification. And there is also a domestic political interest served by the policy in that it enables a consensus to exist in support of overall U.S. China policy. The broad range of U.S. interests served by the current policy is the best explanation, and best guarantee, for its continuity.

Based upon the above analysis, it appears likely that the current U.S. policy towards China's reunification will remain in place unless compelling circumstances force a change. The concluding section (Chapters 12 and 13) examines some of these circumstances and draws several conclusions of interest to students of Sino-American relations in general.

Notes

1. *Washington Post,* July 25, 1985, p. A4.
2. CNA, October 9, 1985, in *FBIS-China,* October 10, 1985, p. V3.

3. *Xinhua,* October 15, 1985, in *FBIS-China,* October 16, 1985, p. B1.

4. Zi Zhongyun and Zhuang Qubing, "Opportunities and Potential Crisis," *Beijing Review,* October 14, 1985, pp. 21-24.

5. *Zhongguo Xinwen She,* October 13, 1985, in *FBIS-China,* October 16, 1985, p. B3.

6. Mark Pratt, "The Future of Taiwan," paper presented at the Conference on Major Current Issues in East Asia, St. John's University, Jamaica, New York, October 24, 1985, ms.

7. "Speech by U.S. Ambassador to China Winston Lord to the National Council on U.S.-China Trade, Washington, D.C., May 28, 1986," pp. 7-8, ms.

8. "Deng Xiaoping on Sino-U.S. Relations," Embassy of the People's Republic of China, Press Release, September 6, 1986, pp. 1-2.

9. See Gaston J. Sigur, Jr., "China Policy Today: Consensus, Consistence, Stability," U.S. Department of State, *Current Policy,* No. 901 (December 1986).

10. *Washington Times,* March 6, 1987, p. 6A.

11. See "Remarks by the Honorable George P. Shultz, Secretary of State, Shanghai Banquet, Shanghai, China, March 5, 1987," Department of State, *Press Release,* No. 59 (March 10, 1987).

12. Contained in a letter from Secretary Shultz to a conservative political organization asking for an explanation of his remarks in Shanghai.

13. Gaston J. Sigur, Jr., "U.S. Policy Priorities for Relations with China," paper presented to the National Issues Forum on the Outlook for U.S.-China Trade and Economic Relations, Washington, D.C., Brookings Institution, April 22, 1987, ms.

14. Interviews by the author in Washington, D.C., March-April 1987.

15. Interviews by the author in Taipei, Beijing, and Shanghai, March 1987.

16. The text of Pell's speech can be found in *Taiwan Communiqué,* 30 (May 28, 1987), pp. 13-15.

17. Interview by author in Washington, D.C., April 1987.

18. "Speech by Vice Chairman Yang Shangkun at Welcoming Dinner Hosted by World Affairs Council in Los Angeles," May 26, 1987, p. 10, ms.

19. *Xinhua,* May 19, 1987, in *FBIS-China,* May 19, 1987, p. B2.

20. CNA, May 21, 1987, in *FBIS-China,* May 22, 1987, p. V1.

21. *Far Eastern Economic Review,* July 24, 1986, p. 27. See also Zhang Jingxu, "A Preliminary Analysis of the 'Taiwan Straits Military Power Balance' Theory," *Liaowang,* July 28, 1986, in *FBIS-China,* August 1, 1986, pp. B2-B4.

22. *Washington Post,* April 25, 1986, p. A32.

23. *Far Eastern Economic Review,* July 3, 1986, p. 11.

24. *Xinhua,* August 9, 1986, in *FBIS-China,* August 12, 1986, p. B1.

25. *Far Eastern Economic Review,* August 28, 1986, pp. 26-27.

26. *Navy News & Undersea Technology,* 4, 13 (June 19, 1987), p. 1.

PART FOUR

U.S. Policy Options

12

Alternative Futures and Policy Options

At the end of 1987, U.S. policy toward the reunification of China was firm on principle but somewhat flexible in application. The principles included several found within the three U.S.-PRC joint communiqués, including: recognition of the PRC government as the sole legal government of China; acknowledgement of the Chinese position that Taiwan is part of China; assurance that the U.S. did not seek to create "two Chinas" or "one China, one Taiwan"; and maintenance of close but unofficial relations with the people of Taiwan. More specific principles of U.S. reunification policy were:

1. The U.S. will not become a mediator between Beijing and Taipei.
2. The U.S. will not pressure Taiwan in any way to contact or negotiate with Beijing or to accept PRC proposals.
3. The U.S. will not support a specific outcome of the reunification issue, but may act to ensure that the resolution of the issue is arrived at peacefully by the two Chinese sides.

Flexibility existed in U.S. policy to the degree that Washington can passively or actively pursue its interest in seeing the reunification issue settled peacefully. From 1979 to 1987 the U.S. actively pursued this interest by selling Taiwan defensive weapons and technology to ensure that Taipei fielded an adequate deterrent capability. U.S. efforts to create an enduring friendly relationship with Beijing contributed to this interest by lowering PRC incentives to attack Taiwan. In 1987 an important new step was taken in pursuit of this interest, when the Reagan administration indicated that it would, in response to increased contact between the two Chinese sides, more actively encourage those contacts.

As described by Secretary of State George Shultz and other officials, U.S. policy in 1987 supported an "evolutionary process" toward a peaceful resolution of the Taiwan issue. The U.S. role was to facilitate an "environment" in the Taiwan Strait in which this evolution could take place. In effect, this meant that U.S. policy toward China's reunification had moved into an evolutionary stage, the direction of which was to be determined largely by interaction between Taipei and Beijing.

The logic of this multifaceted policy becomes clearer when the incentives and disincentives for the U.S. to play a role in China's reunification are examined. Since U.S. policy is closely tied to the reunification policies of Beijing and Taipei, speculation as to their respective incentives and disincentives is also in order. This exercise, while imperfect, nonetheless provides fairly good insight into the reasons why, at the end of 1987, the PRC strongly promoted peaceful reunification, whereas Taipei and Washington sought to preserve the status quo in the Taiwan Strait while exploring the merits of increased contact between the two Chinese sides.

Incentives for China's Reunification

In terms of incentives to promote the reunification of China, Beijing's reasons seem overwhelming:

- Reunification would enhance the national power and prestige of the PRC, and benefit the country economically.
- Reunification with the KMT recognized as a local government on Taiwan and the CPC as the national government in Beijing would end the Chinese civil war and signal the final victory of the communists.
- Reunification would eliminate Taiwan's potential for becoming independent in the future or for playing host to bases of the superpowers.
- Reunification would be a magnificent victory for Deng Xiaoping personally and appease conservative critics of some of his domestic reforms.
- Control over Taiwan would give Beijing access to the excellent airfields and ports on the island, thereby greatly strengthening PRC geopolitical power in East Asia.

There are also a few potential incentives for Taiwan to move toward peaceful reunification with China, although these are much less compelling than PRC incentives. Taiwan's incentives include the following:

- Signals that Taiwan would accept reunification with the mainland might lower the probability of a PRC use of force against the island in the future.
- Commercial contacts with the PRC would stimulate Taiwan's exports and benefit the island's economy.
- Helping to achieve China's reunification would fulfill a desire shared by most Chinese to unite the motherland.
- Reunification would prevent Taiwan's independence in the future.
- Movement toward reunification would satisfy some Chinese nationalistic elements on Taiwan who do not want to be politically dominated by Taiwanese in the future.

Disincentives for Reunification

Turning to Chinese disincentives for reunification, it is difficult to find reasons why the PRC should not want to promote wider contact with Taiwan. But a few hypothetical disincentives can be suggested which might cause Beijing to slow down the process of reunification. These disincentives include:

- Wider contact with Taiwan might increase dissatisfaction on the mainland for CPC policies, as the Chinese people compare their standard of living with that on Taiwan.
- Absorbing Taiwan into China's political and economic systems might disrupt other PRC priorities, particularly if difficulties are experienced over Hong Kong's transition to Chinese sovereignty.
- Closer contact with Taiwan might put too much pressure on Beijing to increase the pace of its economic and political reforms at a time when retrenchment is deemed a necessity.

Disincentives for Taiwan even to discuss reunification with the PRC are many and profound:

- Entering into talks with Beijing could lead to a loss of the ROC's remaining diplomatic status.
- Such talks might have the effect of undermining confidence in local and foreign businessmen and investors, leading to a withdrawal of capital and a major downturn in Taiwan's economy.
- The acquisition of weapons from the U.S. and other countries might prove more difficult, since foreign governments would not want to be perceived as interfering in the negotiation process between Taipei and Beijing.

- Official contact with the mainland might cause serious domestic political and social problems for the ROC government. The talks might exacerbate latent tensions between the Taiwanese and mainlanders and alienate KMT members firmly opposed to negotiations with the CPC.
- Talks would signal that the KMT had rejected Chiang Kai-shek's anti-communist stand and given up Sun Yat-sen's hope of a united China under a democratic regime.
- Despite whatever assurances Beijing might give, reuniting with China would turn Taiwan's fate over to the CPC, which may not keep its word.
- Talks between the KMT and CPC might precipitate a last-ditch effort by Taiwanese separatists to declare an independent Taiwan.

From the above analysis, it can be seen that Beijing has tremendous incentives to pursue reunification and few compelling disincentives. Taipei, on the other hand, has few incentives and powerful disincentives. Taiwan might receive some benefit from closer contact with the mainland, but it might also suffer major damage. In terms of policy decisions, therefore, it is perfectly reasonable for PRC leaders to pursue reunification, while ROC leaders preserve an official "three-no" policy but with some low-level contacts with China to explore options. This indeed would characterize the reunification policies and behavior of China and Taiwan at the end of 1987.

U.S. Incentives and Disincentives

The U.S. also faces incentives and disincentives to assume a more active role in promoting China's peaceful reunification. The incentives include the following:

- Sino-American relations might improve if the Taiwan issue were resolved with U.S. help.
- U.S. involvement might enable Washington to maintain continued friendly relations with both sides if reunification were achieved peacefully.
- Regional peace and stability might be enhanced if the Taiwan issue were resolved satisfactorily.

The disincentives for U.S. involvement stem largely from uncertainties. These disincentives include:

- U.S. involvement would have an uncertain impact on Taiwan's economic future. Many would interpret U.S. involvement as meaning that Taiwan's fate had been sealed and that reunification with China was inevitable. Investor confidence might be undermined, leading to severe economic problems for Taiwan and adversely affecting U.S. investments and trade.
- U.S. involvement would likewise have uncertain impact on Taiwan's social and political stability. Social and political disruption might occur since reunification with the PRC is clearly opposed by the vast majority of the people on Taiwan. The PRC has said it would intervene on Taiwan if this occurred. Hence, U.S. involvement might help destabilize the Taiwan Strait region rather than contribute to regional stability.
- Washington's involvement might not be supported by U.S. allies in the region, many of whom look to Washington's support of Taipei as proof of America's commitments to its friends. An effort to bring the two Chinese sides together—especially against Taipei's will—would be viewed as a further betrayal of a faithful ally. This would damage U.S. credibility in the region and perhaps adversely affect the network of U.S. security alliances in Asia.
- Reunification would add to China's national power and thus affect the regional balance of power. China's neighbors would not like this, and the PRC might act in ways not necessarily in U.S. interests in the future.
- Washington's involvement in China's reunification would be politically divisive in the U.S. Conservatives would consider such a move tantamount to pushing Taiwan into the hands of the communists; liberals would decry the lack of opportunity for self-determination on the part of the Taiwanese people. The consensus on U.S. China policy would quickly unravel.

Weighing the incentives and disincentives for broader U.S. involvement in China's reunification, there does not seem to be compelling reasons to change current U.S. policy. There is no incentive to abandon Taiwan and very few incentives to encourage it to reunify with China. Taipei does not want the U.S. to become involved in the reunification issue. And there is no assurance that Sino-American relations will improve if Washington does encourage Taipei to negotiate. It is unlikely, for example, that Beijing will change its "independent" foreign policy; nor can the PRC dramatically increase its purchases of American products because of China's lack of foreign exchange. Only the atmosphere of Sino-American relations might improve.

But are the advantages of an improved atmosphere in Sino-American relations justification to accept the risks involved in playing a more active role in China's reunification? Based upon the analysis presented in this book, the answer has to be "no," at least until the U.S. has had an opportunity to observe the fate of Hong Kong under the "one country, two systems" formula and the fate of China's current economic and political reforms. And even if these observations indicate that reunification can occur under favorable circumstances, the U.S. should not assume the initiative in attempting to draw the two Chinese sides together. China's reunification remains a Chinese problem; Washington's role should be strictly limited to supporting a peaceful resolution of the issue.

The above approach characterized the Reagan administration's reunification policy at the end of 1987. There is a very strong possibility that future administrations will share that assessment, unless major changes occur in the reunification policies of Taipei and Beijing. Before drawing this study to a close, however, some alternative futures for Taiwan should be considered, along with several U.S. policy options. The various scenarios these combinations create will not be examined, but rather remain areas for future study.

Alternative Futures for Taiwan

In general terms, there are three possible alternative futures for Taiwan: (1) Taiwan independence, (2) an indefinite continuation of the status quo, or (3) reunification with China.

Most people on Taiwan—and analysts in the U.S. for that matter—prefer the continuation of the status quo. But, as noted by Secretary Shultz in 1987, the status quo does not mean that the situation in the Taiwan Strait is static. In fact, both Chinese sides are in the midst of remarkable political and economic transformation. Despite these internal changes, it is unlikely that Taipei will seek either independence or reunification, and it is improbable that Beijing will be able to force Taiwan to give up its sovereignty. Thus, there is high probability Taiwan will retain its political independence from Beijing at least until the end of this century.

But other alternatives for Taiwan's future are also possible. Taiwan could become an internationally recognized independent state under certain circumstances. This development could occur, for example, if:

- The PRC unsuccessfully attacked Taiwan.
- Taiwanese gained control of the island's political processes and declared independence.

- The U.S. decided to support Taiwan's independence and convinced Taipei to pursue this course of action.
- Reforms in the PRC collapsed, making peaceful reunification impossible, and Taiwan elected to pursue a separate diplomatic status from China.

A third alternative future for Taiwan is eventual reunification with China. This might occur under the following circumstances:

- The KMT determined that the only way to prevent Taiwan independence was to reunify with the mainland.
- Beijing offered Taipei such generous terms and international guarantees were so unconditional that Taiwan saw its interests served by unifying with China.
- The two sides gradually narrowed their differences and expanded contacts until eventually their governments decided to unite formally.
- The U.S. forced Taipei to reach an accommodation with Beijing.
- The PRC achieved reunification by force of arms.
- The KMT was invited back to the mainland by an anti-communist faction successful in overthrowing the CPC.

Since the future of Taiwan is heavily influenced by U.S. policy, alternative U.S. policies toward China's reunification should be noted as well.

U.S. Policy Options

Essentially, there are three policy options open to the U.S. in regards to the Taiwan issue. These are (1) support for a specific *outcome* of Taiwan's future, such as Taiwan's independence, maintenance of the status quo, or support for Taiwan's reunification; (2) adherence to the current U.S. policy of noninvolvement save to support the *process* of peaceful resolution of the Taiwan issue by the Chinese themselves; and (3) total disengagement from the Taiwan issue.

As shown by the analysis presented in this book, there is high probability that the U.S. will continue its present policy of supporting the evolutionary processes now underway in the Taiwan Strait without becoming more directly involved. This gives the U.S. considerable flexibility and also maximizes U.S. interests in preserving close, friendly ties with both Beijing and Taipei. But alternative policies are possible.

The U.S. might decide, for example, to support a specific outcome of the Taiwan issue if a future President wanted to play a personal role in China's reunification, or if circumstances forced the U.S. to become more actively involved. In the case of U.S. support for Taiwan's independence, such a policy might be adopted under these circumstances:

- The PRC attacked Taiwan.
- The people of Taiwan determined in a plebiscite that they wished to become an independent state.
- Taipei declared itself independent and asked for U.S. recognition.
- The "one country, two systems" formula for Hong Kong proved to be unworkable.
- Reforms in China collapsed and a more radical style of communist leadership emerged in Beijing.

In the case of support for an indefinite prolongation of the status quo in the Taiwan Strait, the U.S. might choose this policy option if:

- Developments in Taiwan and the mainland became too uncertain and the U.S. desired more time to assess the situation.
- Taipei and/or Beijing reversed their policies of gradually expanding contact and chose instead to limit or curtail interchanges.
- The U.S. became convinced that Taiwanese interests were being sacrificed in KMT-CPC discussions over the future of Taiwan.

The U.S. might actively support the reunification of China if the following occurred:

- An administration came to office determined to resolve the Taiwan issue once and for all by pressuring Taipei into reunification talks with the mainland.
- Taipei asked Washington to play some role in reunification such as mediation or to guarantee an arrangement worked out with Beijing.
- U.S. friends and allies in the region convinced Washington that it should change its policy and support China's reunification.
- The U.S. became convinced that the only way to prevent Sino-Soviet relations from improving to the point of harming U.S. interests was to support China's reunification.

The third broad policy option for the U.S. is to disengage entirely from the Taiwan issue. This might occur if:

- The U.S. undertook a major withdrawal from Asia as a result of isolationist sentiment, budgetary constraints, the loss of critical bases in the region, or the loss of national will to sustain a presence in the Far East.
- Anti-American feeling on Taiwan increased to the point where the U.S. decided to cut itself free from the Taiwan situation once and for all.
- Events occurred on Taiwan and/or China that led the U.S. to conclude that there was no useful policy which Washington could pursue.

Of the possible futures for Taiwan and the policy options available to the U.S., it seems reasonably apparent that current U.S. policy is well-matched to realities in the Taiwan Strait. A change in that policy should not be initiated by the U.S., but made only in response to substantial changes in the reunification policies of either Taipei or Beijing. Since both Chinese societies are rapidly changing due to internal political and economic developments, and since both are slowly working out mechanisms for increased contact across the Taiwan Strait, it behooves Washington to remain in the background on the reunification issue. To do otherwise would be premature and probably harmful to U.S. interests.

13

Conclusion

U.S. policy toward the reunification of China has changed in both direction and nuance over the years. This chapter will summarize the evolution of that policy and suggest various lessons which might be drawn.

Evolution of U.S. Reunification Policy

During the 1940s, when the Nationalists were the sole recognized government of China, the U.S. supported China's unification under the ROC. The U.S. agreed in the 1943 Cairo Conference that Taiwan should be returned to China at the conclusion of World War II. Nationalist soldiers occupied Taiwan immediately following the war and established ROC control.

U.S. support for the ROC gradually diminished following the resumption of the Chinese civil war. By late 1949 there was no U.S. military and economic assistance to the Nationalists. After the ROC government fled to Taiwan, the Truman administration considered the fall of Taiwan to the communists to be imminent and decided not to intervene. By default, the U.S. was allowing China to be reunited under the Communist Party of China (CPC).

The North Korean invasion of South Korea in June 1950 and the subsequent introduction of PRC forces into that conflict dramatically changed U.S. reunification policy. The Truman administration interposed the Seventh Fleet into the Taiwan Strait to prevent either Chinese side from attacking the other. In effect, the U.S. policy was to prevent China's reunification and to encourage the rapid recovery of the Nationalists on Taiwan.

For the next twenty years, Washington included the ROC in U.S. strategy to isolate the PRC and to contain the spread of communism in Asia. A U.S.-ROC mutual defense treaty was signed in 1954, and the U.S. recognized Taipei as the sole legal government of all of China.

Washington extended billions of dollars in economic and military assistance to the ROC, and Taiwan became an important U.S. logistics base during the Vietnam War.

During the 1970s, the U.S. made major changes in its China policy. The Nixon administration determined that U.S. efforts to isolate China had failed. In a dramatic reversal of that policy, the U.S. began to draw the PRC into the international community and to explore the prospects for Sino-American strategic cooperation against the Soviet Union. For its own interests, China was willing to improve relations with the U.S.

As the PRC's international role grew, that of the ROC diminished. This was demonstrated by the 1971 expulsion of Taiwan from the U.N. and the admission of Beijing as the sole representative of China. During the early 1970s, the Nixon administration followed a "two Chinas" policy, advocating official U.S. relations with both Beijing and Taipei. The ROC and PRC rejected this approach, however.

Nixon started the process of normalization of Sino-American relations with the Shanghai Communiqué of February 1972. In an important statement of policy, the U.S. acknowledged that both Chinese sides maintain there is but one China and Taiwan is part of China. The communiqué said the U.S. does not challenge that position but does affirm its interests in a peaceful settlement of the Taiwan issue by the Chinese themselves. With only slight—but important—modifications, this statement remains U.S. policy today.

In large part because of the Watergate scandal and the Cultural Revolution, normalization of Sino-American relations did not proceed until the election of Jimmy Carter and the rehabilitation of Deng Xiaoping. After 1978 both sides moved expeditiously. In 1979 the U.S. recognized the PRC as the sole legal government of China and ended all official relations with Taipei. In the normalization agreement, the Carter administration acknowledged once again the Chinese position that Taiwan is part of China. The U.S. did not attempt to secure from Beijing a promise not to use force against Taiwan, but Carter did tell the Chinese that the U.S. would continue to sell Taiwan defensive weapons. Carter also encouraged the PRC to adopt a policy of "peaceful reunification" instead of "liberation" in respect to Taiwan. This the PRC was willing to do as part of its pragmatic policy package of economic and political reforms.

Also in 1979 the U.S. Congress passed the Taiwan Relations Act (TRA), which links a peaceful resolution of the Taiwan issue to U.S. security interests in the Far East. The TRA provides an open-ended commitment to sell Taiwan defensive articles and services to enable Taipei to maintain an adequate defense against a PRC attack.

The passage of the TRA angered the PRC, as did presidential candidate Ronald Reagan's calls for the reestablishment of "official" relations with Taiwan. When Reagan assumed office, Beijing exerted tremendous pressure on the new administration to restrain its support of Taiwan. If it did not, the PRC threatened to downgrade Sino-American relations, which were seen by the conservative administration as crucial to its policy of stopping Soviet expansion. To preserve Sino-American relations, the U.S. in 1982 denied Taiwan the FX fighter and agreed to the August 17 Communiqué.

The communiqué was another important statement of U.S. reunification policy. In it, the U.S. once again acknowledged the Chinese position that there is but one China and Taiwan is part of China. Also, for the first time, the U.S. said in an official document that it does not intend to pursue a policy of "two Chinas" or "one China, one Taiwan." Regarding future arms sales to Taiwan, the U.S. promised to reduce gradually such sales and to limit their quantity and quality so long as China pursues a peaceful resolution of the Taiwan issue.

No change occurred in U.S. reunification policy from 1983-1986, although at least two reviews of that policy took place following the 1984 Hong Kong Agreement and the 1986 speech of General Secretary Gorbachev in Vladivostok.

The next significant step in U.S. reunification policy was the March 1987 statement by Secretary of State George Shultz in Shanghai. By encouraging increased contact between the two Chinese sides and by defining the U.S. objective as facilitating an "environment" in which the Taiwan issue can be settled peacefully, the U.S. for the first time became supportive of Beijing-Taipei interaction. Both Chinese sides interpreted Shultz's remarks as moving the U.S. in the direction of supporting China's reunification. The administration claimed this was not its intent.

Next Step in U.S. Policy

What is the next step in the evolution of U.S. policy toward China's reunification? Will a future administration move beyond support of the "process" of a peaceful resolution of the Taiwan issue to support of reunification itself?

There is reason to believe U.S. support of Chinese interaction will increase. This is because the trends underway in the Taiwan Strait point to more, not less, contact between the two Chinese sides. In the months just preceding the completion of this book, for example, the following were reported in the Taiwan press:

- China is receiving about $100 million each month from Taiwan through visitors and other channels.[1]
- Taiwan's ban on mail to and from the mainland is being lifted, if the mail is routed through a special post office box in Taipei.[2]
- Taipei is seriously considering allowing people from the mainland to visit Taiwan under certain circumstances.[3]
- Taiwan is considering the importation of raw materials from China, if these are purchased through third countries.[4]
- In mid-1988 China became Taiwan's fifth largest trading partner and is projected to become its third largest in the next decade.[5]
- There is overwhelming support on Taiwan to allow direct trade with China and to permit Chinese cultural, academic, and sports groups to visit Taiwan.[6]

Trends toward increased contact between Taipei and Beijing are undeniable. The increased interaction across the Taiwan Strait may indicate that the two Chinese sides are gradually working out their differences. Eventually, Taiwan may unify with the mainland under very favorable conditions of maximum autonomy. It can be argued that U.S. interests might be served by this type of an arrangement, since the Taiwan issue would be removed as an "obstacle" in Sino-American relations and the U.S. would likely have continued access to the Taiwan market. The appeal of this optimistic scenario may one day cause it to become an objective of U.S. reunification policy.

Need for Caution

But there are several reasons why the U.S. should avoid this potential shift in reunification policy.

First, there have not been adequate studies made of the impact of China's reunification on U.S. strategic, political, and economic interests. The costs and benefits of reunification to the U.S. should be assessed well in advance of any potential move to support China's reunification.

Second, a consensus does not yet exist on Taiwan about its future relationship with the mainland. Until the people of Taiwan have an opportunity to explore various options open to them, it would be premature for the U.S. to assume that reunification is the preferred choice.

Third, Beijing has not yet worked out the mechanisms for handling capitalist regions in the "one country, two systems" model. The exodus of capital and trained personnel from Hong Kong is largely in response to unexpected PRC intervention in Hong Kong affairs since 1984. Until the Hong Kong model has proven itself workable, the U.S. should not see reunification as a preferable solution for the Taiwan issue.

Fourth, China's economic reforms are entering a crucial stage, the outcome of which is not yet apparent. At the time of writing (June 1988), the CPC's Politburo was meeting to discuss the many problems facing the reform program, particularly inflation. If the reformists are unable to solve these problems, there is a good chance their program will be discredited. If this should occur at a time of Deng Xiaoping's passing, the reformists' continued leadership of the CPC would be open to question. Until the reforms prove capable of surviving in the post-Deng era, the U.S. should not urge Taipei to unify with the mainland.

Fifth, although Taipei is permitting unofficial contact with China, its motives for doing so may not be to reach an accommodation with Beijing. Several other explanations—more in keeping with KMT anti-communist traditions—could be offered. These include a bargaining attempt to reduce the PRC military threat to Taiwan, a political move designed to acquaint the Taiwan people with true conditions on the mainland and thus earn broader support for KMT policies at home, a diplomatic effort to improve Taiwan's international image by appearing reasonable on the reunification issue, and an ideological offensive to prove the superiority of the KMT system on Taiwan to that of the CPC system on the mainland. Until the U.S. is sure of what Taipei's motivations are, it would be a mistake to assume Taiwan is moving toward re-unification.

Sixth, even if Taiwan does intend to unify with China, the U.S. should not publicly promote reunification because it would weaken Taipei's bargaining position. Beijing knows that the U.S. is Taiwan's strongest friend in the international community. A U.S. gesture in support of reunification would be viewed in the PRC as depriving Taiwan of its other options. Hence, Beijing could offer Taiwan less in negotiations and still be confident of eventual reunification. A premature U.S. support of reunification could harm the interests of the people of Taiwan.

Seventh, the status quo in the Taiwan Strait is of great value to the U.S. and should not be easily changed. Among the advantages the U.S. gains from having a friendly government in Taipei are an inducement for Beijing to continue its market-oriented reforms and political lib-eralization, something of a "brake" on improving Sino-Soviet relations (Beijing has to wonder what the U.S. might do regarding Taiwan if the PRC proceeds too rapidly in improving relations with Moscow), and—theoretically speaking—possible alternative basing should U.S. bases in the Philippines be closed. Moreover, the U.S. enjoys a healthy trade and investment relationship with Taiwan under the KMT. No one knows what that relationship would be like if the PRC controlled Taiwan. U.S. support for China's reunification would give away these assets with very little in return.

All of these reasons strongly suggest that the U.S. should proceed very cautiously in contemplating a change in its present policy toward China's reunification. The safest approach is simply to follow the lead of the Chinese on both sides of the Taiwan Strait, while protecting U.S. interest in a peaceful settlement of the Taiwan issue. The most dangerous approach is to assume the initiative on the reunification issue, or to back a specific proposal advanced by only one side.

Notes

1. *Free China Journal,* March 28, 1988, p. 4.
2. *Free China Journal,* April 25, 1988, p. 3.
3. *China News,* April 13, 1988, p. 12.
4. *Free China Journal,* May 16, 1988, p. 1.
5. *Free China Journal,* May 2, 1988, p. 4.
6. Author's interviews with visiting Taiwan scholars in Washington, D.C., May-June 1988.

Bibliography

A Draft Agreement between the Government of the United Kingdom of Great Britain and Northern Ireland and the Government of the People's Republic of China on the Future of Hong Kong. London: Her Majesty's Government, 1984.

Baker, Howard H. *The United States and China: A Report to the United States Senate by the Senate Majority Leader.* Washington: GPO, 1982.

Barnett, A. Doak. *The FX Decision.* Washington: Brookings Institution, 1981.

————. *U.S. Arms Sales: The China-Taiwan Tangle.* Washington: Brookings Institution, 1982.

————, and Ralph N. Clough. *Modernizing China: Post-Mao Reform and Development.* Boulder: Westview, 1986.

Bonds, Ray. *The Chinese War Machine.* London: Salamander Books Ltd., 1979.

Bullard, Monte R. *China's Political-Military Evolution.* Boulder: Westview, 1985.

Bunge, Frederica M. and Rinn-sup Shinn. *China: A Country Study.* Washington: American University, 1981.

Camilleri, Joseph. *Chinese Foreign Policy: The Maoist Era and Its Aftermath.* Seattle: University of Washington, 1980.

Carpenter, William M. *Long-Term Strategic Forecast for the Republic of China.* Arlington: SRI International, 1980.

Carter, Jimmy. *Keeping Faith: Memoirs of a President.* New York: Bantam Books, 1982.

Chaffee, Frederick H. *Area Handbook for the Republic of China.* Washington: American University, 1969.

Chang, Jaw-ling Joanne. *United States-China Normalization: An Evaluation of Foreign Policy Decision Making.* Baltimore: University of Maryland School of Law, 1986.

Chang, King-yuh. *A Framework for China's Unification.* Taipei: Kwang Hwa Publishing Co., 1986.

China: U.S. Policy Since 1945. Washington: Congressional Quarterly, Inc., 1980.

Ching, Frank. *Hong Kong and China: For Better or For Worse.* New York: China Council of The Asia Society and the Foreign Policy Association, 1985.

Clough, Ralph N. *Island China.* Cambridge: Harvard University, 1978.

Copper, John F. and George P. Chen. *Taiwan's Elections: Democratization and Political Development in the Republic of China.* Baltimore: University of Maryland School of Law, 1984.

Deng, Xiaoping. *Selected Works of Deng Xiaoping: 1975-1982.* Beijing: Foreign Languages Press, 1984.

Domes, Jurgen. *The Government and Politics of the PRC.* Boulder: Westview, 1985.

Downen, Robert L. *The Taiwan Pawn in the China Game.* Washington: Georgetown University, 1979.

———. *To Bridge the Taiwan Strait.* Washington: Council for Social and Economic Studies, 1984.

Ellison, Herbert J. *The Sino-Soviet Conflict: A Global Perspective.* Seattle: University of Washington, 1982.

Fairbank, John K. *The United States and China.* Cambridge: Harvard University, 1979.

Furuya, Keiji. *Chiang Kai-shek: His Life and Times.* New York: St. John's University, 1981.

Garrett, Banning N. *Soviet Perceptions of China and Sino-American Military Ties.* Arlington: Harold Rosebaum Associates, 1981.

Garver, John W. *China's Decision for Rapprochement with the United States, 1968-1971.* Boulder: Westview, 1982.

Gelber, Harry G. *Technology, Defense, and External Relations in China, 1975-1978.* Boulder: Westview, 1979.

Gilbert, Stephen P. *Northeast Asia in U.S. Foreign Policy.* Beverly Hills: Sage Publications, 1979.

Godwin, Paul H. B. *The Chinese Defense Establishment: Continuity and Change in the 1980s.* Boulder: Westview, 1983.

Goldwater, Barry M. *China and the Abrogation of Treaties.* Washington: Heritage Foundation, 1978.

Gottlieb, Thomas M. *Chinese Foreign Policy Factionalism and the Origins of the Strategic Triangle.* Santa Monica: Rand Corporation, 1977.

Gregor, A. James. *The China Connection.* Stanford: Hoover Institution, 1986.

———, and Maria Hsia Chang. *The Republic of China and U.S. Policy.* Washington: Ethics and Public Policy Center, 1983.

———, and Andrew B. Zimmerman. *Ideology and Development: Sun Yat-sen and the Economic History of Taiwan.* Berkeley: University of California, 1981.

Han, Lih-wu. *Taiwan Today: 1986.* Taipei: Cheng Chung Book Co., 1986.

Heaton, William R., Jr. *A United Front against Hegemonism: Chinese Foreign Policy into the 1980s.* Washington: National Defense University, 1980.

Hinton, Harold C. *Communist China in World Politics.* Boston: Houghton Mifflin Co., 1966.

———. *Peking-Washington.* Beverly Hills: Sage Publications, 1976.

———. *The Sino-Soviet Confrontation.* New York: National Strategy Information Center, 1976.

———. *The China Sea.* New York: National Strategy Information Center, 1980.

Hsiung, James C. *The Taiwan Experience: 1950-1980.* New York: American Association for Chinese Studies, 1981.

Jacobsen, Carl G. *Sino-Soviet Relations Since Mao.* New York: Praeger, 1981.

Jencks, Harlan W. *From Muskets to Missiles: Politics and Professionalism in the Chinese Army, 1945-1981.* Boulder: Westview, 1982.

Joffe, Ellis. *The Chinese Army After Mao*. Cambridge: Harvard University, 1987.

Johnson, Stuart E. *The Military Equation in Northeast Asia*. Washington: Brookings Institution, 1979.

Johnson, U. Alexis, George R. Packard, and Alfred D. Wilhelm, Jr. *China's Policy for the Next Decade*. Washington: Atlantic Council, 1984.

Kenny, Henry J. *The American Role in Vietnam and East Asia*. New York: Praeger, 1984.

Kim, Samuel S. *China and the World: Chinese Foreign Policy in the Post-Mao Era*. Boulder: Westview, 1984.

Kintner, William R. *A Matter of Two Chinas*. Philadephia: Foreign Policy Research Institute, 1979.

Kissinger, Henry A. *White House Years*. Boston: Little, Brown and Co., 1979.

Kuo, Shirley W. Y., Gustav Ranis, and John C. H. Fei, *The Taiwan Success Story*. Boulder: Westview, 1981.

Lardy, Nicholas R. *China's Entry into the World Economy*. New York: The Asia Society, 1987.

Lasater, Martin L. *The Security of Taiwan*. Washington: Georgetown University, 1982.

———. *The Taiwan Issue in Sino-American Strategic Relations*. Boulder: Westview, 1984.

———. *Taiwan: Facing Mounting Threats*. Washington: Heritage Foundation, 1987.

Lieberthal, Kenneth. *Sino-Soviet Conflict in the 1970s*. Santa Monica: Rand Corporation, 1978.

———. *The Strategic Triangle*. Colgne: Federal Institute for East European and International Studies, 1979.

Nixon, Richard M.. *RN: The Memoirs of Richard Nixon*. New York: Grosset and Dunlap, 1978.

Pollack, Jonathan D. *The Sino-Soviet Rivalry and Chinese Security Debate*. Santa Monica: Rand Corporation, 1983.

Pye, Lucian W. *Chinese Commercial Negotiating Style*. Cambridge: Oelgeschlager, Gunn and Haig Publishers, 1982.

Rees, David. *Soviet Border Problems: China and Japan*. London: Institute for the Study of Conflict, 1982.

Republic of China in 1986: A Reference Book. Taipei: Government Information Office, 1986.

Robinson, Mary Ann. *The American Military and the Far East*. Colorado Springs: USAF Academy Library, 1980.

Rothenberg, Morris. *Whither China: The View from the Kremlin*. Miami: University of Miami, 1977.

Shaw, Yu-ming. *The Prospects for ROC-US Relations under the Reagan Administration*. Taipei: Asia and World Institute, 1983.

Shen, James. *The U.S. and Free China*. Washington: Acropolis Books, 1983.

Snyder, Edwin K., A. James Gregor, and Maria Hsia Chang. *The Taiwan Relations Act and the Defense of the ROC*. Berkeley: University of California, 1980.

Solomon, Richard H. *The China Factor: Sino-American Relations and the Global Scene*. Englewood Cliffs: Prentice-Hall, 1981.

————. *Chinese Political Negotiating Behavior: A Briefing Analysis.* Santa Monica: Rand Corporation, 1985.

Stuart, Douglas T. and William T. Tow. *China, the Soviet Union, and the West.* Boulder: Westview, 1982.

Sullivan, David S. *Redressing the Strategic Nuclear Imbalance in Northeast Asia.* Arlington: SRI International, 1982.

Sutter, Robert G. *Future Sino-Soviet Relations and Their Implications for the United States.* Washington: Library of Congress, Congressional Research Service, 1982.

————. *The China Quandary.* Boulder: Westview, 1983.

Swanson, Bruce. *Eighth Voyage of the Dragon.* Annapolis: Naval Institute Press, 1982.

The Military Balance, 1986-1987. London: International Institute of Strategic Studies, 1986.

The Twelfth National Congress of the CPC. Beijing: Foreign Languages Press, 1982.

U.S. Congress, House of Representatives. *The United States and China: Communication from the Speaker Transmitting a Report.* Washington: GPO, 1983.

————, Committee on Foreign Affairs. *China-Taiwan.* Washington: GPO, 1982.

————, Subcommittee on Asian and Pacific Affairs. *Implementation of the Taiwan Relations Act.* Washington: GPO, 1980.

————. *The United States and the People's Republic of China.* Washington: GPO, 1980.

————. *The New Era in East Asia.* Washington: GPO, 1981.

————. *United States-China Relations Eleven Years after the Shanghai Communiqué.* Washington: GPO, 1983.

————. *Political Developments in Taiwan.* Washington: GPO, 1985.

————, Subcommittees on Asian and Pacific Affairs and on Europe and the Middle East. *The Soviet Role in Asia.* Washington: GPO, 1983.

U.S. Congress, Senate, Committee on Foreign Relations. *Taiwan.* Washington: GPO, 1979.

————. *Implementation of the Taiwan Relations Act, the First Year:A Staff Report.* Washington: GPO, 1980.

————. *East-West Relations: Focus on the Pacific.* Washington: GPO, 1982.

————. *U.S. Policy toward China and Taiwan.* Washington: GPO, 1982.

————. *The Future of Taiwan.* Washington: GPO, 1984. , Subcommittee on East Asian and Pacific Affairs. *Oversight of Taiwan Relations Act.* Washington: GPO, 1980.

————, and Library of Congress, Congressional Research Service. *The Implications of U.S.-China Military Cooperation: A Workshop.* Washington: GPO, 1981.

U.S. Congress, Senate, Committee on the Judiciary, Subcommittee on Separation of Powers. *Taiwan Communiqué and Separation of Powers.* Washington: GPO, 1983.

U.S. Congress, Joint Economic Committee. *China's Economy Looks Toward the Year 2000.* Washington: GPO, 1986.

U.S. Congress, Office of Technology Assessment. *Technology Transfer to China.* Washington: GPO, 1987.

U.S. Department of Defense. *Soviet Military Power: 1988.* Washington: GPO, 1988.

Wheeler, Jimmy W. and Perry L. Wood. *Beyond Recrimination: Perspectives on U.S.-Taiwan Trade Tensions.* Indianapolis: Hudson Institute, 1987.

Whiting, Allen S. *The Chinese Calculus of Deterrence: India and Indochina.* Ann Arbor: University of Michigan, 1975.

Wich, Richard. *Sino-Soviet Crisis Politics.* Cambridge: Harvard University, 1980.

Wolff, Lester L. and David L. Simon. *Legislative History of the Taiwan Relations Act.* New York: American Association for Chinese Studies, 1982.

Zagoria, Donald S. *The Sino-Soviet Conflict: 1956-1961.* Princeton: Princeton University, 1962.

Index